Essays on money and inflation

Studies in inflation

This is the third volume in a
series of studies in inflation
under the general editorship
of D. E. W. Laidler and J. M. Parkin

The first two volumes are

Incomes policy and inflation
edited by J. M. Parkin and M. T. Sumner

Inflation and labour markets
edited by D. E. W. Laidler and D. L. Purdy

Essays on
money and inflation

D. E. W. Laidler

The University of Chicago Press

The University of Chicago Press,
Chicago 60637

Manchester University Press,
Manchester M13 9PL

© 1975 by D. E. W. Laidler

Published 1975

Printed in Great Britain by
Unwin Brothers Limited

Library of Congress Cataloging in Publication Data

Laidler, David E. W.
 Essays on money and inflation.

 Bibliography: p. 228
 Includes index.
 1. Inflation (Finance) 2. Monetary policy—
Mathematical models. I. Title.
HG229. L2   332. 4'1   75-22170
ISBN 0-226-46793-7

Contents

Foreword to the series

In July 1971 a group of some twenty economists, econometricians and accountants, financed by the Social Science Research Council began work at the University of Manchester on a five year research programme on the problem of inflation. The research consists largely of a series of self-contained investigations of various aspects of the inflationary process. In order to ensure that our own work does not develop in isolation from that being carried out elsewhere, it is the policy of the Manchester-S.S.R.C. Inflation Programme regularly to invite scholars from other Universities in the United Kingdom and elsewhere to present papers at Manchester. Though our own work, and that of our colleauges at other institutions, consists of self-contained projects, certain common themes continue to emerge as research progresses.

The purpose of this series of volumes is to bring together in a convenient form papers on related aspects of inflation so that other research workers and students will have easy access to a relatively integrated body of material. Though each volume will contain a large proportion of previously unpublished work, previous publication in a learned journal will not disqualify an otherwise relevant paper from being included in this series.

In promoting a wider understanding of the inflationary process original research is vital, but the dissemination of the results of that research is just as vital. It is our hope that this series of volumes will enable the results of our own work at Manchester, and that of our colleagues elsewhere, to reach a wide audience.

D. E. W. Laidler
J. M. Parkin

Introduction

For the last fifteen years the academic literature on inflation has been dominated, particularly in Britain, by analysis of the determinants of the rate of change of money wages. Concentration on the explanation of wage inflation in academic discussion has been paralleled in the policy field by an emphasis on wage and price controls as the principal component of anti-inflation policy. At first sight concentration on *wage* inflation is rather strange, given that it is *price* inflation which produces the undesirable social consequences that make the control of inflation an important policy issue. However, given the nature of the short-run macro-economic theory widely taught in the 1950's and 1960's, this emphasis on wage inflation is not so hard to understand.

Post-Keynesian macro-economics, whose major characteristics are embodied in the IS-LM, or Hicks-Hansen, analytic framework, was designed principally as a theory of the determination of the level of real income, and hence of employment. Given the policy problems of the 1920's and 1930's, this emphasis is perfectly understandable and sensible, and it is not my purpose here to question the suitability of this framework as a tool for analysing such problems. However, whatever its merits as a means of organising discussion about causes of and policies towards depression, the IS-LM framework is not well adapted to deal with inflation. The theory of the price level emboided in it is rudimentary in the extreme.

The model treats the level of money wages as exogenously given and then determines the general price level, either by a simple mark-up pricing theory or, in its more sophisticated aggregate demand-aggregate supply formulations, as a result of perfectly competitive firms setting prices equal to short-run marginal labour costs.[1] In either case the main determinant of

---

[1] A lucid and brief account of the properties of this macro model is to be found in the 'Appendix' by Marcus H. Miller to Harry G. Johnson, *Macroeconomics and Monetary Theory*, London, Gray-Mills, 1971.

the price level is an exogenously given level of money wages. Such a model is obviously not much help in understanding situations in which variations in the price level are the principal policy problem, but it does prompt those seeking a greater understanding of inflation to look in a particular direction. If the major determinant of the price level is the money wage level, then an explanation of money wage inflation will provide the necessary foundation for a theory of price inflation. This is why so much attention has been given to money wage inflation among both academic economists and policy makers.

Now the last few years have seen vigorous and continuing debate about the determinants of money wage inflation. One side in this debate has related the rate of change of money wages to the state of supply and demand in the labour market. The principal analytic and empirical device deployed here is the inverse relationship between the level of unemployment and the rate of wage inflation known as the Phillips curve. The unemployment rate stands in this analysis as a proxy for the excess demand for labour, but it is important to appreciate that there is nothing in the Phillips curve to rule out the possibility of a shift on the *supply* side of the labour market leading to excess demand for labour and hence to wage inflation. Moreover the inclusion of inflationary expectations in recent versions of this analysis introduces a factor which may be thought of as affecting both the supply and demand schedules for labour, and hence the rate of wage inflation, independently of current excess demand for labour. Thus the Phillips curve is a 'demand pull' theory of wage inflation only in the sense that it regards one proximate cause of wage inflation to be the market force of excess demand; it does not, in and of itself, say anything about how that excess demand is generated.

Nevertheless this approach stands in sharp opposition to the main alternative view, which attributes wage inflation to the militancy of trade unions that exercise power to raise money wages quite independently of the state of supply and demand in the labour market and independently of the current state of expectations about price or wage inflation.[2] This latter view attributes wage inflation to factors quite exogenous to any orthodox macroeconomic model and hence leads its proponents to look for sociological or socio-psychological explanations of the phenomenon. In contrast, more orthodox economic explanations point to the overall

---

[2] A. G. Hines, 'The determinants of the rate of change of money wage rates and the effectiveness of incomes policy', in Harry G. Johnson and A. R. Nobay (eds.), *The Current Inflation,* London, Macmillan, 1971, provides a relatively recent account of this point of view.

level of aggregate demand for goods and services as an important influence on the inflation rate; the demand for labour is, after all, derived from the demand for goods and services.

The first two volumes in the Manchester Inflation Workshop series have reflected the general emphasis in contemporary literature on understanding wage inflation.[3] One of them has concentrated solely on problems associated with the behaviour of labour markets in the inflationary process, while the analyses of incomes policies dealt with in the other were all carried out within a framework that gave heavy emphasis to the behaviour of money wages. The work included in these two volumes has tended on the whole to favour an economic explanation of inflation and to cast grave doubts upon the likely efficacy of any anti-inflation policy that relies upon wage and price controls. But if it is the case that the supply and demand for labour are important determinants of the rate of wage inflation, and if it is the case that the demand for labour is heavily dependent upon the aggregate demand for goods and services, then certain important questions arise.

The proposition that variations in the level of demand for labour cause variations in the rate of wage inflation is not an explanation of wage inflation; it is, as already noted above, a theory of the proximate cause of wage inflation, a piece of partial analysis concerning the behaviour of one market. Nor is wage inflation necessarily explained if we argue that the demand for labour is derived from the demand for goods and services unless it can be shown that the direction of causation here is purely one-way. If variations in aggregate demand affect wage inflation, which in turn affect price inflation, then this might constitute something approaching a complete explanation of inflation only if variations in aggregate demand are independent of the variations in the inflation rate which they are supposed to be explaining.

A moment's reflection will convince the reader that the level of aggregate demand is very unlikely to be independent of the inflation rate. If private expenditure is at all sensitive to interest rates, then unless economic agents suffer from money illusion, or unless they never adapt their expectations about the likely future course of inflation to experience, then the inflation rate will influence the level of aggregate demand through its influence on the real value of interest rates. Again, if there does indeed exist a stable demand function for real balances, then, given the behaviour of the nominal money supply, different rates of inflation imply a

---

[3] *Cf.* J. M. Parkin and M. T. Sumner (eds.), *Incomes Policy and Inflation,* Manchester University Press, 1972, and D. E. W. Laidler and D. L. Purdy (eds.), *Inflation and Labour Markets,* Manchester University Press, 1974.

different time path for the real money supply. Hence, unless
aggregate demand is quite unaffected by the supply of real
balances, we have another route whereby the inflation rate can
effect aggregate demand. Moreover in an open economy the
behaviour of the price level can affect the balance of payments
and hence aggregate demand. Thus models which deal with the
generation of wage and price inflation while treating the level of
excess demand in the economy as exogenous, although they can
yield much valuable insight and information about how wages and
prices interact, cannot constitute an explanation of the time path
of either variable. The level of aggregate demand and hence of
excess demand is in fact determined in part by the inflation rate
itself and ought not to be treated as an exogenous variable.

All this suggests that analyses of wage and price inflation such
as those contained in the first two volumes of this series must, if
we are to get full benefit from them, be complemented by work
which studies inflation in the context of a complete macro-
economic framework. One way in which this might be accomplished
would be to construct a large-scale econometric model which
included explicit wage and price inflation equations, or perhaps
sets of such equations. However, such models are typically so
complex as to require computer simulation exercises in order to
reveal anything about their properties; in thinking about them and
trying to understand them the economist must always have in his
mind, either consciously or unconsciously, a much simpler and
more aggregated model.[4] The model most readily available for
the purpose is, of course, the static IS-LM framework, but, as we
have already seen, it is not a helpful device when it comes to
thinking about problems concerning inflation. It is the search for
an alternative simple macro-economic viewpoint better adapted
to helping us think about inflation which provides the basic theme
of this volume.

The emphasis in the following pages is on price inflation
rather than on wage inflation because it is price inflation that
interacts with interest rates, the nominal money supply and the
balance of payments to influence aggregate demand. Moreover,

---

[4] Only the so-called St Louis econometric model approaches
the degree of analytic simplicity that enables its structure to be
grasped without recourse to such simplification, but even this
model, conceived very much in the same spirit as some of the
work included in this volume, is much too complex for its dynamic
properties to be analysed without the aid of computer simulation.
Cf. L. C. Andersen and K. M. Carlson, 'A monetarist model for
economic stabilization', *Federal Reserve Bank of St Louis
Monthly Review,* April 1970.

because inflation involves prices rising over time, it seems
unlikely that a model which does not encompass the passage of
time will be very helpful in dealing with it; thus the analysis concentrates on dynamic models which take explicit account of the
fact that the current decisions of economic agents are made upon
the basis of imperfect information on the likely outcome of their
actions. Expectations must play a key role in determining
behaviour when the future is uncertain, and money plays a key
role in co-ordinating the behaviour of individuals in such circumstances. Hence there is a heavy emphasis in the following pages
on disappointed and changing expectations and on monetary disequilibrium.

Chapters 1 and 2 are survey papers, one written very recently
and the other written in 1970, but the recent advances in theory
dealt with in chapter 1 and the mainly empirical work described in
chapter 2 both point to the necessity of looking at macro-economic
problems from the essentially dynamic viewpoint sketched out
above. Chapter 3 works out the dynamics of real income when
expectation and adjustment lags, so important in empirical work
on particular structural relationships, are introduced into
orthodox IS-LM macro-economics. This model holds prices constant, but chapter 4 sets out the basic properties of an expectations-augmented Phillips curve, the type of mechanism that is
used in most subsequent chapters to link output fluctuations with
variations in the price level. Chapter 5, which deals with some
aspects of Wicksell's economics, sets out a model which, in
certain respects, is complementary to that of chapter 3. Here
prices fluctuate but income and employment remain constant, and
the reasons for this are analysed in some detail.

Chapter 6 represents my first effort at producing a model
capable of generating simultaneous fluctuations in prices and output. Like most first efforts at solving a problem, it is by no means
totally satisfactory, but, in terms of this volume, it provides an
important link between the earlier and later chapters. Chapter 7
presents a much simpler and more manageable version of the
same type of model, along with some empirical evidence which
suggests that the model in question is worth taking seriously.

Up to this point the essays all deal implicitly or explicitly
with the economics of a closed economy. However, whether or not
the economy under analysis is open or closed makes a vital difference to its macro-economic and monetary behaviour. The relative
neglect of this point in earlier British literature stemmed, of
course, from applying to Britain results derived from studies of
the relatively closed United States economy. The last four chapters of this book attempt to make amends for my own earlier
neglect of the openness of the British economy. Chapter 8, written
jointly with Mr A.R. Nobay, surveys the issues raised by analysing

inflation in the context of an open economy. Chapter 9 presents
what amounts to an open-economy version of the closed-economy
model set out in chapter 7. This model, ignoring as it does the
role of international capital markets, is too simple for direct
empirical implementation, but chapter 10 does deal, in an informal
way, with some of its basic implications for recent British
economic history, and finds them not without empirical support.

Finally chapter 11 is about an earlier controversy over the
relationships between money, the balance of payments and inflation-
namely the currency school-banking school debate. This essay was
written between 1966 and 1969, before the current literature on
the monetary approach to balance of payments theory appeared.
Thus the vocabulary it uses is not very contemporary, but the
ideas with which it deals are topical in the extreme; they concern
the extent to which an open economy operating a fixed exchange
rate with full convertibility can pursue an independent monetary
policy. Hence my decision to include the paper in question in this
collection.

With the exception of chapter 11 the essays in this book have
been written since the beginning of 1970. Most of this work has
been carried out under the auspices of the SSRC-University of
Manchester Inflation Workshop; that which was completed before
the programme formally began - Chapters 2, 4 and 11 - along with
Michael Parkin's early work on incomes policies played an important role in generating the original research proposal out of which
the workshop grew. It is precisely because this work has formed
an integral part of the workshop's output that it has been decided
to gather it together in one volume and publish it as part of our on-
going series; this despite the fact that there is a higher proportion
of reprinted articles here than in other volumes in the series.

The essays collected together here are to be read not as a
definitive statement of a particular position but as a series of
accounts of work in progress, written at particular moments and
often with quite specific audiences in mind. I have not edited them
with a view to producing a spurious harmony of ideas between them;
there are places where I contradict myself, and that is because my
views on certain issues have not stood still over the last five years.
Such continuity as exists in the volume arises from the basic point
of view stated earlier in this introduction rather than from any
careful co-ordination of analytic detail. However, I have made
minor changes to nearly all the essays reprinted. Some of them
contained analytic errors when they first appeared, and I have
removed such of these as I have tracked down. Several essays
use the same mathematical techniques; where mathematical
detail was needlessly repetitive between essays I have made
appropriate amendments. The only major changes have been made
to chapter 2, which, when it first appeared, contained a fairly

lengthy account of some empirical work on the demand for money in the United Kingdom. Since those results are not central to the essay, particularly in the context of this volume, and since it was in any event very long, I have deleted this section from the version of it reprinted here by permission of the Clarendon Press, Oxford.

The reader is warned of deletions from the original version of any essay by the appearance of three dots . . . He will recognise additions or amended sections by their being enclosed in square brackets[ ].

Many people have contributed to the work presented in this volume, and their help is acknowledged at the beginning of individual essays. However, George Zis deserves special thanks for having read through the contents and made many helpful suggestions both on detailed amendments and on the general layout of the essays included. Michael Parkin and Bob Nobay were also most helpful in this respect. Finally, I am deeply in the debt of Mrs Vicki Whelan for her help in getting the volume ready for the press. All errors and omissions are, of course, to be blamed on the author, indeed doubly so, for I have, after all, had a second chance to get right all but one of the papers printed here.

David Laidler

1 Information, money and the macro-economics of inflation[1]

I

Recent years have seen a spate of work on a set of interrelated problems; work that has gone under a variety of headings: 'the economics of information', 'the new micro-economics', 'the reinterpretation of Keynesian economics', to name but three of the more popular titles.[2] It deals with one of the oldest problems in our subject: the way in which a market economy co-ordinates the activities of economic agents, each of whom is pursuing his own self-interest so as to produce a coherent social solution to the problem of scarcity.

In this paper I shall describe how this work departs from older approaches to the problem, and show how a potentially far greater degree of integration between micro-economics and macro-economics is permitted by the insights it yields, this intergration hingeing on the role played by money in the economic system. I shall then argue that such integration implies a considerable modification of prevailing macro-economic orthodoxy and one that completely breaks down the distinctions between the economics of inflation and depression. I shall sketch out the salient features of this 'new macro-economics', particularly as it applies to the problem of inflation, showing how it permits an economic — as opposed to sociological or socio-psychological — explanation of this phenomenon, an explanation that assigns a key role to monetary factors. Thereafter I shall not end with any set of neatly drawn conclusions, for perhaps the strongest theme of all those running through the following pages is that this new work puts us in possession not of any new set of established truths but of a set of insights which provide the foundations upon which much economics can be reconstructed. Such reconstruction has hardly begun.

II

The question of the dissemination of information has long been central to economics. It has seldom, if ever, been the case that a model of an economy has been built upon the explicit assumption of complete and costless information.[3] The 'economic problem' concerns the allocation of scarce resources among competing ends. We want an economic system to solve for a set of quantities. Prices are of no intrinsic importance from this point of view. Consider Robinson Crusoe's economic life: he has to allocate the resources available to him in order to satisfy his wants, but he has no one to trade with, no one with whom he must co-ordinate his activities. The solution to his maximisation problem will, to be sure, yield a set of prices along with a set of quantities, but there is no question of those prices helping him to solve his maximisation problem. They simply exist as part of its solution. The economist looking from the outside at a general equilibrium system made up of many economic agents, and finding its equilibrium properties, will solve simultaneously for quantities and prices, and, since it is the quantities that go to satisfy wants, it is the quantities that are the important part of the solution. If every agent within the economy had the same information as that economist looking in from the outside he could perform exactly the same calculation and immediately act in a way that was consistent with equilibrium overall.

Prices are important in the analysis of allocation precisely because information is not perfect in the sense just outlined. In traditional accounts of a market economy, prices convey both information and incentives to economic agents in order that they will act in a fashion that is consistent with general equilibrium in the absence of complete information about the nature of that equilibrium. Analysis of Walrasian *tâtonnement* is, then, concerned with the existence and stability of general equilibrium, not in a situation of complete knowledge, but in a situation of highly imperfect knowledge. There is no other way to justify the key role played by prices in that analysis. Each individual knows about the technology available to him and the resources with which he is initially endowed, but nothing about the endowments or tastes of other members of the economic system. It is solely through market prices that his activities are co-ordinated with the activities of orders. The basic social role of prices is to economise on costly information about the possibilities open to economic agents, and to provide the incentives for them to harmonise activities.[4]

But Walrasian economics does not get to the root of the social problem of co-ordinating economic activity. One symptom of its inadequacy is the difficulty of reconciling the existence and use of money with such a view of the world. A numeraire, a unit of account, may be introduced on the grounds that it economises on computation costs, but in a Walrasian economy in static equilibrium—and trade takes place under no other circumstances in such an economy

—it is difficult to see why an intermediate good should enter naturally into the process of exchange.[5] After all, one interpretation of
static general equilibrium is that the same exchanges take place
time and time again between the same agents. It is difficult to
apply to such circumstances the usual arguments about the greater
costs of direct barter, most of which stem from the costs of finding
the appropriate set of trading partners; but even if some such
artificiality as uncertainty about the precise timing of meetings
between pairs of traders during the market period is introduced,
this only opens up the possibility of intermediate trades taking
place; it stops far short of explaining why it is sensible to hold
inventories of any good, and money in particular, between market
periods.[6] It makes sense to do this only if the individual sees some
chance of his receipts in the market not being equal to his out-
goings, and this possibility does not arise when all trades are taking place, and are known to be taking place, at equilibrium prices.
Only if individuals come to market uncertain of the prices at which
they are going to trade or uncertain about the likelihood of expenditures and receipts balancing does it become sensible to hold
inventories of goods and money between visits to the market.[7]

We frequently talk about how supply and demand in the market
determine prices, but this is precisely what they do not do in
Walrasian analysis. *Ex ante* supply and demand information are
used by the auctioneer to determine prices, and then the market
opens up for trade. The prices of the Walrasian model economise
information costs for participants in the market but they are not
determined by anything, or anybody, within the economy. They are
given, costlessly, from the outside. From an empirical viewpoint
it is difficult to take seriously the proposition that a market
economy functions with everyone aware of all the prices that are
ruling, and it is even more difficult to believe that all the prices
ruling at a particular moment are compatible with the market
being cleared overall. As time passes, tastes and technology
change, equilibrium quantities of goods and services change, and
so does the structure of equilibrium prices. Beyond the question
of whether, at a particular moment, a set of prices exists, knowledge of which on the part of economic agents would cause them to
act in a manner compatible with the existence of general equilibrium, lie the questions of how, or even whether, those prices are
set in the first place, and how information about them is dissemin-
ated. The very existence of the phenomenon of unemployment
among scarce resources makes it impossible to hold to the comfortable proposition that any market economy behaves 'as if'
equilibrium prices always rule and are known to all agents.

That the failure of prices adequately to convey information and
incentives lies at the root of the problem of unemployment has long
been a commonplace of macro-economics. The reasons typically

advanced for inappropriate price patterns have to do with institutional rigidities associated with monopoly and with various forms of irrationality that go under the general heading of 'money illusion'. In any case, these reasons have never been central to orthodox macro-analysis, which concentrates upon the consequences rather than the causes of these rigidities. This analysis is enshrined in the LM-IS or Hicks-Hansen macro-model. In its usual textbook formulation this model presents an account of the determination of an *equilibrium* situation in which, because of wage and price rigidities, real output lies below the maximum that would be permitted by the full employment of available resources.[8]

The existence of money in the LM-IS model, as it is usually interpreted, is no easier to explain than it is in terms of Walrasian analysis. To say that prices are rigid does not mean that they are unknown to anyone, and to postulate that the economic system is in equilibrium, even at less than full employment, would appear to involve all participants in market activity being able to undertake all their planned exchanges of goods and services in a manner consistent with given expectations. All the factors that make it difficult to explain why money should exist in the context of a smoothly functioning Walrasian system are present in the LM-IS model even though its very structure, and many of the apparently most empirically relevant propositions that may be derived from the framework, are critically dependent on the existence of an asset that goes by the name 'money' and purports to correspond to some easily recognised empirical conterpart.

That neither the Walrasian nor the Hicks-Hansen model can provide any compelling explanation for the existence of money is particularly disconcerting when we try to deal with the contemporary problem of inflation. A theory of inflation must explain variations in the ratio in which money exchanges for goods and services, but neither of these models even explains *why* money should be exchanged for goods and services in the first place. It is hardly surprising that there is widespread doubt about the capacity of orthodox economics to deal with inflation. However, the new approaches, alluded to at the outset of this paper, to the problem of how a decentralised market economy goes about disseminating the information concerning the behaviour that is required for general equilibrium to prevail are putting us in a position to get to grips with the problem of inflation. The new micro-economics enables us to begin constructing a new macro-economics whose relevance to the way in which a market economy deals with the problem of scarcity is far clearer than was that of the old macro-economics.

III

This 'new micro-economics' rests on three obviously true premisses, from which the old micro-economics, in its more rigorous
formulations, nevertheless abstracted. First, once they are com-
mitted to a certain course of behaviour, economic agents may not
instantaneously and costlessly change that commitment; thus the
passage of time and its irreversibility are matters of paramount
importance in understanding economic activity. Second, prices are
not 'determined by markets' but are set by individual agents. Third
information about prices that currently rule is not freely available
but must actively be sought at a cost in real resources. Based on
these premisses we have models in which members of the labour
force remain unemployed while they seek information about wage
levels in various employments, at each moment deciding to remain
unemployed or not, depending upon whether the expected return
from further search is enough to compensate for the income fore-
gone by not taking the highest-paying job currently known to be
available; we have models in which firms set prices on the basis
of expectations about the time path of sales and hence of profits
that various pricing policies will generate, and in which they adjust
prices as those expectations fail to be fulfilled; we have models
in which the costs of adjusting prices result in their being changed
at discrete intervals rather than continuously; and so on.[9]

At present it is far from clear how these various models of
individual behaviour might fit together into a coherent whole; indeed, it is not even clear that they do all fit together. However,
certain themes run through them all. Most obvious is the paramount importance of expectations. To offer goods at a certain
price, to accept employment at a certain wage, and so forth, all
involve making commitments for the future and hence involve
closing off alternatives. Such choices cannot be made in an uncertain world unless expectations about the future are formed;
but because expectations cannot be formed with certainty, and
because current and past experience is not a thoroughly reliable
guide to the future, behaviour will not immediately respond to current changes in circumstances. A firm will not immediately cut
its prices and reduce its output when demand falls, since it is
costly to do either and not immediately obvious that the fall in
question is anything but temporary. Nor will a worker faced with
a choice between a lay-off or a wage cut necessarily take the
wage cut. It might, given his expectations of his earning power
elsewhere, seem to pay him to accept unemployment while looking
for another job. Only if his search activity reveals to him that he
was unduly optimistic about the alternatives will be become willing to accept a lower wage. We have a picture, then, of an economic
system in which people form expectations, act upon them, and as a

consequence of acting receive information in terms of which they will eventually modify both their expectations and their future behaviour. Equilibrium in such a system thus requires not only that everyone's plans to be compatible at a particular moment but also that the outcome of everyone's action be what he expected. Only in this way is there no incentive for behaviour to change over time.[10]

It is relatively easy to rationalise the use of money in such an economic system. If the future pattern of prices is unclear, so that what any economic agent might expect to realise from the sale of goods and services is uncertain, and if it is costly to change production and consumption plans, then it might pay to hold various buffer stocks rather than engage in the costly search activities needed to reduce uncertainity to negligible proportions. Moreover it is not hard to see that a buffer stock of an asset that is readily exchangeable with anyone for anything is particularly desirable. Money is just such an asset, since virtually every trade involves an exchange of goods and services against money. By holding money the economic agent can reduce the amount of resources he devotes to generating information for himself, since it reduces the cost which ignorance and errors impose upon him. For example, it enables him to undertake various market transactions at discrete intervals - to engage in indirect trade - rather than to devote time and effort to the costly business of seeking out just those people whose trading plans perfectly complement his own so that he may then engage in simultaneous direct barter. Once a general means of exchange is established in use, then, it pays everyone to maintain it in use and to hold inventories of it.[11]

Equally, it is reasonable for those fixing prices to fix them in terms of the item against which they exchange so that the unit of account and the means of exchange in the economy are usually the same asset. The basic fact of the allocative mechanism is not the determination of a set of relative prices by markets - which may, trivially, be converted to money prices by using a numeraire - but the fixing of money prices by economic agents - which may, of course, be converted into a set of relative prices whose significance is far from trivial. When put in these terms the difference in perspective between the new and the old micro-economics is sharp indeed. Money now enters at the beginning of the analysis with a fundamental role to play rather than entering at the end as an afterthought.

Money plays two interlinked roles in this new approach to economics. Individuals may economise on gathering information by holding money as an inventory of generalised purchasing power, while the volume of money that flows between agents conveys information to them about whether the expectations upon which they have planned their market activities were correct.

Excess demand (or supply) for a good manifests itself as more money (or less) than expected being offered in exchange for it at the going price. The use of a price system and the use of money are inextricably linked up with the transmission of information between economic agents. To return to Robinson Crusoe for a moment, his economic life needs neither prices nor money. Both are social institutions whose role is to contribute to the co-ordination of economic activity where information is imperfect and costly.[12]

All this points to money being a very special good indeed and suggests that to treat it in analysis as if it were no different to any other good is likely to be fraught with difficulties. In particular it suggests that to treat the general price level, which is the inverse of the price of money, as if it were directly determined by the supply and demand for money just like the price of any other good is misleading. Even in terms of the new micro-economics one would expect an excess demand for a particular good to lead those selling it to revise its price upwards relative to what it otherwise would have been, but it is of the very essence of the foregoing analysis that no one sets the 'price' of money relative to goods in general. There is no unique market for money, and its 'price' emerges as the result of economic agents each setting the price of the particular good he is supplying in terms of money. Thus there is no question of inflation being understood in terms of the supply and demand for money alone.[13] A satisfactory theory of inflation must take into account the factors that influence the price-setting activities of individual agents *vis-à-vis* particular goods and services.

The very body of analysis that poses the problem of explaining price level fluctuations in these terms, however, puts us in a position to deal with it, as I shall now show. The resulting approach to macro-economic disturbance still assigns a key role to money's behaviour, but not the least of its advantages over the old macro-economics is that it explains why money should be so important. The importance of money for macro-economic phenomena stems from its role in the transmission of information and incentives between economic agents.

IV

So long as macro-economics is based on the postulate that factors such as monopoly and money illusion are the main determinants of price level behaviour it cannot provide a coherent explanation of inflation in terms of economic factors. Sociological and socio-psychological explanations thus become popular for want of an alternative. It is the peculiar contribution of the new micro-economics to macro-economics that it explains the time

path of prices and their potential incompatibility with full employment as the result of rational behaviour in the face of the imperfect and costly information that is inherent in a market economy.
It thus opens the way to a truly economic explanation of the inflationary process in which output and employment fluctuations
play a key role. This is not to say that, in the current state of
knowledge, such an explanation can explicity and rigorously be
deduced from the new micro-economic models referred to earlier.
The discussion of aggregative policy problems will not wait for this
difficult task to be accomplished; moreover the present generation
of micro models which attribute imperfect information to individual agents also attribute to them unlimited and costless access
to computational skills, and hence are unlikely to represent anything like the last word to be said on the relevant problems at
the micro level.[14]

Nevertheless, it does appear to be possible to describe the
process of inflation in a way that seems consistent with what we
know of the micro-economics of price formation. The basic
postulates about behaviour that underly the analysis of the
allocative mechanism in the absence of costless knowledge about
which prices are ruling and which prices it would be appropriate
to set provide the ingredients of such a description. Firms set
the money prices of both inputs and outputs.[15] Their ability to do
so implies that, over some relevant time horizon, they exercise
both monopoly and monopsony power; along with the prices they set
must go certain expectations about both the volume of sales that
will be realised and the volume of factor services that will be
offered to them for employment. Disappointed expectations about
quantities cause prices to be revised upwards if more output is
demanded or fewer factors supplied than expected and vice versa.
Firms meet unexpected discrepancies between the volume of sales
and that of factor payments by permitting inventories of goods and
money balances to vary, and by varying the intensity with which
inputs are utilised, thus gaining time to revise their price and output plans. Households search for prices and wage offers and revise their expectations about the terms that can be had in the light
of that search; search activities are supported both by cutting
down on current consumption expenditure and by running down
assets, including money balances. An important factor in the determination of the wages and prices that firms think it appropriate
to set any any moment, and households expect to find at any moment, is the recent history of wages and prices as perceived by
the agents in question as a result of their search activities.
Finally, both firms and households find it sensible to maintain, on
average (but obviously not at each and every moment), an inventory of cash balances whose purchasing power bears a stable

relationship to the real volume of market transactions in which they expect to be involved.[16]

The foregoing specifications are broadly drawn and, clearly, a wide variety of particular macro models could be constructed within the boundaries that they lay down. We may, nevertheless, make the following general observations about the nature of the inflationary process.[17] When the rate of change of money wages and prices is just what economic agents expect it to be, and when it also generates the volume of sales and availability of inputs that firms expect, then there will be no forces at play to cause those rates of change to vary over time. Such an equilibrium rate of inflation - including a zero or negative one - is compatible with a certain level of unemployment, because one would always expect to find a certain fraction of the labour force involved in wage and price searching rather than in employment.[18]

Any rate of inflation may be an equilibrium rate provided that it is anticipated and generates the appropriate level of output and employment. However, for a given level of real output and trans-actions, and hence for a given demand for real cash balances, a different inflation rate requires a different rate of growth of the nominal money supply. The proportionality of the rate of inflation to the rate of monetary expansion, a key proposition of the 'old macro-economics' as far as inflation is concerned, emerges from the newer framework as a proposition about *equilibrium* inflation.[19] Though the "old macro-economics" usually had causation clearly running from money to prices, there is no such direct implication in the foregoing argument. Firms, on the basis of expectations, think it appropriate to raise prices; firms and households finding themselves with growing money balances attempt to exchange them for goods and factor services, but the prices of these are rising at just that rate which absorbs the growth in money balances and keeps them at an equilibrium level. The flow of money between economic agents informs them that the expectations upon which they set prices and wages were valid. There is no suggestion of 'demand pull' or 'cost push' here: this traditional dichotomy has no meaning in the present context.

If an equilibrium inflation rate is one in which expectations are always justified, then a disequilibrium rate involves disap-pointed expectations. Suppose wages and prices are rising at the expected rate but that this is in excess of what can be suppor-ted by the current rate of monetary expansion. In order to main-tain inventories of real cash balances at desired levels households must cut expenditure. Firms' inventories of goods will begin to accumulate unexpectedly and their cash balances will run down as households restore theirs. The shortfall of cash flowing into firms signals to them the desirability of revising prices and wages downward relative to what was planned as well as the desirability of cutting output and employment. Lowered wage offers will persuade those engaged in job search to prolong that search, finance it in part by cutting back on expenditure, and thus reinforce the tendencies already set in motion by what amounts to the first round of the Keynesian multiplier process.

Now to cut prices, wages and employment is just what we require a firm to do when a shortfall of cash inflow signals that demand has shifted away from what it has to sell towards some-one else's product. But a firm cannot immediately distinguish between a general fall in demand and one specific to its own product. Nor can a member of the labour force immediately distinguish between a shift in the structure of the demand for labour and a shift in its overall level. An overall fall in output and employment is thus an integral part of the mechanism where-by it is signalled to firms that their pricing policies have been inappropriate and to firms and households that their wage and price expectations have been erroneous, given the rate of monetary expansion. An exactly similar argument, but with signs reversed, goes through if we start with wages and prices rising too slowly for the rate of monetary expansion. Not the least appealing characteristic of this new approach to macro-economics is that it enables us to use the same theory to deal with both inflation and depression. In disequilibrium prices and output fluctuate together. Even if it is output fluctuations that are important in a particular instance, it is impossible to analyse the behaviour of output without reference to the behaviour of prices. Similarly, if price level behaviour is of most concern it cannot be understood unless attention is paid to the time path of output. Instead of having an economics of depression and an economics of inflation we simply have macro-economics.[20]

The framework which I have outlined in the last few pages is not irrevocably tied to any particular view of the original source of specific macro-economic disturbances, but it does assign a key role to the behaviour of the money supply. It tells us first of all that a necessary condition for an equilibrium rate of inflation to exist is that there must be a constant rate of monetary expansion. But the properties of equilibrium inflation *per se* are, perhaps, of more academic than practical interest. Equilibrium inflation, being fully anticipated, has none of the socially disruptive con-sequences for the distribution of income and wealth that are the prime reason for regarding price level fluctuations as undesirable. As is well known, the only consequences of having one equilbrium inflation rate rather than another is a tendency for equilibrium cash balances to be of a different order of magnitude and for this to be associated with a different long-run equilibrium capital stock. Even these consequences hinge upon cartel arrangements in the banking system preventing a competitive rate of return being paid on money balances.[21] The predictions of the quantity theory of money, then, an important component of the old macro-economics, are, according to the new, likely to be consistent only with the facts of what is in many ways the least interesting aspect of the inflationary process.

Nevertheless, this new approach assigns money a key role in disequilibrium too. It views incompatibility between the rate of monetary expansion on the one hand and the actual and expected inflation rates on the other as lying at the heart of the process whereby output, employment and prices fluctuate together, while simultaneously suggesting that the very characteristics of this process will tend to distract attention from its fundamentally monetary nature. Suppose that, in a condition of full equilibrium, the rate of monetary expansion increases. There is no reason to believe that excess cash balances will initially spill over equally into each and every sector of the economy, nor is there any reason to believe that, if such a disruption were to take place a number of times, the same sectors would be affected in the same order and to the same extent on each occasion. Much would depend on the way in which new money found its way into the system. Thus it would be all too easy to infer from observation that the inflation rate was changing as a result of special circumstances affecting specific sectors of the economy at a particular moment. Such observations as these surely lie at the root of the widespread acceptance of structuralist explanations of inflation. The proximate cause of price and wage level changes is, after all, not some auctioneer declaring the price of money balances to be falling relative to goods and services but the actions of specific firms in raising the prices of particular goods and the wages of particular classes of labour.[22]

It is also an inherent property of a disequilibrium inflation in which the actual rate exceeds the expected rate that those whose money incomes are increasing are surprised to find that rising prices prevent real incomes from increasing at the same rate. This surprise is an integral part of the mechanism whereby inflationary expectations are brought into harmony with what is actually happening. While expectations are catching up with events, however, there is inevitable disappointment about realised real income levels.[23] It would be easy enough to take such a symptom of inflation for a fundamental cause and it is not surprising that competition over real income levels is often looked upon as lying at the root of the inflationary process. After all, it is another inherent property of disequilibrium inflation that real income and interest rates also fluctuate along with prices so that there is unlikely to be any close correlation between the rate of monetary expansion and the rate of inflation. The old macro-economics would have us read such a lack of correlation as evidence against a monetary explanation of a particular inflationary episode, but not the new.[24]

It has already been observed that, in terms of this new analysis, the economics of inflation and depression are the same, and the arguments of the last two paragraphs are easily enough adapted to the case of an economy in the process of contracting as a result of the slow-down in the rate of monetary expansion. There is no reason to suppose that the impacts of such a slow-down should be equally spread across all industries, and again there is considerable potential for confusion of cause and effect: the reader hardly needs reminding that recessions are frequently attributed to causes specific to particular industries. There is also something to be said about the behaviour of income relative to expectations in economic contraction. Money incomes fall or fail to rise as quickly as before, but it is not immediately apparent to households that the behaviour of prices will tend to offset the effects of this on real income. Thus expenditure plans are cut by more than is justified by events. In this light the 'hoarding' that so often accompanies recession and is frequently regarded as being one of its causes is more appropriately regarded as a symptom.[25]

Now the old macro-economics does not confine itself to situations in which the major influence on economic activity is an *exogenous* rate of monetary expansion. In the Wicksellian analysis of inflation the value of the so-called 'money rate of interest' is set by the banking system at such a level as to result in excess demand at full employment. Prices rise and the money supply simultaneously expands to validate this. Where the monetary theory of the balance of payments is applied to a small economy operating a fixed exchange rate, the domestic price level rises in harmony with world-wide trends and the balance of payments instantaneously adjusts in order to provide the required expansion of the money supply. The new macro-economics no more than the old can afford to ignore the relevance of the institutional assumptions that underly such pieces of analysis as these. However, it would stress that the validation of price level behaviour by that of the money supply is likely to be a state of affairs approached only in the long run rather than something which can be relied upon to occur immediately.

In the Wicksellian case the initial response to the appearance of a discrepancy between the money rate of interest and the 'natural' rate - which must now be redefined as that rate of interest compatible with the maintenance of the natural rate of unemployment - would be an increase in output followed by an increase in the inflation rate and only then by an increase in the rate of monetary expansion. Moreover changes in inflationary expectations over time would alter the real value of the money rate

of interest for a given nominal value, and hence the level of aggregate demand and the inflation rate itself. All in all, there would
appear to be plenty of scope for both output and the inflation rate
to fluctuate once the lags in behaviour inherent in the new macro-
economics are put into a Wicksellian framework.

The same can be said of the application of the monetary
theory of the balance of payments to the problem of inflation in
a small open economy. Instead of all firms being 'price takers'
in a competitive world market, it becomes appropriate to think of
those firms selling abroad or buying from abroad searching out
and taking account of world price level trends when forming the
expectations upon which their own price and output decisions are
made. There is no need to expect them to do this continuously,
completely and accurately; while we might expect firms who deal
only in the domestic market to be even slower in adapting their
plans to what is happening in the world at large. Moreover, along
with capital account adjustments, it requires a change in the
composition of output between these two groups of firms to
generate the balance of payments effects by which the rate of
monetary expansion is adapted to changed circumstances. The
new macro-economics naturally focuses our attention upon the
time required for the necessary re-allocation of productive
resources to take place. This new analysis would seem to have an
important role to play in illuminating the potentially confusing
disequilibrium dynamic process whereby a small economy
adapts its inflation rate to that ruling in the rest of the world.[26]

V

In this paper I have tried to show that recent analysis of the way
in which a market economy deals with the problem of disseminating
information among economic agents puts us in a position to build
a micro-economics of allocation and distribution and a macro-
economics of inflation and depression which are consistent with
one another and which assign a key role to money. I have also
sketched out some properties of the relevent macro-economic
system, arguing that the basic advance has been to make endogenous to the macro-economy the behaviour of the general price
level so that the problem of explaining price level behaviour becomes one of economic rather than sociological or socio-psychological analysis. Nevertheless my account of this new macro-
economics has indeed been a sketch, and for reasons that are not
hard to find. It has been fundamental to my argument that the
appropriate formulation for a model of the macro-economic
system is a dynamic one in which the time paths of key variables
interact over time. The precise behaviour of dynamic economic
systems is notoriously dependent upon the quantitative as well

as upon the qualitative characteristics of the structural relationships that they encompass.

We would like to know how long it takes to get back to an
equilibrium inflation rate after disturbance and we would like
some idea of how large are the real income fluctuations relative
to the fluctuations in the inflation rate that they accompany. There
is always the possibility of outright instability in a dynamic
system, to say nothing of proneness to cyclical behaviour, and it
would be desirable to know something of the circumstances under
which any actual economy might display such characteristics. Such
problems as these are immediately raised by the conclusion
that the appropriate formulation of macro-economics is dynamic.
Only by building and analysing explicit models can we begin to get
to grips with them, but *a priori* analysis alone is hardly likely to
prove enough. The general outlines laid down by the analysis set
out in this paper would permit an extremely wide variety of
models. The only way to narrow down the field is by the test
of empirical content. Thus the building up of new macro-economics is likely to be a process of formulating hypotheses about
particular aspects of macro-economic behaviour, testing them
against available data, and ruling them out or including them in
the new structure, depending upon their performance. The basic
theme of this paper has been that new work on the manner in which
a market economy disseminates information has permitted a far
greater integration of micro and macro-analysis than did earlier
approaches. Almost as important, it looks like requiring a much
greater degree of integration between theoretical and empirical
work in economics than has previously existed.

NOTES

[1]   This paper was prepared for the Symposium on the Economics
of Information held at the University of Lund from 22 and 24
August 1973. It is reprinted from the *Swedish Journal of
Economics,* January 1974. I am grateful to John Foster, Malcolm
Gray and George Zis for reading and commenting on an earlier
draft.

[2]   The basic ideas of this branch of the literature are crystallis-
ed in two books; Leijonhufvud (1968) and Phelps (1970), but
important papers by Clower (1965) and Stigler (1961) ought also to
be mentioned. Once a particular viewpoint becomes clearly
established in economics it is inevitable that particular aspects of
it will be found to have been present in earlier writings. The new
micro-economics is no exception, but in this paper I hope to avoid
dealing with the history of economic ideas for its own sake.

[3]   The analysis of 'recontracting' based on Edgeworth's work
involves economic agents being informed about allocations of goods

and then accepting or rejecting such allocations. This analysis
comes as close to assuming complete and costless information
as does any. I am indebted to Alan Feldman for drawing my
attention to this point.

4   That prices are an economical way of conveying information
and instructions is basic to the Lange-Lerner defence of the
viability of a socialist economy. Frank Knight's still widely read
account of the functions of a price system (1933) makes much of
this point also. However, the author of *Risk, Uncertainity and
Profit* was by no means unaware of the problems that the passage
of time and the difficulty of forecasting the future raise for the
smooth functioning of a price system.

5   The very role of a numeraire in economising computation is
another example of the way in which Walrasian general equilibrium economics recognises the problem of economising on
information costs.

6   In trying to integrate money with a simple Walrasian analysis of exchange Patinkin (1965) introduces the notion that though
trades all take place on a particular day, the actual settling of
accounts takes place between market days and with an uncertain
time pattern. The very artificiality of this construction provides
an excellent example of the difficulty of bringing money-holding
into Walrasian economics.

7   This is not to say that there exists a particular degree of
uncertainty beyond the control of the economic agent. The point
is that he may both reduce uncertainty by devoting real resources
to information gathering and reduce the costs of uncertainty by
holding and trading with money. Money holding is, up to a point,
a cheaper alternative to incurring search costs, and this is an
important reason why money holding is associated with the per-
sistence of market uncertainty. On this matter see Brunner and
Meltzer (1971). See also below, pp. 6-7 where the role of money
is further discussed.

8   The typical contemporary textbook simultaneously contains
an account of how the behaviour of prices is a key factor in
ensuring an appropriate allocation of productive resources, and
an account of a model premised on the downward rigidity of
prices which, if taken seriously, demonstrates that a market
economy cannot even guarantee full employment of resources,
let alone an appropriate allocation of them: hardly a comfortable
pair of positions to hold simultaneously, and made not easier to
reconcile by sometimes being accompanied by a third view to
the effect that, if by good luck or wise management full employment does prevail, then the price mechanism can, after all, play
its allocative role! Finally, it should be noted that whether the
Hicks-Hansen model is what Keynes 'really meant' or not is not
an issue which I wish to raise here. The way the model is utilised

in orthodox analysis and not its historical origins is what matters
in the current discussion.

9   Labour market search analysis underlies the work of
Alchian, Lucas and Rapping, Mortenson and Phelps. Phelps and
Winter, (1970) Carlson (1972) and Barro (1972) deal with the
pricing behaviour of firms. All except the last two cited pieces of
analysis are to be found in papers included in Phelps (1970).

10   Hicks defined equilibrium in this was as long ago as 1932.
It is also worth noting that Robbins (1935) regarded uncertainty as
a basic postulate of theories both of economic dynamics and of
money.

11   The foregoing analysis of the role of money draws heavily on
the analysis of Brunner and Meltzer (1971). Note that though it
provides a rationale for the use of money it does not explain
how the use of money develops in the first place.

12   Which is not to say that it is always preferable to use money
in trading activities. Specialised dealers, for example in used
cars, often find it appropriate to indulge in barter. Moreover
when long-established trading relationships exist the information
that these provide about the reliability and probity of particular
economic agents makes the institution of trade credit a viable
proposition. This is *not* to say that either used cars or trade
credit are money, but only that they may substitute for money,
the *general* means of exchange, in certain *specific* transactions.

13   The argument here has something in common with earlier
work on the validity of the so-called classical dichotomy; *cf.*
Brunner (1951) and Patinkin (1965).

14   The emphasis in these models is on the maximising behaviour of individual agents rather than on the interaction over time
of the market behaviour of many such agents. To maintain rigour
at the level of the analysis of the individual while dealing with
market activity presents formidable technical problems, and hence
it may be appropriate to characterise individual agents as operating by simple rules of thumb when dealing with market activity.
Whether it is or not is basically an empirical question. I am
indebted to Sidney G. Winter for helpful discussion on this point.

15   [This statement tends to obscure a potentially important gap
in the new micro-economics. Over a large range of industries,
firms do not set wages but negotiate them with trade unions.
Moreover, closely related, members of the labour force do not
respond to wage offers simply by accepting a job or continuing
their search; there is always the possibility of strike or similar
action. In addition, the decision to leave employment is not always
at the discretion of the worker; involuntary lay-offs do take place.
Thus there appears to be an interrelated set of labour market
phenomena which the new micro-economics as yet leaves unexplained. The extent to which this might vitiate the macro-

analysis which follows in this paper must remain to be seen.]
16   A stable, and not a constant, relationship is postulated here,
and there is a great deal of evidence in favour of this. Not the
least thing that we require from the new macro-economics is
that it explain and be consistent with the empirical evidence
amassed to support the old.
17   Again, there is a good deal of empirical evidence that people
do form expectations about the rate of inflation and act upon
them when it comes to money holding. The same expectations
ought to inform the fixing of prices and money wages.
18   This, of course, is the so-called 'natural rate of unemployment' hypothesis. There is no need to think of this rate as a constant that never changes. Presumably the faster tastes and technology change the more worthwhile an activity will search be,
while, given that people have memories, the more search there
has been in the recent past the less valuable might it be at present. Even though the natural rate of unemployment may be
expected to vary over time, however, this does not seriously
affect the current analysis. Phelps (1972), chapter 2, presents a
most useful discussion of the determinants of the natural unemployment rate.
19   Strict proportionality here is only a prediction in the case of
a non-growing economy. In general the quantity theory prediction
is that the rate of inflation will equal the rate of monetary expansion minus the income elasticity of demand for real balances
times the growth rate of real income.
20   The foregoing can all be cast in LM-IS terms. So long as the
rate of monetary expansion and the rate of inflation are equal -
I assume zero real growth for simplicity - the LM curve is
stationary, and if it intersects the IS curve at that level of real
income at which the natural rate of unemployment prevails we have
full macro-economic equilibrium. If it does not, then disappointed
expectations about sales and job prospects cause the rate of inflation to vary relative to the expected rate of inflation and relative to the rate of monetary expansion. Hence the LM curve
begins to shift and the level of real income to change affecting in
turn the rate of inflation. The model as usually presented may
then be reinterpreted as showing a point on a disequilibrium path
at a moment in time rather than a situation of macro-equilibrium.
The so-called 'full employment' version of the model becomes
nonsense in terms of this analysis and the usefulness of the whole
LM-IS system as an expositional device is sharply reduced.
21   See Patinkin (1972), chapters 10 and 11, for a lucid exposition
of the issues at stake in the analysis of the long-run neutrality of
money.
22   Note, though, that the faster the pace of structural change in
an economy the higher will be the natural rate of unemployment.

Hence a speed-up of technical change combined with a policy of maintaining a given unemployment rate will inevitably prove inflationary. This point is made by Alchian (1969)

23   This is a modern verision of Hume's wages lag hypothesis. Though real wages do not necessarily fall, they do fail to rise as fast as was expected.

24   One must be careful here not to carry this argument to the point of rendering a monetary explanation of inflation irrefutable. A well specified dynamic model would, of course, make precise predictions about the relationship between the inflation rate and the rate of monetary expansion that would be open to test.

25   Note that this argument implies that income expectations are formed on the basis of expectations about money incomes and of expectations about price level behaviour rather than being derived directly from past evidence on the behaviour of real income itself. The relationship between this argument and more usual formulations of the permanent income hypothesis would be well worth investigating. Disappointed income expectations are one aspect of the more general distributional consequences of the actual inflation rate differing from that which was expected. Such consequences, though their social importance has long been recognised, have occupied a rather minor role in the traditional economic analysis of inflation. The tendency has been to regard them as an unfortunate by-product of inflation about which economics has little to say. The new analysis stresses that these distributional effects arise because economic agents act on faulty information and that the latter are likely to alter their expectations and future actions as a result. Thus such distributional effects can influence the future course of the economy and should, perhaps be assigned a much more central role in the analysis of macro-economic disequilibrium than has usually been accorded them.

26   Laidler (1972c) presents one attempt to come to grips with this problem. The monetary theory of the balance of payments is really based on the proposition that the relevant market for analysing inflation is more widespread than the boundaries of a particular nation State. These boundaries are, after all, political rather than economic. The analysis of what happens in one small economy is inherently a partial equilibrium exercise which perhaps ought to be complemented by an analysis of the causes of inflation at the level of the world economy.

2 The influence of money on economic activity: a survey of some current problems[1]

I

The growth of knowledge about monetary phenomena over the last fifteen years or so has been enormous, and recent literature is almost embarrassingly rich in surveys of that knowledge.[2] To write yet another survey paper needs a good reason, and mine is this. Over the past fifteen years the main task which monetary economists have set themselves has been to convince their, by and large sceptical, colleagues of the importance of the influence of monetary factors not only on real variables but also upon the variable whose determination was at one time regarded as a purely monetary phenomenon, the price level. The tendency, therefore, whether in research articles or in surveys, has naturally and rightly been to stress what has been learnt rather than to draw attention to what is yet to be found out. Moreover research strategy has hardly been uniform, and there has been remarkably little debate as to which strategy is likely to be most fruitful. Again, this has been understandable and desirable; had monetary economists permitted themselves to become involved in methodological debate our stock of positive knowledge about monetary phenomena would be significantly smaller than it now is.

However, it is no longer necessary to be defensive about working in monetary economics. The importance of the field is well established, and it seems worth while to draw attention to those questions which we have not yet answered, and to look at past work to see whether there is anything to be learnt from it about what particular research strategy is worth following in attempting to deal with these unsettled questions. In this paper, then, there will be more emphasis on what we have not yet learnt about money than on what we know, and more explicit attention than usual will be paid to matters of method.

The more important questions at issue are as follows. Is it possible that variations in the quantity of money can have a systematic influence upon the level of real income and prices? Is it the case that there are episodes of economic history which can be interpreted in terms of such influence? Is this influence more predictable than that of variations in autonomous expenditure? If there could, or does, exist such systematic influence, through what channels might, or does, it get transmitted? Are there any significant time lags involved in this transmission mechanism? If there are, are these lags constant? If they are not constant, are they systematically related to any economic variables in a manner that would enable variations in lag effects to be predicted?

In order to organise these questions in a manner that will enable empirical evidence to be brought to bear on them in a systematic way some formal model is required. One cannot have an hypothesis about the answer to any of these questions without a theoretical framework that will yield testable predictions. As we shall see, the greatest difficulties arise in connection with those questions about which we lack formal theories because these are the problems about which we do not yet know which empirical questions to ask. However, a well known and simple theoretical framework will take us quite a long way. The Hicks-Hansen macro-model is part of the basic toolkit of every economist and has underlain a great deal of work in monetary economics. The model may be set out as follows, linear in the variables for simplicity.[3]

E is real expenditure, Y is real output, r is the rate of interest, M is the quantity of nominal balance and P the general price level, and with bars over variables indicating that they are exogenous, we have

$$Y = E = \overline{A} + kY - ar \tag{1}$$

$$M = Md = (mY - lr)\, P \tag{2}$$

As it stands, the model is underdetermined. One, though not the only, solution to this problem is to postulate two distinct situations, one characterised by unemployed resources in which the price level is fixed at an historically given value (call it P^+) so that the model determines the level of real income, and the other characterised by fully employed resources which fix the level of income (at Y^+), leaving the model free to determine the equilibrium price level.[4]

It is worth noting explicity that this model does not enable us to deal with all the questions posed above: the model is static and tells us about the equilibrium relationships between variables. It does not enable us to formulate questions about the time paths whereby endogenous variables approach new equilibrium values when exogenous variables change. [Nor does it enable us to deal satisfactorily with the interaction of real income and prices.]

Nevertheless this model does yield predictions about the relationships between the equilibrium level of income or prices and variables potentially under government control, such as the money stock and the level of government expenditure (subsumed into A in equation 1) or tax rates (here ignored for simplicity or perhaps subsumed into the parameter k as suits the reader's taste), and, since a great deal of work over the last fifteen years has been devoted to testing predictions yielded by models of this type, any account of unsolved problems in monetary economics is best begun with a brief review of the results achieved by these tests.

II

At the very outset of this survey we are faced with a methodological question. Given that we are interested in finding out about the stability of the relationships between equilibrium levels of income and prices and such variables as the quantity of money and the level of autonomous expenditure, we can proceed in two distinct ways. We may either test hypotheses about the relationships between income, interest rates and expenditure, and those about the relationships between the demand for money and income and interest rates, and then see what the results of these structural tests imply about the relationships that ultimately interest us; or we can take a short cut and attempt to estimate directly the reduced form relationships that exist between the exogenous variables and the target variables such as income and prices.

Now both kinds of study have been carried out, but at least one economist has expressed a preference for reduced form estimates.[5] I shall argue in this section that in fact we have learned a good deal less from studying reduced forms than is often supposed, because the actual statistical hypotheses tested have been ill devised to discriminate between the economic hypotheses that were alleged to underly them. The tests in question are supposed to distinguish between simple 'Keynesian' and 'Classical' accounts of the income determination process. The 'Keynesian' hypothesis at stake is that all, or at least most, fluctuations in income and prices are the result of fluctuations in autonomous expenditure, while the 'classical' hypothesis attributes such fluctuations to variations in the quantity of money.[6]

Now if we start from the Hicks-Hansen model there are three ways to produce a simple 'Keynesian' model. Two of them involve the assumption that the rate of interest is an exogenous variable. This may be justified on the grounds that the demand-for-money function becomes perfectly elastic with respect to the rate of interest at some positive, exogenously given value which happens to be ruling in the circumstances being analysed. This assump-

tion is also appropriate if the monetary authorities choose to
control the rate of interest and hence permit the nominal stock
of money to become determined by the level of nominal income.
In either event the supply and demand for money are rendered
irrelevant as far as the income determination process concerned;
equation 1 forms a complete income determination model by itself,
a model often presented in the form of the famous 'Keynesian
cross diagram'. The 'Keynesian' simplification may also be obtained by assuming that expenditure is independent of interest
rates. In this case equation 1 still determines real income, and
equation 2 determines the interest rate.

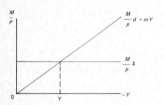

Figure 2.1 A 'classical cross' diagram to determine real income.
See footnote 7, p. 52.

Alternatively one may make the assumption that the velocity
of circulation is independent of the rate of interest, that the parameter l is equal to zero. In that case, income (or the price level
in full employment situations) is determined solely by equation
2; equation 1 determines only the rate of interest. This particular
assumption yields a naive 'classical' model.[7]

So long as raising the question of which of these simple
models has the more empirical content is not read as forbidding
one to ask at the same time whether more complicated models
do not have more empirical content than either naive model—and
it certainly should not be so read—there can be no objection to
the issue being put in this way. Indeed, given the methodological
precept that a 'good' theory is one that can predict 'much' from
'little', there is a great deal to be said in favour of this exercise:
certainly one would be hard put to it to find two models based
on 'less' than these two, and if either of them did prove to be
empirically useful this would be an important discovery. The
trouble is that, as I have already indicated, comparing the reduced
forms of these two models is not a very useful test of their
relative empirical relevance.

The procedure typically followed has been to divide expenditure between an induced (i.e. income-dependent) component,
usually referred to as 'consumption', and the rest, so that our

expenditure function becomes, with C being consumption and I other expenditure, two relationships.[8]

$$C = kY \tag{3}$$

$$I = \bar{A} - ar \tag{4}$$

Regressions of the forms

$$PC = b_0 + b_1 PI + v \tag{5}$$

$$PC = d_0 + d_1 \bar{M} + u \tag{6}$$

are then performed and the explanatory power of these two equations over time series data is compared, using both R^2 and the consistency of parameter estimates between separate sub-periods as criteria. The use of the money value of the 'consumption' as a dependent variable rather than the money value of income is of no particular significance. Given that investment is a component of income, the use of PY as the dependent variable in equation 5 would lead to spurious correlation between Y and I biasing the outcome of the tests in question in favour of the 'Keynesian' view of the world. Consumer expenditure, which apparently bears a close proportional relationship to income in aggregate time series data, is used as a proxy for income to avoid this problem.[9]

Now we may ask what naive 'Keynesian' and 'classical' models might lead us to predict about the empirical performance of equations 5 and 6. The answers we may give will depend upon whether we are dealing with an unemployment situation, in which variations are predominantly in real variables, or with a full employment situation in which it is the price level that is varying. Let us consider the unemployment case first of all.[10]

Our version of the Hicks-Hansen model, modified to make the income determination process independent of the quantity of money, yields either

$$P^+C = \frac{k}{1-k} (A - \bar{ar}) P^+ \tag{7}$$

if we assume that the interest rate is exogenous, or simply

$$P^+C = \frac{k}{1-k} (A) P^+ \tag{8}$$

if we assume that the interest rate is irrelevant to real expenditure. In either event, mere inspection of equations 7 and 8 ought to convince the reader that, if the 'Keynesian' model is true, equation 5 ought to provide strong evidence of a close relationship between consumption and 'investment'. The trouble is that, were velocity constant, so that real income was determined solely by the quantity of money, equation 5 would perform equally well, provided only that there was a stable marginal propensity to consume. The equilibrium level of real income, even if a constant velocity of circulation ensures that it is proportional to the quantity of money, must, after all, still satisfy the relationship

$$Y = \frac{1}{1-k}\, I \tag{9}$$

All that is required for equation 5 to provide a good empirical performance is a stable value of k.[11]

Moreover, equation 5 could still perform 'better' than equation **6** even if all systematic variations in real income were attributable to variations in the quantity of money. In the type of model we are considering here, in which there is neither interest elasticity of consumption nor a 'wealth effect', changes in the quantity of money cause changes in income by way of their effect on interest rates and hence on investment. The quantity of money variable of equation 6 is further removed along the causal chain from income and consumption than is the investment variable of equation 5 and hence might well be found to be less closely related to them even though it was the variable that was solely responsible for determining the latter.

Now we have shown that equation 5 will perform well in unemployment situations as long as the consumption function is stable. What about equation 6? If the demand for money is independent of the rate of interest, then equation 2 yields

$$P^+Y = \frac{1}{m}\, \overline{M} \tag{10}$$

and, provided that there is a stable average propensity to consume to permit the substitution of consumption for income, equation 6 ought clearly to perform well, though not necessarily better than equation 5, as we have already argued.[12] On the other hand, if income is determined independently of the quantity of money, whether or not equation 5 will perform well depends upon which version of the 'Keynesian' model it is that is operative. If the level of income were determined independently of the quantity of money because of a 'liquidity trap', then the well known result that such a 'trap' permits velocity to vary in order to adapt any quantity of money to any level of income implies that only by the most unlikely mischance would equation 6 perform well. Were the level of expenditure altogether independent of the rate of interest, and provided that there was some interest elasticity to the demand for money, equation 2 would yield

$$P^+Y = \frac{1}{m}\, \overline{M} + P^+ \frac{l}{m}\, r \tag{11}$$

Since P^+, Y and $\overline{M}$ would all be determined independently of the demand for money, only the rate of interest could vary to equili-

brate this market. Equation 6 would be unlikely to provide a convincing explanation of the observations that would be generated
in such circumstances.

Even so, equation 6 is quite capable of producing 'good'
results when the 'Keynesian' account of the income determination
process is correct. This would happen in a situation in which the
monetary authorities were seeking to control the rate of interest
but in which there also existed a stable demand for money function in which the level of income entered as an important argument. In such circumstances a stable relationship between the
quantity of money and the level of income might well be observable, but the direction of causation involved would be from income to money rather than vice versa.[13]

To summarise the last few paragraphs: as far as unemployment situations are concerned, there are circumstances in which
the income determination process can be purely 'Keynesian' and
in which both equation 5 and 6 will simultaneously produce 'good'
results, while equally 'good' results could be obtained with both
expressions when the income determination process was purely
'classical' in nature. Indeed, regardless of what it is that determines income, equation 5, which purports to embody a 'Keynesian'
model, will show up badly only if the conventional consumption
function is unstable, whereas the 'classical' model will tend to
perform well whenever there is a stable relationship between
the demand for money and the level of income. A comparison of
equations 5 and 6 could actually be misleading, because it is
quite possible that equation 5 will produce the better statistical
results even when faced with data generated by a world in which
income is primarily determined by the quantity of money. Thus
the fact that periods of relatively heavy unemployment, notably
the 1930's for the United States and the 1920's and 1930's for
Britain, produce statistical results that show equation 5 to be
superior to equation 6 in no sense implies that either economy
should be characterised as having been predominantly 'Keynesian'.
All such a result shows is that the marginal propensity to consume
was reasonably stable over the periods in question. The fact that
equation 6, though performing less well on the whole than equation 5, nevertheless gave reasonable results when faced with the
same data is enough to prevent our disqualifying a 'classical'
account of the income determination process during these
periods.[14]
This evidence does at least suggest that the 'liquidity trap' was
not a phenomenon of any particular importance during the years
in question, but, *taken by itself,* it still leaves open the possibility
that changes in the quantity of money were the consequence
rather than the cause of changes in the level of income. This
point will be taken up later.

As far as underemployment situations are concerned, then,
tests of the relative stability of money and investment multipliers
of the type described seem to be ill devised to answer the questions with which they were supposed to deal. None of this evidence
tells us anything about cause and effect. The situation is even
worse when we come to ask what these same tests might reveal
in a situation of full employment. In such circumstances our
simple model tells us to treat the level of real income as given,
and it becomes a price level determination model.[15] Problems
arise the moment we make the 'Keynesian' simplifying assumptions; equation 1 does not permit us to determine the price level.
Either aggregate demand is equal to output, in which case the price
level will remain at whatever its historically given level might
be, or it exceeds it, in which case there will be an 'inflationary
gap' which cannot be closed by any mechanism embodied in
equation 1; it is nonsensical to treat the simple 'Keynesian model'
as having any relevance at all to the determination of the level
of *money* income in a fully employed economy.

As Johnson (1967) has pointed out, all this was well enough
known during the early post-war period and led many 'Keynesian'
economists to superimpose wage cost theories of the price level,
and its rate of change, upon this simple macro-economic model
in order to deal with the problem of inflation. However, this
problem seems to have been forgotten by their successors, who
were only too eager to accept the proposition that regression
results based on equations implied by an expression like

$$PkY^+ = PC = \frac{k}{1-k} \ (I)P \tag{12}$$

would shed some light upon the money income determination process, the only proviso being that the division of national income
between 'induced' and 'autonomous' components was done on
some basis other than that proposed and adopted by Friedman and
Meiselman.

This does not mean, of course, that one cannot get close cor-
relations between the money value of consumption and the money
value of 'autonomous' expenditure during periods of full employment. To begin with, the price levels of these two components of
national income would tend to move together in inflationary
periods, while, to the extent that the economy was growing in real
terms, one might expect real consumption and investment to
grow together—particularly if the former is indeed proportional
to real income.

Now Friedman and Meiselman (1963) found, overall, a poor
fit between consumption and 'autonomous' expenditure measured
in nominal terms, and the fit was particularly bad in periods of

relatively full employment. This result is perhaps a little surprising in view of the foregoing arguments, and it is not to be wondered at that different definitions of autonomous expenditure produced closer statistical relationships for the United States, or that similarly close relationships seem easy enough to discover for Great Britain. What is perplexing, however, is that anyone should have suggested that the existence of a well determined statistical relationship between nominal consumption and the money value of 'autonomous' expenditure, however defined, could tell us anything about the money income determination process in a fully employed economy.

As far as the fully employed economy is concerned, the simple 'classical' model wins the contest with the simple 'Keynesian' construction by default. Equation 2 implies

$$PY^+ = \frac{1}{m} \, \overline{M} \tag{13}$$

and we need only call $1/m$ by another symbol, V, to realise that we are applying the quantity theory of money in its income velocity form to the very problem with which it was originally designed to deal—namely that of the determination of the price level in a fully employed economy.

This, of course, is not to say that the model will perform well empirically—only that it is applicable to the explanation of fluctuations in the level of money income in a fully employed economy.[16] An exogenously given level of output is only one condition for this model's success—velocity must be stable, and if in fact the rate of interest is an important variable in the demand-for-money function the more variation there is in the rate of interest the less satisfactory will be the performance of equation 6 when faced with evidence drawn from a fully employed economy. Thus testing equation 6 against such data can reveal inadequacies in the simple 'classical' model, but since we have no alternative model with which we can compare its results this does not get us very far. How 'inadequate' we judge the 'classical' model must always depend upon whether or not it does better than a rival, and we have no rival in this case. At the same time, *taken by themselves,* 'good' statistical results are open to the objection that they tell us nothing about the direction of causation.

As far as a fully employed economy is concerned, then, the tests we are discussing are even less revealing than they are in an unemployment context. The simple 'Keynesian' model should not be applied to such data, since it is not a theory of the determination of the level of money income at full employment. All that 'good' results obtained with equation 5 reveal is that the average propensity to consume is relatively stable and that, over the periods to which the equation has been fitted, the relative

price of consumption and investment goods has not varied much.
They reveal nothing about the role played by variations in so-
called autonomous expenditure in determining the level of money
income. What we can learn about equation 6 is also limited. It
is reasonable enough to apply it to full employment data, but in
the absence of a properly conceived rival theory there is no yard-
stick by which we may judge the adequacy of its performance.
Moreover, even the 'best' statistical fit imaginable would still
tell us nothing about cause and effect in the income determination
process.

Studies of reduced form equations have not only concerned
themselves with asking which of these two simple models is the
better approximation to reality. Attempts have also been made
to allow for the fact that shifts both in the quantity of money and
in autonomous expenditure can contribute to variations in the
level of money income. Again using consumption as an income
proxy, regressions of the form

$$PC = b_0 + b_1 PI + b_2 \overline{M} + \epsilon \tag{14}$$

have been run and the magnitudes and stability (usually as
measured by T statistics) of the parameters b_1 and b_2 have been
interpreted as yielding information about the relative importance
and predictability of monetary and real effects in the income
determination process. As far as unemployment situations are
concerned, this *appears* to be a reasonable enough procedure,
for our version of the Hicks-Hansen model yields, without the
simplifying 'Keynesian' or 'classical' assumptions, the following
expression for money income:

$$P^+Y = \left[\frac{1}{(1-k) + \frac{a}{l}m}\right] \overline{A}P^+ + \left[\frac{1}{(1-k)\frac{l}{a} + m}\right] \overline{M} \tag{15}$$

It would be easy to confuse this expression with equation 14, for
it implies a linear relationship between autonomous expenditure,
the money supply and money income. However, the term 'autonomous' tends to be used ambiguously in macro-economics. Sometimes it is taken to mean expenditure whose value is determined
independently of income (I in equation 14) and sometimes it is
used to describe expenditure that is independent of income *and
the interest rate* (A in equation 15). The empirical studies we
are discussing here have used variants of equation 14, and this
expression is at best a misspecified version of equation 15. If
monetary policy worked entirely through interest rate effects on
investment, as our simple model implies, then to fit equation 14,
when I is given by equation 4, would ensure that all monetary
effects were already embodied in the so-called 'autonomous

expenditure' term; nothing would be left over for variations in
the money supply to explain, even if it was in fact the dominant
variable in the income determination process. It is small
wonder, then, that for both Britain and the United States, and
independently of the exact breakdown of national income made
between C and I, variations in autonomous expenditure turned
out to be the most important variable when equation 14 was
confronted with data from unemployment periods.

When we come to deal with full employment, matters are
again worse. With real income fixed exogenously, our simple
model yields as an expression for the price level

$$P = \frac{\overline{M}}{Y^+ \left[m + \dfrac{l}{a}(1 - k) \right] - \dfrac{l}{a}\overline{A}} \tag{16}$$

'Autonomous' expenditure clearly effects the level of money
income in a positive direction, but once more this is 'autonomous' expenditure in the sense of expenditure that is independent
of both income *and the interest rate*. Moreover it is *real* autonomous expenditure that appears in equation 16. This equation is
distinctly non-linear and shows clearly that the effects of changes
in the quantity of money and of changes in real autonomous
expenditure do not interact in a simple additive way in determining
prices and hence money income. Though the relationship between
prices and the quantity of money is linear, the 'money multiplier'
in this case has a value that depends, among other things, upon
the level of real autonomous expenditure. The more unstable is
autonomous expenditure, the more unstable will be the money
multiplier. The inclusion of the money value of investment as an
additive variable in equation 14 represents a considerable misspecification of the 'true' Hicks-Hansen model as it applies to a
fully employed economy, and it is not clear what there is of value
to be learnt from fitting equation 14 to such data.

Now the last few pages argue that, in terms of the Hicks-
Hansen framework, reduced form studies do not tell us much. They
provide some evidence about the stability of a simple aggregate
consumption function, thus giving us some information about the
structure of the underlying model, while, for most times and
places, they also betray signs of a stable relationship between
the quantity of money and the level of nominal income. This
latter result suggests some sort of presumption in favour of the
proposition that changes in the quantity of money could have a
stable predictable effect on the level of income, but they stop far
short of establishing it, particularly since the relationship in
question is by no means observed consistently, its absence being
particularly notable as far as Britain in the 1950's and 1960's
is concerned.

If changes in the quantity of money can cause, or have caused, changes in the level of income, then it takes far more than evidence of a statistical association between the two variables to convince anyone of this. First, a plausible transmission mechanism must be demonstrated to exist in order to establish the *possibility* of variations in the quantity of money being able to influence the level of income; second, in order to establish that such influence *has in fact taken place during particular historical episodes,* it must be shown that the variations in the quantity of money that are supposed to have been the cause of variations in the level of income were not rather their consequence.

As far as problems at hand are concerned, then, viewed even in the most favourable light, reduced form studies can only complement an examination of structural relationships and are in no way a substitute for it. In terms of the Hicks-Hansen model, mere inspection of equations 15 and 16 tells one that the parameters of all the behaviour relationships in the model are potentially relevant to the transmission mechanisms whereby changes both in the quantity of money and in autonomous expenditure affect the level of real income and prices; the strict implication of this observation would be that this survey should now branch out to consider in more or less detail the evidence on each of these structural relationships and then go on to ask about the implications of this evidence for the Hicks-Hansen model. Obviously it would take far more than the space of one paper to carry out this task, and so, as far as the next section of this paper is concerned, I shall confine the discussion mainly to the demand for and supply of money. It is no more justifiable to do this than to concentrate on, say, the investment function. The division of labour is the only viable defence for thus narrowing down the paper's scope at this point.

III

The importance of a stable demand for money function for the workings of monetary policy should be self-evident. If the demand for money is a predictable function of a few variables, then changes in the supply of money must result in at least one of those variables changing in order to maintain equilibrium in the money market. Though the demand for money function does not provide the whole transmission mechanism whereby changes in the quantity of money might lead to changes in income, employment and prices, it provides a vital link in that mechanism. Moreover most of the scepticism concerning the efficiency of monetary policy that is still enshrined in so many textbooks was based on the proposition that the demand for money was highly interest-elastic and likely to be unstable. It is not surprising, then, that a great deal of the work that has gone into re-establishing the quantity of money as an important economic variable has concentrated on this particular functional relationship.

Most of the work in question has been carried out using United States data, even though two of the earliest modern studies of the demand for money dealt with Britain (Brown, 1939, and Khusro, 1952). The American evidence has been surveyed in a fair amount of detail elsewhere (*cf.* Laidler, 1969a), and it will suffice here to summarise the conclusions that have emerged from it. The evidence in favour of the existence of a stable relationship between the aggregate demand for real balances and a few variables is overwhelming. The variables in question appear to be an interest rate, which is interpreted as measuring the opportunity cost of holding money, and 'permanent' real income, or the real value of non-human wealth, either of which variables performs consistently better than current real income.[17] Moreover there is a good deal of evidence that the demand for real balances is independent of the price level. In short, there appears to be no empirical basis for the view that the nature of the demand for money function precludes the money stock from having an important and systematic influence on aggregate demand.

Now data for the United States go back a hundred years, and the demand for money function has not remained immutable over so long a period. For example, the elasticity of demand for real balances with respect to permanent income as computed for time series data has fallen from about 1·6 for the pre-first world war period to somewhere in the region of 0·7 over the years since the second world war. These figures are, of course, but a statistical reflection of the fact that the often noted secular decline in the velocity of circulation was particularly pronounced in the late nineteenth century and has actually reversed itself since 1945. They suggest that there has been a slow shift over time of the demand for money function, a shift that has yet to be explained but which may well be the result of the increasing financial sophistication of the American economy.

The interest elasticity of demand for money has been more stable, particularly with respect to short rates of interest; this parameter seems to have lain consistently between −0·05 and −0·20 over the period for which data are available, but there is a growing body of evidence that those assets which are particularly close substitutes for money have changed over time. Since the second world war the demand for money appears to have become particularly stably related to the interest rate paid on the liabilities of non-bank financial intermediaries (*cf.* Lee, 1967, and Hamburger, 1968) rather than to rates on such assets as short-term commercial paper.

That there should be some secular shifts in the demand for money function ought not to be too surprising in an economy that has changed as much as that of the United States, and in any event these shifts are largely irrelevant as far as assessing what are essentially short-run propositions about the interaction of monetary and real phenomena. From this point of view the demand for money function does indeed appear to be a stable function of a few variables, though it is worth noting that the replacement of current income with permanent income turns out to be of some significance for our assessment of the manner in which monetary policy is likely to work, as we shall see later on in this paper.

Now it is worth asking whether the stability of the demand for money function over such a long period is a fairly general phenomenon or whether it is unique to the United States. No economy has been as thoroughly studied as the United States, but what evidence there is for other economies certainly suggests that a stable demand function for money is far from being a purely American phenomenon.[18] Few countries provide a run of data that is long enough for studies comparable to those done for America to be carried out, but Britain does yield such data. However, as we have seen above, most work done on the British economy has attempted to estimate directly money and autonomous expenditure multipliers: it has not, on the whole, dealt with structural relationships.

An important exception is Walter's (1969) presentation of results on the determinants of the money to income ratio over the period 1878-1961. Walters examined the relationship between the money to income ratio and interest rates and the level of income. He found relationships that are tantalisingly like those which have been well established for the United States. He found a stable negative relationship between this ratio and interest rates, implying a stable negative relationship between the demand for money and the rate of interest, whether he dealt with the levels or the first differences of the data. However, he also found that this ratio was positively related to income when he used the levels of the data and negatively related when first differences were employed.

If we postulate for a moment that the variances of both the level of income and the money to income ratio are dominated by their secular trends, and that the variances of their first differences are dominated by cyclical behaviour, then this evidence produced by Walters suggests that, *even when allowance is made for the influence of interest rates,* velocity in Britain has tended to decline secularly but has conformed to the cycle. This, of course, is precisely the characteristic of United States data that caused Friedman (1956, 1959) to formulate his permanent income hypothesis of the demand for money, and Walters's evidence suggests that the same hypothesis ought to deal with British data.[19] ...

Over the long run the demand for money function for Britain does not appear to be very different from that for the United States though whether this conclusion will withstand further investigation must remain to be seen. However, post-war British data have already been analysed with considerable care and nothing has emerged from the analysis that would lead one to question it. This is a result of considerable importance, because this post-war period is one for which money multiplier studies of the kind dealt with earlier found no stable relationship between the quantity of money and the level of money income.

Three separate studies by Fisher (1968), Laidler and Parkin (1970) and Goodhart and Crockett (1970) found that the key to getting sensible-looking results on the demand for money for post-war Britain with quarterly data was to pay attention to the presence of time lags in the relationship. To use a permanent income variable constructed as a weighted average of past and present levels of income is, of course, to introduce implicit time lags into the relationship, but what is an adequate procedure when dealing with annual data need not necessarily be adequate when it comes to quarterly observations. As Friedman (1959) suggested, in presenting the earliest results on the permanent income hypothesis of the demand for money, quarterly data might be expected to reflect not only time lags in the adjustment of income expectations to current experience but also lags in the adjustment of actual cash balance to desired balances.[20]

Work on British data certainly seems to bear this suggestion out, for the time lags measured by Goodhart and Crockett seem implausibly long if one interprets them, as they do, as being solely adjustment lags. The results suggest that only just over 10 per cent of any discrepency between actual and desired cash balances is made good over three months.[21] Laidler and Parkin found similarly long lags and were able to show that the somewhat shorter and *a priori* more plausible lags presented by Fisher were probably the result of biases resulting from the specification of the function he fitted.[22] They were also able to show that much more plausible results were obtainable when the lag effect was shared between an expectations lag and an adjustment lag.

In principle there is no difficulty in sorting out these two types of lag. Feige (1967) successfully did so using annual data for the United States, confirming Friedman's contention that for annual data it was the permanent income lag that was all-important. Laidler and Parkin's results for Britain are a good deal less clear-cut then Feige's but, taken at face value, they seem to show that the equilibrium demand for money in Britain depends upon permanent income and that over 80 per cent of any discrepency

between actual and desired cash balances is made up over a
three-month period. [23]

Finally it is worth noting that these quarterly results for the
1950's and '60s also throw some light on the question of the
homogeneity of the demand for money in the general price level.
Laidler and Parkin found evidence of a proportional relationship
between the demand for nominal balances and the price level—
indeed, this was the most definite conclusion to emerge from
that study—while Goodhart and Crockett, who constrained their
functions to produce the same lag in the adjustment of nominal
balances to changes in real income, the interest rate and the
price level, nevertheless obtained results consistent with a long-
run price level elasticity of about unity.[24] These two sets of
results are not directly comparable, since Laidler and Parkin did
not investigate the question of lagged response to price level
change, while Goodhart and Crockett did not attempt to test
hypotheses about different speeds of the demand for money's
response to changes in different variables, but they do provide
evidence in favour of the homogeneity postulate; Goodhart and
Crockett's results in particular add weight to Friedman's (1959)
suggestion that the notion of a 'permanent price level' measured
as some average of current and lagged values of prices might
well prove helpful in explaining the demand for nominal balances.

Now this evidence for Britain certainly points to the existence of a stable demand for money function in that economy. If
this matter is not as well established as it is for the United
States it is likely that this is the result rather of less work having
been done on the problem for Britain than of there being any
fundamental difference between the two economies. At least
the evidence seems to be strong enough to warrant my continuing
this paper 'as if' the existence of this particular link in the
causal chain between the quantity of money and the level of
economic activity was well established. For the United States the
evidence is overwhelming, and for Britain it is at the very least
highly suggestive.

What of the other links? To establish the *possibility* of the
quantity of money affecting the level of economic activity we
require evidence both of the existence of a demand for money
function and, if we are to stay within the Hicks-Hansen framework, of a relationship between expenditure and interest rates.
That there also exists the possibility of a direct wealth effect
between the quantity of money and expenditure whenever the
money stock does not bear interest at the competitive rate has
recently been demonstrated by Pesek and Saving (1967) but,
in the absence of any evidence as to the empirical significance of
such a wealth effect, those who want to establish the potential
importance of the quantity of money must rely on the expenditure—

interest rate relationship. Given a stable demand for money
relationship, and given that there is evidence enough that changes
in the quantity of money have not always been the consequence of
changes in the level of income (a matter I shall take up below),
then the existence of stable money multiplier relationships provides strong indirect evidence that some classes of expenditure
at least are interest-sensitive. However, direct evidence has
always been less easy to come by, and this has been troublesome
to monetary economists.

This paper cannot now turn into a survey of theories and
evidence on expenditure functions, but it is worth while at least
pointing out that this particular gap does now seem to be in the
process of being filled. In a series of papers Jorgenson (*cf.* 1963
for the most accessible of these papers) has presented a theory
of business investment in which the interest rate figures and
which copes reasonably well with explaining a good deal of
observed behaviour; Hamburger (1967) has produced evidence
of the influence of interest rates on consumer demand for durable
goods; Wright (1969) reports the existence of a relationship
between consumption and interest rates. Less direct evidence
comes from Cagan (1969a), who shows that there is a systematic
relationship between the lag between economic activity and
interest rates at business cycle turning points and the length of the
subsequent cycle phase. He interprets this relationship as reflecting the—albeit considerably lagged—influence of interest
rates on economic activity. The picture that is beginning to
emerge here is one of a widely diffused influence of interest rates
on expenditure. If their influence on any one class of expenditure
is not great the breadth of the area over which they do have an
influence nevertheless makes them a potentially significant
determinant of the level of economic activity. The evidence cited
here is all for the United States; there appears to be growing up
no such systematic body of knowledge about the role of interest
rates in expenditure functions in the British economy. Again
we have a problem area that requires some work.[25]

Taken all in all, the evidence on the demand for money function, that on the money multipliers and that on the role of interest
rates as an influence on various classes of expenditure at the very
least puts the burden of proof firmly upon those who would deny
the possibility of the quantity of money having a systematic
influence on economic activity. However, the question of what
can happen is not the same question as what *did* happen at any
particular moment in time. Before it can be concluded that the
quantity of money has had a systematic effect on economic activity
it must be shown that variations in the quantity of money to which
variations in the level of economic activity are attributed have

not come about as a result of the very variations they are supposed to explain.

This is not a matter about which one can generalise. The very
nature of the problem requires careful study of specific cases, and,
as far as Britain is concerned one of the consequences of the
until recently prevailing view among economists of the basic
irrelevance of money has been the historical studies of the
determination of the quantity of money have been a relatively
neglected problem. For the United States this is far from being
the case, and that country's economic history provides us with
what have become classic test cases in the shape of the episodes
1929-33 and 1933-41. That there was a close relationship between
the quantity of money and the level of money income during both
these periods is now well known, but the standard interpretation
given to this association until recently has been that it demonstrated conclusively that (a) it was impossible to use monetary
policy to offset a downturn (1929-33) and (b) it was impossible
to use monetary policy to promote an upturn once the trough was
reached. Variations in the quantity of money, in short, were looked
on as being the consequences of changes in the level of income
during these episodes.

It is now widely accepted that the direction of causation was
just the opposite, that the downturn was the consequence of
monetary changes, and that lack of sufficiently expansionary
monetary policy prolonged the trough; but since Professor
Kaldor (1970) has challenged these views, particularly about the
1929-33 episode, in a recent and widely publicised lecture, it is
probably worthwhile going quickly over the sequence of events
again.[26] A falling off in the rate of growth of the money supply
beginning in mid-1928 preceded a mild cyclical downturn which
the National Bureau dates as having started in August 1929.
October saw the stock market crash, which was followed by a
contraction in the stock of high-powered money and in the money
stock itself.[27] The former fell by 4·6 per cent of its 1929 value
between October 1929 and October 1930, and the latter by 3·3
per cent, while the deposit—currency ratio of the public and the
deposit-reserve ratio of the commercial banks stayed roughly
constant, changing from 11·13 to 11·29 and from 12·723 to 12·716
respectively over the same period. The first of a series of banking crises occurred in October 1930 and immediately thereafter
both ratios, particularly the deposit-currency ratio, began to fall
steeply, setting off a series of further crises, the last of which
occurred in January 1933. June 1933 saw the public's deposit-
currency ratio at 5·08 and the commercial banks' deposit-
reserve ratio at 8·15, so that although the quantity of high-powered
money had by the time increased by 10·1 per cent since October

1929 (15·2 per cent since October 1930) the money stock had fallen by 35·3 per cent since October 1929.[28]

The interpretation put upon this sequence of events by Friedman and Schwartz is that a mild downturn was transformed into a major catastrophe by the failure of the central bank to act as a lender of last resort during the series of banking crises and by its failure to increase the quantity of high-powered money sufficiently to offset the shifts in the deposit-currency ratio consequent upon the public's loss of faith in the banks' ability to redeem their deposits if asked and the shift in the deposit-reserve ratio that reflected the banks' loss of faith in the public's willingness to maintain their deposits. According to Friedman and Schwartz the disturbances orginating in the monetary sector were the cause of disturbances in the level of economic activity.

According to Kaldor, on the contrary, the downturn originated in the real sector, and happened despite a monetary expansion, his evidence of this being the increase in the quantity of high-powered money between 1929 and 1933 already alluded to. The fall in the public's deposit-currency ratio he attributes to the changing pattern of transactions as income fell and in particular to the fall-off in financial transactions after the stock market crash, while the fall in the banks' deposit-reserve ratio is put down to their inability to make loans in the face of contracting demand for credit. The public's loss of confidence in the banking system seems to be of little significance for Kaldor, but since he does not explain, nor indeed attempt to explain, why a downturn that began in August 1929 and a stock market crash that occurred in October 1929 should not begin to have any significant effect on either of these ratios until November 1930, which just happens to be the month immediately following a series of important bank failures—a piece of timing he fails to mention—there seems to be no reason to take his interpretation of the events of 1929-33 very seriously.[29]

Matters are less clear-cut when it comes to dealing with events in the years following 1933, for although 1933-37 was the longest peace-time expansion until the 1960s, and although it was accompanied by an increasing money stock, the quantity of high-powered money increased more rapidly than did the money stock over the period; much of the effect of its growth was offset by a continued fall in the banks' deposit-reserve ratio. The traditional explanation of this is that the recovery originated on the real side of the economy, that the money supply increased in response to the growth in income, but that the ever-growing quantity of free reserves held by the banking system was evidence of monetary policy's inability to speed up the expansion. It is not immediately obvious that the growth in the free reserve ratio that continued in 1936 is interpretable as reflecting the banks' response to the shocks of the 1930-33 period, particularly since the public's deposit-currency ratio had stabilised itself by the end of 1934; thus the proposition that monetary policy was 'pushing on a string' over the 1933-37 period has a good deal of superficial appeal.

There are, however, two crucial facts with which this explanation fails to deal. First, a slow-down in the rate of growth of the money stock preceded the sharp downturn of 1937, when the 'pushing on a string' argument should have had it following. Second, although the time path of the money supply partly followed that of high-powered money, the monetary tightening was greatly accentuated by a series of increases in required reserve ratios which began in 1936 and continued into 1937. These changes should have simply had the effect of turning free reserves into required reserves if the existence of free reserves was due to a lack of investment opportunities for the banks. In fact the changes in question were met by attempts by the banks to restore their free reserve ratios to 1936 levels, attempts which by 1940 had met with success and are explicable only in terms of the free reserves in question performing an economic function for the banks that held them, a function that was sufficiently valuable for those banks to forego earning opportunities in order to acquire and hold free reserves.[30]

For the United States in the 1930s, then, I would argue that the case for variations in the quantity of money as a cause rather than a consequence of variations in economic activity is clear for the 1929-33 episode, and at least plausible—more plausible than the contrary case, in my view—for the 1933-40 period.[31] Since this has always been *the* case cited to prove the ineffectiveness of monetary policy, *the* period during which, despite the efforts of the authorities, the chain of causation could, allegedly, most clearly be seen to run from changes in the level of economic activity to the money stock rather than vice versa, and since Friedman and Schwartz, in addition to having decisively refuted this view, have been able to show just as decisively for many other episodes that the main line of causation has gone from money to economic activity, it is safe to conclude that as far as that economy is concerned the *possibility* of money affecting economic activity exists, in the shape of a well established transmission mechanism, while there is no shortage of evidence of historical episodes in which the direction of causation *has* gone in that direction.

For Britain, not only is the case of the possibility less well established—though it is, as I have argued above, plausible enough—but we do not as yet possess the kind of detailed historical analysis which would enable us to argue that such possibility has turned into actuality in any particular episode. Indeed, for one episode

at least, namely the years since the revival of 'monetary policy'
in the early 1950s, what we know suggests that the quantity of
money has had little if any causative role to play, however
important a variable it could have been and whatever role it
might have played as an *indicator* of policy. All this is a direct
consequence of 'monetary policy' in post-war Britain having
been an interest rate policy.

What is being argued here is not just that the quantity of
money has been an endogenous variable, in the sense that variations in it are the result of fluctuations elsewhere in the economic
system, over the period in question. For example, variations
in the quantity of high-powered money can be the consequence of
balance of payments fluctuations under a fixed exchange rate
system, and can still lead on to variations in the quantity of
money and hence in the level of economic activity.[32] What is at
issue is the special nature of the endogeneity of the money
supply when a central bank decides to act in the open market so
as to achieve a given interest rate pattern on government securities and hence on securities generally.

A central bank can carry out such a policy only by standing
ready to buy and sell securities at a given price, and since it
must carry out its transactions in terms of high-powered money
it necessarily gives up all control of the money supply when it
seeks a peg interest rates. In terms of the Hicks-Hansen model,
the quantity of money ceases to be an exogenous variable and
the rate of interest takes its place; instead of a causative chain
running primarily from the quantity of money through interest
rates to aggregate demand, we get a system in which the interest
rate directly affects the level of economic activity so that, the
two principle determinants of the demand for money being
determined, the money supply passively adjusts in order to
maintain equilibrium in the money market.[33] In such a system
as this the rate and direction of change of the money supply will
usually be reliable indicators of the ease or tightness of monetary
policy—they may indeed by more reliable indicators than the
level of interest rates that the bank is trying to maintain—but this
is a far cry from variations in the money supply causing anything.

That the control of interest rates has been the Bank of
England's primary concern over the last twenty years or so
seems to be widely recognised by participants on all sides of
contemporary monetary debates. Though Mrs Schwartz (1969)
finds some evidence of recognition of the importance of the
quantity of money on the Bank's part in its evidence to the Radcliffe committee, she concedes that the publication of the Report
of the committee seems to have finally enshrined the structure of
interest rates as the centrepiece of monetary policy. At the same

time, some model similar to that which I have sketched out above must surely underlie Kaldor's insistence that the main determinant of variations in the money supply of Britain since the war has been fluctuations in government borrowing. The money supply must fluctuate in tune with such borrowing if the price of government debt is not permitted to vary in order to equilibrate its supply and demand.[34]

None of this means, of course, that had the quantity of money been determined independently of the level of economic activity it could not have exerted an important influence on that activity. Whether or not it would have done so depends upon the existence or otherwise of a stable demand for money function and a relationship between interest rates and aggregate demand.[35] It does, however, mean that it did not do so during this particular episode, though the recent revival of interest in the quantity of money as an instrument of economic policy still makes it worthwhile to ask further questions about the way in which this variable might operate if used. The evidence of this and the preceding section of this paper, though there are still formidable gaps in it, is surely strong enough to persuade even quite sceptical readers that the possibility of the quantity of money having a systematic effect on economic activity certainly exists, and that it certainly has in fact had such effects in some, if not all, episodes of recent economic history. However, fundamental to the question of using the quantity of money (or any other variable, for that matter) as a policy variable is the question of the time lags involved in the processes whereby it has its effect. It is no use manipulating a policy variable, no matter how sure one may be of its effects, if one does not know when those effects will occur. I shall turn to a discussion of these lag effects in section IV of this paper, where I shall once more seek to demonstrate the importance of discussing such questions with the help of an explicit model.

IV

The model with which this paper started has not, as we have seen, emerged totally unscathed from empirical investigation. For one thing, there are time lags in the demand for money relationship, and whether one cares to think of them as being mainly adjustment lags or expectation lags is secondary to the general point that their existence, and that of similar lags in the expenditure function, must yield implications about the time path along which the economy adjusts to policy changes. There is, of course, a substantial literature on the subject, particularly on lag effects in monetary policies (*cf.* Mayer, 1967, for a survey), but the bulk of this work is based on only the most flimsy theoretical foundation.

Some of it, (Friedman, 1958, is the most famous example) is concerned mainly with comparing the timing of turning points in various time series, and the hypothesis underlying such time series comparisons seems to be no more formal than that changes in the quantity of money (or its rate of change) lead eventually to changes in the level of economic activity.[36] The transmission mechanism is spelled out clearly enough in more than one place, contrary to what is all too frequently alleged, but there is nothing in the account of this mechanism that tells us explicitly upon what factors the length of the lag depends; there seems to be just a general presumption that in the world, as opposed to a comparative static economic model, causes take time to have effects.[37] Any length of time lag, and any degree of variability in this lag, seem to be compatible with the transmission mechanism that is described.

Most work subsequent to Friedman's has been prompted by dissatisfaction with one aspect or another of his procedures. The most widely known of this work is that of Kareken and Solow (1963). They produce estimates of lag effects at least as long as those presented by Friedman, despite statements to the contrary in the introduction to their study (*cf.* Mayer, 1967). They broke down the transmission mechanism of monetary policy into component stages - change in reserves to change in quantity of money, change in quantity of money to change in interest rates, change in interest rates to change in investment - and attempted to measure the time lags involved at each stage. For some reason that is not explained they did not proceed along this sequence to investigate the length of the lag involved in the working out of the multiplier effect of a change in investment on a change in income; they did not, therefore, have to face up to the difficulties involved in investigating the feedback effects of changing income on interest rates.[38] Their underlying model, in short, appears to have been a sequential one, in which cause and effect move in a unique direction, rather than being one in which goods and money markets mutually interact: this despite the fact that the analysis of such interaction is central to post-Keynesian macro-economics, even at the simple level of the Hicks-Hansen type of model set out at the beginning of this paper.

Indeed, most of the work on lag effects seems to suffer from a fundamental methodological defect, whether it follows Friedman's example or that of Kareken and Solow. This defect, which probably lies at the root of the dissatisfaction which many - not least those who have carried out the work in question - feel about our current state of knowledge on the question of lag effects, is that the work lacks an explicit theoretical basis. It has concerned itself with asking empirical questions about how long are the time lags between changes in variables without first

concerning itself with the more basic theoretical questions of
why there should be time lags in the first place, and what factors
might be expected to determine their length. Thus, at best, this
work provides economists with a set of facts. Without an explicit
theoretical framework within which these facts may be organised,
it is impossible to analyse them, fit them together or assess their
significance.

Those empirical results on structural equations which show
that permanent income, rather than measured income, belongs in
the demand for money function tell us about one particular lag
effect, and they explain its existence in terms of people being
slow to adjust their long-run income expectations to current
experience. The hypothesis that there are lags in the demand for
money function because people find it too costly to adjust their
money holdings fast enough to maintain them constantly in
equilibrium also provides a theory about the existence of a particular time lag. Such lags have been found to exist elsewhere
than in the demand for money function, and analysis of the way in
which such lagged functions interact in a model based on the Hicks-
Hansen framework seems to me to represent a promising way of
investigating the whole leads-lags problem. In principle this line
of work opens up the prospect of an explicit theory of income
determination that has time lags between changes in policy
variables and changes in the level of income as an integral part
of its structure.

A little work along these lines has already been done, on
quite a simple level, and it would be wrong to look for much in
the way of a direct empirical applications for the results so far
achieved. However, even when treated as analytic exercises,
such models can produce quite startling and counter-intuitive
results. They totally undermine the fundamental assumption underlying most measuring exercises that the time path of income towards a new equilibrium after some policy change is smooth and
unidirectional. It may not be. They show that the simultaneous
interaction of real goods markets and money markets makes it
just as impossible to treat lag effects of fiscal policy as being
independent of money market behaviour as it is to treat monetary
policy lags as being independent of real goods market behaviour.
Moreover time lags turn out to depend upon the parameters of the
underlying static equilibrium relationships as well as upon the
parameters of the lag processes themselves, while apparently
slight changes in the specification of lag processes turn out to
lead to major changes in the behaviour of the complete model.

With expenditure functions and the demand for money function as candidates for the inclusion of lag effects, and with expectations lags and adjustment lags to choose between, or even to
use simultaneously, the number of models that could be built and

analysed is large. However, what is required here is illustration of the results stated above, rather than a complete and tedious taxonomy, and the results in question can nearly all be derived from a model which was first set out, mainly in geometric terms, in Laidler (1968).[39] The model in question is simply a linear in the real variables version of the Hicks-Hansen model, with permanent income replacing measured income in the expenditure and demand for money functions, though later it will be necessary to replace the expectations lag implicit in the use of permanent income in the demand for money function with an adjustment lag in order to derive the final result asserted in the previous paragraph, namely that such an apparently minor change makes an important difference to the model's behaviour.

Since the price level is to be held constant in the following analysis it is notationally convenient to give it a value of unity, and, with all other symbols having their usual meaning, the model may be set out as follows.

$$Y_t = E_t = kY_t^e + \overline{A}_t - ar_t \tag{17}$$

$$\overline{M}_t = M_{d_t} = mY_t^e - lr_t \tag{18}$$

$$Y_t^e = bY_t + (1-b)Y_{t-1}^e \tag{19}$$

It yields, as a reduced form for income...

$$Y_t = \frac{1}{1-bz}\,\overline{A}_t - \frac{1-b}{1-bz}\,\overline{A}_{t-1} + \frac{1}{\dfrac{l}{a}(1-bz)}\,\overline{M}_t$$

$$- \frac{1-b}{\dfrac{l}{a}(1-bz)}\,\overline{M}_{t-1} + \frac{1-b}{1-bz}\,Y_{t-1} \tag{20}$$

where

$$z \equiv (k - \frac{am}{l}). \tag{21}$$

Since $0 < k < 1$ and $0 < b < 1$ it follows that $z < 1$ and

$$0 < \frac{1-b}{1-bz} < 1 \tag{22}$$

A solution for steady state income $\hat{Y}$ is easily obtained by substituting $\hat{Y} = Y_t^e = Y_t$ for all t into equations 17, 18 and 19. It is

$$\hat{Y} = \frac{1}{1-z}\,\overline{A}_t + \frac{1}{\dfrac{l}{a}(1-z)}\,\overline{M}_t \tag{23}$$

Because the model converges smoothly on this steady state solution after any disturbance it is possible to analyse qualitatively the length of the lags involved in the response of income to changes in the money stock and to changes in autonomous expenditure by comparing the 'impact multipliers', the coefficients of A_t and M_t, in equation 20 with the "steady state multipliers", the coefficients of the same variables in equation 23. The bigger is a steady state multiplier relative to an impact multiplier, the 'longer' will we call the lag effect in the response of the level of income to the variable in question. We may thus treat L_m as an index of the time lag involved in the operation of monetary policy, and L_a as a similar index for fiscal policy (in as much as this involves changing autonomous expenditure); we get

$$L_a = L_m = \frac{1 - bz}{1 - z} \qquad (24)$$

In this model—and it cannot be too much stressed that this property belongs to one particular model rather than to any actual economy—the lag effects of monetary and fiscal policy are identical.[40] Their interdependence is, of course, a more general phenomenon. . . .

Perhaps the first thing to note [about the ratios implicit in equation 24] is that it is only if z is positive that we have a unidirectional time path of income towards its new equilibrium value after a change in the money stock or in autonomous expenditure. If z is negative, the impact multipliers are actually larger than the steady state multipliers. The more sensitive is the demand for money to income and the less sensitive it is to the interest rate (the higher is m and the smaller is l), and the less sensitive is expenditure to income and the more sensitive it is to interest rates (the smaller is k and the larger is a), the more likely is this to happen. Thus at least one important characteristic of the lag pattern with which income responds to a change in an exogenous variable is dependent on the characteristics of the steady state behaviour equations and not on the time lags involved in the short-run versions of those relationships.[41]

It is obvious from equation 24 that the length of the lag effect always depends upon the value of the parameters of these basic behaviour relationships, so that if the parameters of the basic steady state relationships of our model vary, then so will the lags we are analysing. For example, if the relationship between expenditure and income is unstable, then so are the lag patterns with which the economy will respond to monetary and fiscal policy. Indeed, policy itself might affect the lags: if changes in tax rates alter the propensity to spend out of income, then the lags in the model's behaviour will also be affected.

What about b, the parameter of the expectations formation mechanism, which alone is responsible for introducing lags (as opposed to determining the length of those lags) into the model under analysis? Even here there is not much to be said in general. From equation 21 we can derive

$$\frac{\delta L}{\delta b} = \frac{-z}{(1-z)} \quad \begin{array}{l} < 0 \text{ if } z > 0 \\ = 0 \text{ if } z = 0 \\ > 0 \text{ if } z < 0 \end{array} \qquad (25)$$

The sign of this derivative depends upon the sign of z; if the lag is long already, in the sense that the impact multiplier is small relative to the steady state multiplier, then the longer is the expectations formation lag (the smaller is b) the longer will the lag be. This idea is intuitively appealing enough, but it is not so obvious, though equally true, that, if the lag is already so short that the impact multiplier is bigger than the steady state multiplier, then a lower value of b implies a still shorter lag.

Now of course all the foregoing results have been derived in terms of a very special model, in which the only source of time lags is the income expectations formation mechanism of equation 3. We must be particularly careful about generalising from this special case because it is easy to show that only a slight change in the model is needed to alter its characteristics in an important fashion.

If we replace the expectations lag in the demand for money function with an adjustment lag, so that the demand for money function becomes

$$M_{d_t} = cmY_t - clr_t + (1-c)M_{t-1} \qquad (18a)$$

we do not alter the steady state solution of the model at all. .. However, the impact multiplier that we get for autonomous expenditure becomes

$$\frac{1}{1 - kb + \frac{a}{l}m}$$

It is crucially different from that contained in equation 20. The existence of time lags in the money market now has no effect at all on its value and it is unambiguously smaller than the steady state multiplier. This result suggests that it is of extreme importance to distinguish between adjustment lags and expectation lags in the demand for money function, and, as already noted, it should make us wary indeed of treating the specific results generated in this section of the paper as having significance other than that which may be attached to them as the outcome of an analytic exercise.

However, even looked at in this rather narrow light the results in question do seem to yield important lessons for work in
the general area of the analysis of the lag effects of policy. First,
they suggest that when the interaction of real goods and money
markets is taken account of, as surely it should be, the practice
of treating the causative mechanism of either monetary or fiscal
policy as a purely sequential one, with no feedback effects, comes
to appear suspect, to say the very least. They also suggest that to
treat the time lags which appear in the world as if they were
purely the result of the fact that it 'takes time' to approach a
steady state solution, and to treat the analysis of steady state
solutions and of time lags as independent problems, is misleading.
There is a strong interdependence here. Finally the fact that
apparently relatively small changes in the specification of a model
can make an important difference to the time lag patterns implicit
in it suggests that we shall have to do a great deal of careful
empirical work, and not only on the structure of the monetary
sector, before we can be even remotely confident that the model
which gets pieced together as a result of that work will give us
an accurate picture of the lag effects present in any economy.[42]

Not only does the foregoing analysis give us some tentative
insight into the empirical questions that need to be asked when
considering the length of the lag effects of monetary and fiscal
policy. It is equally informative as to where to look when investigating the variability of those lags effects. Movements in the
values of the parameters of the structural equations of the model
alter not only the amounts by which given policy changes are
likely to affect the level of economic activity but also the speed
with which they do so.

Similarly, variations in the parameters governing the behaviour of the expectations formation and adjustment mechanisms
will also lead to variation in the length of lag effects in the kinds
of model with which we are dealing, and the determinants of these
parameters are certainly worth investigating. I would conjecture
that these parameters are more subject to short-period fluctuations than are those of the steady state structural relationships of
the economy, and there is already a certain amount of evidence to
support the proposition that they do vary importantly.

Consider the expectations lag first of all. This is derived
from an error-learning mechanism whereby economic units revise their expectations about the value of some economic variable
in proportion to the size of the error in their previous prediction.
To suggest that the proportion in question tends to fluctuate about
some mean value is one thing, but to suggest that it is a constant
is quite another. Presumably it is necessary to form expectations
about economic variables because there are costs involved in
acting in ignorance or in error, and there is no reason to suppose

that the costs involved in making an error depend only upon the
size of that error and not upon its sign. Furthermore there is no
reason why the relationship between the costs of making errors
and the magnitude of the errors in question needs to be a simple
proportional one.

This line of argument suggests that, when dealing, for example,
with lags involved in forming income expectations, the parameter
b might depend upon both the magnitude and the sign of the discrepency between expected and realised income. Though this
matter has not been looked into at all in the context of income
expectations, at least as far as this writer is aware, Morrison's
(1966) suggestion that commercial banks tend to 'lengthen their
memories' when forming expectations about 'permanent deposits'
in the wake of heavy unexpected losses of deposits does amount
to applying this kind of analysis to an expectations formation problem.[43] Underlying this suggestion is the by no means unreasonable
argument that heavy unexpected losses of deposits are more
costly to banks than heavy unexpected gains and are hence more
likely to induce them to alter the kind of expectations formation
mechanism that led them into error; the specific alteration that
Morrison suggests they make is to begin giving less weight to
recent experience, to revise their expectations less in the face of
current fluctuations in their deposits. This hypothesis, as I noted
above, enables Morrison to deal with the question of the slow
build-up of large amounts of free reserves by United States commercial banks in the post-1933 period, and deserves attention for
that reason alone. Probably more important, however, is the fact
that it provides a striking example of the way in which the error-
learning type of expectations formation mechanism can be extended and made more flexible in order to widen the class of phenomena with which it is capable of dealing, an example which would
almost certainly be worth following up in other contexts.

The question of the variability of adjustment lags has also
been worked on recently, and in the context of the demand for
money function. Lags in the adjustment of cash balances to
equilibrium arise because, although it it costly to be out of
equilibrium, adjustment itself is not a costless process. A potential source of variations in such lags is not hard to find; the cost
of adjusting cash balances will depend upon what else it is that
must be changed to restore equilibrium. One cannot, after all, have
an individual with too few (or many) cash balances without his
simultaneously having too much (or little) of something else.
For example, if a deficiency in money holdings is matched by too
many building society deposits one would expect the restoration
of equilibrium to be a good deal cheaper and more rapid than if
the matching disequilibrium were too big a house.

This kind of question has been investigated for the household sector in the United States by Motley (1970), who finds that the overall composition of that sector's portfolio does indeed exert an important influence on the speed with which any part of it is brought into equilibrium. The importance of work along these lines should be obvious, and it is intriguing to note the implication that portfolio analysis, far from being an alternative to the demand and supply of money approach to the issues being dealt with in this paper, becomes a necessary complement to this approach once the question of lag effects arises.[44]

Now the analysis of lag effects was carried out above in the context of a model in which the price level is taken as given and all adjustments are in quantities. This is clearly unsatisfactory from any viewpoint but that of an analytic exercise and provides yet another reason for not looking for too much practical significance in its results. This is not to say that the model cannot be extended to deal, in a primitive way, with price level changes. If we postulate, as we did at the outset of this paper, a unique full-employment level of income, then permanent income becomes equal to measured income at a level fixed exogenously by supply side factors and the behaviour of the model is then exactly that of the simple Hicks-Hansen framework; or rather it would be, were it not for a factor that I have so far neglected in this section of the paper, namely the whole area of price level expectations.[45]

We do not yet have the kind of knowledge that would enable us to analyse in terms of a variant of the Hicks-Hansen model the time paths of output and the price level, as they interact in response to exogenous shocks. Indeed, our lack of a satisfactory model of this interaction is now widely recognised as perhaps *the* crucial gap in short-run macro-economic theory. The kind of phenomenon with which any such model would have to deal is the apparently all-pervasive inability of economies to meet a contraction in aggregate demand even in the presence of inflation without important contractions in real output.[46] We observe this phenomenon in both contemporary Britain and the United States, where rising unemployment rather than a falling rate of inflation is the most noticeable short-run response to restrictive policies, and we see it in the history of the inter-war depressions in both countries, where rapid price deflations were nevertheless accompanied by massive unemployment.

Exactly how fluctuations in aggregate demand spread their effects over time between prices and output remains mysterious, though it is coming to look increasingly as if the key to these problems will be found to lie in the analysis of price expectations. Formal analysis of the type presented earlier is out of the question, given the present state of this writer's grasp of the mechanisms involved, but an informal sketch of the kind of process that might be fruitfully analysed is perhaps an appropriate way to close this discussion of the leads and lags problem.

If it is postulated that the price level which is relevant for the demand for nominal balances is a permanent price level rather than a current one, then it is hard to resist the implication that the same concept ought to be relevant as far as the money wage bargain is concerned.[47] If this is accepted, however, and if the money wage determines the *current* supply price of output, then the scene is set for wages, prices and output to behave asymmetrically, depending upon whether goods are in excess demand or excess supply.[48] If we begin with a situation in the region of full employment, with stable wages and prices, then an increase in demand for goods will lead to prices being bid up, and, as higher prices feed into price level expectations, to money wages following.[49]

However, if instead we have a fall-off in demand, caused by either monetary or fiscal contraction — the source is irrelevant — then the resulting downward pressure on prices will meet with resistance from the supply side. There will be no reason for the labour force to accept money wage cuts unless it anticipates price cuts; to do so would be to accept a cut in real wages while there was still full employment. To the extent that price expectations are extrapolated from past experience they will not be modified until prices begin to fall; however, to the extent that on the supply side prices are determined by money wages they will not fall until those money wages start to fall. Hence the initial response to a fall in demand is likely to be a fall in output and employment. Moreover it should be noted that, if we had begun the foregoing analysis in an economy whose past experience led those concerned with the wage bargain to expect a given rate of inflation, then a fall in demand would still lead to a fall in output initially. If real wages were to be maintained stable in such an economy, money wage bargains would be struck for a given rate of change of money wages, and the rate of change of money wages would not fall off until the rate of price inflation began to decline. This in turn would require a slow-down in the rate of money wage inflation to set it in motion.[50]

How long a return to full employment would take in such a situation presumably depends upon how fast the real wage responds to the pressure of unemployment, how fast prices (or their rate of change) respond to money wages (or their rate of change) and how fast price level expectations respond to current price level variations.[51] Given some of the rather startling results that the simple dynamic model dealt with earlier produced, it would be rash indeed to say anything more specific about the manner in which these factors are likely to interact and

the behaviour they are likely to produce without first analysing
an explicit model of the processes I have sketched out in the last
few paragraphs. The reader will not, I hope, hold it against this
writer that he has as yet been unable to work out such a model in
a satisfactory manner.[52]

V

A long summary of the issues dealt with in this paper is hardly
necessary. First and foremost I have argued that, because the
manner in which monetary policy—or fiscal policy, for that
matter—works involves not just one but all sectors of the economy,
some knowledge of the structural relationships that exist in any
economy is needed before monetary policy can be usefully discussed. However suggestive reduced form relationships may
be—and I have argued at some length in part II of this paper that
such relationships tell us quite a lot less than is sometimes
supposed—it is impossible to interpret them fully without independent knowledge of the underlying structure of the economy to
which they appertain.

A stable relationship between the quantity of money and the
level of income taken by itself is open to a variety of interpretations. It is only when we have convincing evidence, as I believe
we do for the United States, if not yet for Britain, that variations
in the quantity of money took place independently of the variations
in the level of income to which they are related, and evidence that
a transmission mechanism working through a stable demand for
money function and a relationship between interest rates and
expenditure can be shown to exist, as once again I think is easier
to claim for the United States than for Britain, that such evidence
falls into place as one piece in a complex pattern of observations
which, taken overall, can firmly establish the importance of the
quantity of money as a determinant of the level of economic
activity. . . . Though this writer is on the whole willing to argue
that variations in the quantity of money can have just as strong
and predictable effects in Britain as they do in the United States,
there is as yet a great deal of room for scepticism about this
conclusion, scepticism which can be worn down (or justified, depending on the results) only by a great deal more empirical work.

However, if we know less about Britain than we do about the
United States, there is still a great deal to be learned about the
latter economy, particularly on the matter of the time lags involved
in the response of the economy to policy measures. Again, I have
argued that the answers to questions in this area are to be sought
in the analysis of structural models of the economy. For one
thing, the very parameters that determine the static equilibrium
properties of the economy also have an important influence on the

characteristics of the time path by which static equilibrium is approached. While we do already have some, albeit simple, economic explanations in terms of learning and adjustment mechanisms of the existence of the time lags, the work that has been done on measuring lag effects, taken by itself, serves mainly to emphasise our ignorance of these matters; it provides a set of facts that need a model to explain them, and we are only just beginning to build up such models. In particular our understanding of the factors that determine the way in which variations in money income divide themselves up between variations in real income and variations in prices is imperfect indeed.

However, the main difficulty in any science is knowing which questions to ask, and how to ask them. If this paper has put a sharper focus upon some of the currently unsettled questions in monetary economics and the methods which might usefully be adopted in solving them, then it will have served the purpose that prompted its being written.[53]

NOTES

[1]   Reprinted from G. Clayton, J. Gilbert and R. Sedgwick (eds.), *Monetary Theory and Monetary Policy in the 1970s,* London, Oxford University Press, 1971. In addition to the official discussants, Frank Brechling and Douglas Fisher, I have received helpful comments on earlier drafts of this paper from Milton Friedman, Charles Goodhart, Richard Harrington, Michael Parkin, David Sheppard, Ian Steedman and John Williamson. A number of important papers appeared while this one was in the course of preparation, leading to a far greater than normal amount of revision and rewriting. Particular thanks are due to my secretary, Mrs Jane Wild, for coping so patiently with the extra burden of typing this produced. Finally, I am deeply indebted to the Houblon-Norman Fund for the generous financial support without which this paper could not have been written.

[2]   Among these surveys may be numbered Goodhart and Crockett (1970), especially appendix 1, Harris (1968), Johnson (1962, 1967, 1970), Laidler (1969a) and Walters (1969, 1970). The Walters references are particularly valuable as guides to work on the British economy.

[3]   In equation 1 the aggregation of expenditure into one category is meant to leave open the possibilities that interest rates affect consumption and income affects investment. As Friedman (1970) recently pointed out, it is an empirical hypothesis that the borderline between those categories of expenditure largely dependent upon income and those largely independent of it corresponds to the consumer expenditure-investment borderline.

4   As the reader will notice, this model is a linearised version of the model set out by Alford (1960) and also used by Friedman (1970). The assumption adopted here to deal with the under-determination of the model is the simplest available way of filling in what Friedman refers to as the "missing equation" (1970, p. 219). The writer prefers this reverse L-shaped aggregate supply curve to the frequently used upward-sloping one whose construction requires the assumption of an aggregate production function in which the capital stock is always fully utilised. This should not be taken as implying that the reverse L is a very satisfactory construction either, however. The relationship between the price level and real income is taken up below in section IV of this paper.

5   *Cf.* Walters (1970), p. 51

6   Friedman and Meiselman (1963) produced the first compre-hensive study of this type for the United States, and their results were challenged by Hester (1964), Deprano and Mayer (1965) and Ando and Modigliani (1965). The latter three papers were almost solely concerned with showing how changes in the definition of 'autonomous expenditure' could improve the performance of the "Keynesian" hypothesis. Only Ando and Modigliani touched upon the more fundamental issues, with which I am concerned here, of the ability of the tests to discriminate between the hypotheses at stake. They did so in an appendix to (1965) which apparently was written after their paper was completed (*cf.* Friedman and Meiselman, 1965, p. 781, for evidence of this) and did not influence the procedures they adopted in the paper. In any event, by failing to distinguish between some real and nominal variables in this appendix they missed some rather serious problems. The re-search staff of the Federal Reserve Bank of St Louis have also done work on multipliers recently (e.g. Andersen and Jordan, 1968) but since this work is aimed more at establishing empirical regularities which may be useful for policy purposes than at testing basic propositions about monetary theory it is less open to criticism than is the earlier work in question; the evidence it provides still cannot be used to distinguish between propositions of economic theory of course.

For Britain, work on Multipliers has been done by Barret and Walters (1966), Sheppard (1970) and Artis and Nobay (1969). It is interesting to note that the latter study, modelled on that of Anderson and Jordan, was unable to produce the kind of stable empirical relationship between the quantity of money and the level of money income for post-war Britain that Anderson and Jordan found for the United States.

7   There is no widely known 'classical' counterpart of the 'Keynesian cross' diagram, though one is easily constructed. Holding the price level constant, if we measure real income on the

horizontal and the real money stock on the vertical axis, then the intersection of the supply and demand for money determines income. Holding real income constant, plotting nominal money on the vertical and the price level on the horizontal axis would turn the diagram into one which determined the price level. In this case, though, the homogenity of the demand function in the independent variable would cease to be simply a matter of geometric convenience as it is in the diagram shown and would instead embody a fundamental hypothesis of monetary theory, namely the proportionality of the demand for nominal money to the general price level.

8   There is, as noted above, an extra empirical hypothesis introduced by this division of expenditure, *cf.* note 3 above. There has been quite a lot of dispute as to where in fact this borderline between 'induced' expenditure and the rest ought to be drawn. The bulk of the 'Friedman-Meiselman' debate centred on this issue, but only Friedman and Meiselman themselves noted that consumer expenditure included expenditure on durable goods which might be better classified as more closely akin to investment than to consumption of non-durables. I am indebted to Michael Hamburger for drawing my attention to this point. His work on the demand for durable goods (1967) lends substance to this suggestion.

9   But there still remains the problem of expenditure on durables; *cf.* note 8. The reader's attention is also drawn to the fact that the relative price of consumption and investment goods can shift. To make the assumption that the prices of both groups of commodities may be represented by the general price level is a simplifying assumption that may not hold true.

10   The $^+$ signs attached to the price variable should be read as indicating that this is to be treated as constant. Thus everything in the discussion that follows applies also to the work of those who have used data cast in real terms in similar tests. (These include Friedman and Meiselman, 1963, and Sheppard, 1970.) This result follows from the assumption of price rigidity in unemployment situations, and this is really a very unsatisfactory assumption. For example, between 1929 and 1933 prices in the US fell by 26·7 per cent while *per capita* income fell by 37·5 per cent. We are faced again with the problem of the missing equation that links output and prices. *Cf.* note 4. The full implication of this observation is that the Hicks-Hansen model is inadequate to explain the data with which it is here confronted, but in the absence of a better model it will have to do.

11   Friedman and Meiselman note this point to some extent when they suggest that the good performance of the 'Keynesian' model in the 1930s may reflect effects of the quantity of money working through its influence on investment, but they do not appear to have

appreciated its full significance for the appropriateness of their
tests. Sheppard (1970) similarly recognises the problem and tests
for the effect. With the money supply lagged, he finds it significant
for the inter-war period for Britain, and recognises its importance
for the interpretation of his results.

12   Given that Friedman's permanent income variable is virtually
a linear transformation of consumption (*cf*. Friedman, 1957), and
given that Friedman found a close relationship between the quantity
of money demanded and permanent income (*cf*. Friedman, 1959), it
is arguable that a good performance on the part of equation 6
merely reflects these relationships and adds nothing to what we
knew from them already.

13   This line of argument seems to have been first brought into
contemporary debates by Hester (1964), who fully recognised the
need to explain the close relationship between money income and
the quantity of money in some way if he wished to adopt a largely
'Keynesian' view of the income determination process.

14   I base this broad generalisation of what the results show on
evidence produced by Friedman and Meiselman (1963), Ando and
Modigliani (1965), Deprano and Mayer (1965) and Hester (1964)
for the US, and by Barret and Walters (1966) and Sheppard (1970)
for the United Kingdom. Note, though, that both Friedman and
Meiselman and Sheppard raised the possibility of causation running from money through 'autonomous' expenditure to income and
'induced' expenditure (*cf*. note 11 above)

15   Thus tests using real variables observed at full employment
periods are, in the context of the model I am using here, fundamentally misconceived. Real income, and hence real 'induced'
expenditure, are determined by supply-side constraints and not
by aggregate demand. It must be borne in mind, though, that a
unique level of full employment output is more a property to the
model we are using than of any actual economy. Again we are
faced with the unsolved problem of the interaction of output and
the price level.

16   This simple 'quantity theory' approach performs extremely
badly for post-war Britain—far worse, indeed, than for the inter-
war years. *Cf*. Walters (1969) for a summary of this evidence.
Note that Laidler and Parkin (1970) have suggested that these difficulties arise from not taking account properly of the lag
structure of the economy rather than from unstable monetary
relationships. The question of time lags is taken up in some
detail in part IV of this paper.

17   Of course, the interest rate does not measure the opportunity
cost of holding money in the Keynesian theory of the speculative
demand for money. However, the absence of evidence for the
existence of a liquidity trap or any marked instability in the
interest elasticity of demand for money, this theory's two charac-

teristic predictions, seems to justify interpreting the interest rate as measuring the opportunity cost of holding money. A simple discussion of the relevant theoretical arguments and of the relevant empirical evidence will be found in Laidler (1969a), pp. 50-6, 97-9.

[18]   For example, Cagan's (1956) study of hyper-inflation suggests that there existed stable monetary relationships in a number of central European countries just after the first world war. Breton (1968) has found stable relationships for Canada, as has Hynes (1967) for Chile. Not all work has been successful in finding stable relationships though. Klein (1956) obtained poor results in studying Germany during the Nazi era, and Friedman's suggestion (1956) that this problem was worthy of further study does not seem to have been taken up as yet.

[19]   Tobin and Swan (1969) put the matter as if interest rate variation and the permanent income hypothesis were alternative explanations of the cyclical behaviour of velocity. Surely this evidence of Walters's for Britain, and evidence produced by Laidler (1966) for the United States, show that both, rather than either, variables are required to provide satisfactory results. There seems to this writer to be a theoretical issue concerning the relationship between the demand for money and interest rates which might repay further investigation. In nearly all theoretical treatments of the demand for money the rate of interest measures the opportunity cost of holding money (the Keynesian speculative demand analysis is an exception). However, as far as empirical studies of the demand for money have been concerned, the choice of which interest rate to use has been dictated as much by what data are available as by any careful consideration of how to measure this opportunity cost.

Now which rate measures the opportunity cost of holding money clearly depends upon how long is the planned holding period of cash balances, upon how long is the horizon over which portfolio compositions are fixed, and this horizon is implicitly or explicity taken as exogenously given in many studies of the demand for money. However, to the extent that one of the motives for holding money as a means of bridging the gap between the receipt of income and the making of expenditures is to avoid the costs involved in buying and selling other assets as cash is received and is needed for disbursement, this holding period is in fact endogenous. The lower is the rate of return *per annum* on an asset the longer must it be held before its ownership covers a given cost of acquiring it and disposing of it. To put the same matter another way, as rates of interest fall the opportunity cost of holding money over any time period falls, so that the demand for money increases; however, an essential aspect of increasing the proportion of money in the portfolio is the lengthening of the horizon over which it is planned to hold money.

The foregoing argument suggests that the very idea of using one interest rate as a measure of *the* opportunity cost of holding money is a simplification. What one has in fact is the whole term structure of interest rates measuring the opportunity cost of holding money over various time periods, with the holding period of money itself being a decision variable. In general, the lower are interest rates the longer is the holding period of money going to be, and hence the longer the rate of interest that measures the opportunity cost of holding money on the margin. This is certainly compatible with the evidence which Cagan (1969b) has recently produced to the effect that longer assets appear to become closer substitutes for money as the level of interest rates falls, and suggests in general that the length of the asset the yield on which measures the opportunity cost of holding money will vary with the level of interest rates in general.

[20]   It might be thought that the existence of all these lags in the demand for money relationship makes the time lag in the effect of monetary policy too long to be consistent with the relatively high short-run multipliers reported by Andersen and Jordan (1968). This is an erroneous conclusion. Tucker (1966) and Laidler (1968) have both shown that to introduce lags into the demand for money relationship, *ceteris paribus*, speeds up the money multiplier process. Friedman (1959) also made this point, though he carried out no detailed analysis of the matter. These points are discussed below in section IV.

[21]   Note that DeLeeuw (1965) got a similarly implausible result with US data.

[22]   *Cf.* Laidler and Parkin (1970), appendix B.

[23]   If we have the following model, with all variables in logs and all symbols having their conventional meaning,

$$m_d^+ = \alpha + \beta y^e + \gamma r$$

$$y^e = \lambda y + (1 - \lambda)y^e$$

$$m = \theta m^+ + (1 - \theta)m_{-1}$$

then successive applications of the Koyck transformation yield

$$m = \alpha\theta\lambda + \beta\theta\lambda y + \gamma\theta r - \gamma\theta(1 - \lambda)r_{-1} + (2 - \theta - \lambda)m_{-1} -$$
$$(1 - \theta)(1 - \lambda)m_{-2}$$

The parameters of this model may be estimated using a constrained least squares technique, and Laidler and Parkin (1970) obtained the following, albeit not very well determined, parameter

estimates: $\alpha = 0\cdot165,\ \beta = 0\cdot673, \gamma = -0\cdot012, \lambda = 0\cdot122,\ \theta = 0\cdot874$.
Cf. Laidler and Parkin (1970), table 2.
24   *Cf.* Goodhart and Crockett (1970), table F, p. 195.
25   Even for the United States, of course, the evidence of the
influence of interest rates on expenditure is the weakest link in the
case for the importance of the quantity of money. The writer is
far from being expert in this literature, but he knows of no study
that finds a predominant effect of interest rates on any particular
class of expenditure. In the face of this kind of evidence the case
for the existence of a transmission mechanism working through
interest rates must rest on the existence of relatively small
effects on widely diffused classes of expenditure, as described by
Friedman and Schwartz (1963b), rather than on a particularly
strong textbook-style influence on business investment. Cagan's
study (1969a) is, to my knowledge, the only one to approach the
empirical evidence from the Friedman-Schwartz point of view and
ought, therefore, to be taken particularly seriously in the present
context.
26   Kaldor attributes the selection of this period as a test case
to Friedman. This is surely to overlook the role that this episode
played as *the* example of the ineffectiveness of monetary policy
in orthodox post-Keynesian expositions of macro-economics.
27   All the figures quoted in the following passage are for three-
month averages centred on the month referred to. To have simply
taken monthly figures would, in this writer's judgement, have unduly exaggerated some of the variations in question, while to
have taken longer averages would have tended to obscure important changes in the series that were taking place extremely
rapidly. All the results quoted are based on figures given in
Friedman and Schwartz (1963a), table A-1, pp. 712-14 (for the
money stock data) and table B-3, pp. 803-4 (for high-powered
money, the deposit reserve ratio and the deposit currency ratio).
     For a period in which events were happening so rapidly it is
difficult indeed to choose summary statistics such as those
quoted here without running the risk of being accused of picking
particular figures to prove one's case where slightly different
data would show matters in a different light. Certainly, by drawing
attention to the timing of events within the 1929-33 period, I am
presenting here a radically different picture to the one which
Kaldor (1970) gives. The reader who wishes to choose between
these conflicting views will find time series charts particularly
revealing. Charts 31 (p. 333) and 64 (opposite p. 684) of Friedman
and Schwartz (1963a) present the relevant data.
28   Thus Kaldor (1970) is correct in picking Friedman (1968) up
for a slip in his American Economic Association presidential
address. High-powered money did indeed increase, not decrease,
over the 1929-33 period. The Friedman and Schwartz's interpre-

tation of this period is in no way dependent on a (false) assertion that high-powered money decreased should, however, be quite apparent to anyone who has read chapter 7 of the *Monetary History*.
[29]   Kaldor (1970, p. 13) makes a great deal of the fact that the deposit-currency ratio in July 1960 was about the same as it was in July 1932, and that this ratio reached a trough during the second world war. He seems to think that this is evidence against the view that the behaviour of the ratio in the early 1930s was the consequence of the public's loss of confidence in the commercial banks. Two observations are in order here. First, what is primarily at stake in the 1929-33 episode is the time path of this ratio, not its level at any moment in time. Second, though Kaldor, in looking for reliable sources on the doctrines of 'the new Monetarism', specifically singles out Cagan as 'someone who can be relied on to follow the master [Freidman] closely ...' (Kaldor, 1970, p. 2), nevertheless ignores his work on the deter- minants of the deposit-currency ratio. Cagan argues that during the war the disruption of normal banking relations caused by increased population mobility, largely due to the expansion of the armed forces, could be expected to increase greatly the demand for cash in a country where banks do not branch across state lines. Cagan also noted the existence of a strong incentive to carry out black-market transactions in terms of currency, and of a related incentive to hide transactions by using currency that arises from high marginal income tax rates. The income tax argument holds for the post-war period as well, of course, while one must not overlook the effects on the deposit-currency ratio of the prohibition of interest payments on demand deposits and the fixing of maximum rates on time deposits. *Cf.* Cagan (1965).
[30]   The most thorough work on this problem (again ignored by Kaldor) is that of Morrison (1966). The most difficult aspect of bank behaviour to explain for those who argue that the build-up of free reserves was the result of purposeful behaviour is the length of time it took. Why was the "shock" of 1931-33 still causing the banks to build up free reserves in 1937? Morrison's explanation is that banks hold free reserves against what they regard as 'transitory deposits', the difference between 'permanent deposits' and actual deposits. He argues that their estimate of permanent deposits is developed from an error-learning mechanism charac- terised by what is usually a rapid rate of adjustment of expecta- tions to experience; Morrison then suggests that this rate of adjustment is significantly slowed down in the face of large and costly errors such as the banks discovered they had made in 1931- 33. This hypothesis about variability in the error-learning mechanism is of potentially much wider application and is discus- sed further in section IV.

31   Kaldor largely confines himself to the 1929-33 episode, and, in
this writer's judgement, weakens his own case by doing so. The
1933-37 period would have provided him with more effective
ammunition with which to attack Friedman, Morrison's work
notwithstanding.
32   [I would not wish to defend this naive comment on the monetary effects of balance of payments disequilibria; *cf.* chapters
8-10 on this and related issues.]
33   The distinction between cause and effect here is to some
extent, though by no means entirely, a matter of semantic convenience. As far as the equilibrium properties of a deterministic
static model are concerned, it makes no substantive difference
whether one thinks of a given quantity of money determining a
given interest rate and level of income or whether one prefers
instead to think in terms of a given interest rate determining
a given level of income and quantity of money. However, if one
introduces a stochastic element into such a model, the distinction
in question might be of some importance in designing a regression experiment, since it would be crucial in determining where
error terms would be found. Furthermore, without introducing
a stochastic element, in a dynamic model where the public has
less than perfect foresight it is not difficult to conceive of an
announced interest rate influencing interest rate expectations in
a different way to an announced money supply policy, even when
there is no difference between the equilibrium situations to which
the policies lead. The time paths of the money supply, the
interest rate, and income towards equilibrium could, then, differ,
depending upon what kind of policy the authorities chose to follow.
This could be an important factor in interpreting observed leads
and lags in time series data.
     It is worth noting that control of the interest rate, rather than
the money supply, is not necessarily a foolish policy in terms of
achieving the traditional goals of full employment and price
stability. As Poole (1970) has argued, in terms of the Hicks-
Hansen framework the less stable is the demand for money function relative to the expenditure function, the more likely it is that
control of the interest rate will be sensible policy, and vice
versa.
     The Bank of England tends to argue that it is instability in
the market for government securities that obliges it to pursue
an interest rate policy. Recent work by Parkin (1970a) and
Parkin, Gray and Barrett (1970) on the portfolio behaviour of both
discount houses and commercial banks suggests that these institutions' demand functions for government securities are stable
enough, while Norton (1969) goes so far as to suggest that what
instability there is in markets for government securities occurs
because of, rather than despite, the authorities' activities.

34   Bank reserves will also fluctuate in order to accommodate fluctuations in bank deposits in such circumstances. Thus there is no contradiction between the foregoing argument and Crouch's (1967) regression results on the relationship between bank reserves and the volume of bank deposits. The interpretation of these results is different, of course, for Crouch has causation running from reserves to deposits, and the foregoing argument would reverse his interpretation of the relationship in question.

It is worth noting that is precisely when a central bank is supporting interest rates that bank holdings of liquid assets become important in the generation of the money supply, since these assets are so readily convertible into high-powered money. The debate in Britain over the question of the role of liquid assets in the generating of bank deposits is a complicated one. Coppock and Gibson (1963) provide perhaps the clearest single guide to the issues involved.

35   Thus to agree with Kaldor's account of post-war British monetary history in no way implies acceptance of his more general conclusions concerning the futility of attempting to use the quantity of money as a policy variable. Kaldor seems to regard the level of money income as something that is always determined independently of the quantity of money, and argues as a general proposition that, if there exists an empirical relationship between the two variables, causation always runs from income to money. I cannot resist pointing out, with tongue only partly in cheek, that Kaldor's line of reasoning would lead to the conclusion that the Conquistadores were induced to establish the Spanish empire and to develop its production of the precious metals by strong inflationary pressures that just happened to be present in Europe during the sixteenth century.

36   This is not the place to go into the details of whether the quantity of money or its rate of change is the relevant variable. Suffice it to note here that Friedman (1958) seems to suggest that the rate of change of the money stock determines the *level* of economic activity but that in Friedman and Schwartz (1963b) and in Friedman (1970) the emphasis seems to shift to relationships between the rate of change of money and the rate of change of income. This writer wonders if he is alone in being somewhat confused by this. [This problem is dealt with in detail in chapter 7 below.]

37   The fullest exposition of this transmission mechanism (until the appearance of Friedman, 1970) is in Friedman and Schwartz (1963b.) It is an interest rate mechanism much like that described earlier in this paper, and, as Kaldor (1970, p. 9) notes apparently with surprise, is not significantly different from that described by Keynes (1936). It is a minor mystery in the recent history of economic thought as to where so many economists have got the

impression that Friedman's view of the monetary mechanism is crucially dependent upon some mysterious 'direct' effect of money on expenditure.

38 Though it is fair to note that the authors in question warned their readers that lack of time has prevented them completing as thorough a study as they had hoped to carry out.

39 A model produced by Tucker (1966) concentrated on adjustment rather than expectations lags, and seemed, as far as substantive implications were concerned, to be the same as my own model. Subsequent work has convinced me that this is not the case; expectations and adjustment lags do have importantly different implications for some aspects of the behaviour of Hicks-Hansen-type models, as I shall show below.

40 This peculiar result arises because the model contains no time lag between changes in interest rates and changes in expenditure. If we replace the expectations lag in the expenditure function with an adjustment lag, and let G be government expenditure,

$$Y_t - G_t = E_t = gkY_t + gA_t - gar_t + (1-g)E_{t-1}$$

this does introduce such a lag, and has the effect of slowing down the effects of monetary policy relative to fiscal policy. If $g = b$ the money impact multiplier here is unambiguously smaller than that in equation 20, while the autonomous expenditure multiplier is greater. Thus we reach the hardly novel conclusion that the existence of an adjustment lag in the expenditure function is crucial to the existence of a slower impact for monetary policy than for fiscal policy. It is also worth noting that the model thus modified becomes second-order. Preliminary analysis suggests that it is impossible to rule out a cyclical response of income to an exogeneous shock in this case, so that the very concept of a unique 'lag' which can be measured by the proportion of the distance towards equilibrium which is covered in a given time period is put in question. I hope to be able to deal with this and related issues in much more detail in a future paper. [The paper referred to is chapter 3 below.]

41 [This equation is analysed in more detail in chapter 3.]

42 Grossman and Dolde (1970) represents a pioneering effort at empirically analysing these lag effects in terms of a completely specified macro-economic model. Their model is similar to, though not the same as, the one set out here.

43 Though it is worth noting that Friedman (1957, p. 152) expressed some disquiet about applying an unvarying set of weights to the computation of permanent income in the 1930s.

44 The basic question is one of degrees of aggregation. Motley's work suggests that vital detail is lost by aggregating into only two categories of assets — money and all others. [Recent work by

Lionel Price suggests that different sectors of the economy respond at different speeds to portfolio disequilibria. This points to another potential source of variability in the lag structure of the aggregate demand for money function. *Cf.* L. Price, 'The demand for money in the United Kingdom: a further investigation', *Bank of England Quarterly Bulletin,* XII, March 1972, pp. 43-56.]

45   There are two distinct but closely interrelated aspects to the price level expectations problem. First there is a matter of the permanent or expected price level. If it is important to distinguish this variable from the current price level, ... then it has a role to play in the demand for nominal balance function, and also perhaps in the explanation of the determination of the *level* of money wages.

There is also the matter of the expected rate of inflation, which has a theoretical role to play in the demand for real balances function as a component of the opportunity cost of holding them. Evidence recently produced by Gupta (1970) strongly suggests that the expected rate of inflation is a component of observed bond yields, so that its failure to appear explicitly in the regression equations dealt with above should not be interpreted as an indication that the variable is not a potentially important determinant of the demand for real balances in either Britain or the United States. Moreover, as far as the money wage bargain is concerned, the existence of an expected rate of inflation of other than zero would presumably turn the bargain into one that set a rate of change as well as a current level of money wages.

Questions arise as to the relationship between these two concepts. If the 'permanent price level' concept turns out to have important empirical content, need it be the case that the expected rate of inflation be measured by the rate of change of the variable? Does it make sense to talk about an expected rate of inflation without also dealing with a permanent price level, or is it possible to measure the latter variable merely by the current price level plus the expected rate of inflation over whatever may be the relevant time period? I do not pretend to have the answers to these questions, but until they are found it is hard to see how much progress can be made in understanding the role that price expectations play in macro-economics.

46   The Phillips curve represents an attempt to deal with this interrelationship, as Johnson (1970) has pointed out. Williamson (1970) has used the Phillips curve to produce results showing that initial responses to changes in aggregate demand tend to come in output, with prices being subsequently influenced. The mechanism sketched out below differs crucially from Williamson's in the emphasis it places on the role played by price expectations in the wage bargain. However, it ought to be noted that Williamson's analysis has the merit of being carried out in terms of a growth model. Once the question of the time path of economic

variables arises, one suspects that the influence of investment
on the capital stock, and hence on output, might be an important
factor. The fact that this influence is neglected in the foregoing
analysis is yet another reason for regarding its likely empirical
content as being small.

47   In the discussion that follows I shall deal only with the
effects of price level expectations on the wage bargain and hence
on the supply side of the economy. The effects of these same
expectations on the demand side of the economy, as transmitted
through the money market both by the influence of the effect of
permanent prices and the expected rate of change of prices
on the demand for money, will be ignored. Obviously, a full analysis of the time path of an inflationary process would have to
consider the interaction of its effects on both aggregate demand
and aggregate supply, and my failure to provide such an analysis
here should not be taken to suggest in any way that I do not regard the problem as important.

48   [I am less convinced now than I was when writing this passage
of the asymmetry of the effects on prices of excess demand and
excess supply. As I have argued in the preceding paper, the
responses in question appear to be *qualitatively* identical. There
may, however, be a certain amount of *quantitative* asymmetry in
the relationship, though the results presented in chapter
7 below suggest that this is not important in the context of post-
war United States data.]

49   Phillips curve analysis would suggest that while wages are
rising in response to excess demand there might be some fall-
off in unemployment. When the price and wage level come to rest
again, unemployment would be back to its old level, again according to Phillips curve analysis, and that is why the phenomenon is
neglected here. Nevertheless, it is important to note that the
asymmetry with which I am dealing here is a product of the price
expectations mechanism postulated and not of any assumption
that there exists a unique level of 'full employment' output that
cannot be exceeded. When dealing with changes in the rate of
change of prices and money wages, rather than in their level,
Phillips curve analysis is not so clear on what we might expect
to observe. This matter is discussed further in note [51].

50   The last few paragraphs described a labour market mechanism that is very much in accord with modern interpretations of
Keynes (1936). The expectations mechanism permits us to produce relative downward rigidity in money wages (or their rate of
change) without having to postulate either trade unions with
monopoly power or irrational 'money illusion' on the part of the
suppliers of labour. This writer's debt to Leijonhufvud (1968)
must be obvious.

51   If money wage bargains were always struck with the aim of achieving a given real wage, if the price indices relevant for the suppliers of labour were the same as those taken into account by its demanders, and if there were no repercussions from the demand side of the economy, then movement from one rate of inflation to another ought to be no different to movement from one price level to another. In equilibrium, when anticipations have again caught up with what is happening, the real wage will be the same, and according to the Phillips curve analysis as modified by Phelps (1967) and Friedman (1968), unemployment ought to have returned to its "natural'. rate. Parkin (1970b) has recently produced evidence for post-war Britain which suggests that this does not in fact happen; a faster rate of inflation reduces unemployment permanently, though not by as much as it does in the short run. Parkin's result may be due to the price expectations mechanism he postulated (an exponentially weighted average of past rates of inflation to yield the expected rate) being a misspecification of the true mechanism at work, to his failure to allow for demanders and suppliers of labour forming expectations about different price indices and at different rates, or to his neglect of the influence of price expectations on the demand for goods. But any empirical study is open to comment that there is more than one interpretation to the results it has produced, and until these suggestions are investigated Parkin's results ought to make us a little hesitant about accepting too readily the assumption implicit in this paragraph that the economy will, in the long run, always return to a unique level of 'full employment'.

52   Note that Friedman (1970, pp. 223-34) sketches the outlines of such a model but that he finds the analysis of the time path of money income a more tractable problem than the division of this time path between variations in prices and variations in real income.

53   [This essay almost entirely ignored the question of the relationship between the openness of the economy and the behaviour of the monetary sector. I trust that chapters 8-10 below compensate for this deficiency.]

3 Expectations, adjustment and the dynamic response of income to policy changes[1,2]

I

The analysis of time lags has played a prominent role in recent work on two apparently distinct problem areas in short-run macro-economics. First, in attempting to reconcile empirical evidence with hypotheses about particular structural relationships in the economy many economists have found it necessary to appeal to lag effects both in the adjustment of variables to equilibrium and in the formation of expectations. Second, the literature on stabilisation policy, and particularly on monetary policy, has for some time stressed that the transmission of the effects of the policy measures to such variables as income, employment and prices seems to be subject to long, and perhaps variable, time lags. The literature on time lags in economic policy initially concerned itself with measuring such lags and with pointing up the consequences of their existence rather than with formal analysis of the reasons for their existence. However, if economic policy works with important time lags this must be because there exist important time lags in the behaviour relationships through which the effects of policy are transmitted, and recent work has recognised that these two branches of the literature deal not with different lag effects but with different aspects of the same lag effects. A number of papers have used the information which econometric work has produced about lags in structural equations in order tc analyse the lag effects that are of concern to those working on policy problems.[3] Structural relationships containing various types of lag effect have been introduced into the Hicks-Hansen model, and the dynamic response of the modified model to changes in such policy variables as the quantity of money and the level of government expenditure has then been analysed.

This paper adopts the same procedure but deals with a rather more complex and general model than has so far appeared in the published literature. Indeed, two of the better-known, simpler models that have been analysed elsewhere are special cases of the one dealt with here, and their predictions about the response of income to policy changes are a sub-set of the range of behaviour dealt with below.[4] The conclusions that this more complex model yields may be summarised as follows.

The existence of time lags in the demand for money function tends to accelerate rather than slow down the impact of monetary policy; this is a conclusion that also emerges from simpler models. In addition, the effects of fiscal policy (at least in as much as this involves changes in government expenditure) and of exogenous shocks to private expenditure may also be accelerated; this result depends not upon the values of the lag parameters but on the interrelationships between the static parameters of the model's behaviour relationships. Again this is a result that carries over from simpler models. The path by which income returns towards equilibrium after a disturbance may be cyclical, rather than, as in simpler models, monotonic. This conclusion, which is a new if not too surprising one, must cast doubt upon procedures for analysing lags in the effects of economic policy that involve attempting to find scalar measures of such lags. Apparently it is possible that the response of the economy to exogenous shocks is too complicated to be so characterised.

Finally, and most interesting, whether or not the model does produce cycles, and the extent to which those cycles are damped, depend critically upon the relative sensitivity of expenditure and the demand for money to the rate of interest. These same factors are crucial in determining the extent to which impact effects of exogenous shocks are accelerated, as they are in determining the relative sizes of autonomous expenditure and money multipliers in the steady state version of the model. The case for regarding the quantity of money as a powerful influence on the level of economic activity turns out to be interdependent with the case for treating it as a built-in stabiliser, while the case for preferring government expenditure as a policy variable is interdependent with the case for using it as a discretionary tool. It is a fair generalisation that advocates of fiscal policy tend to be in favour of its discretionary use and that many of those who prefer monetary policy put their faith in the stabilising effects of holding the quantity of money on a secular time path. I believe that this paper is the first to give an explicit analytic basis to the interconnectedness of these positions on matters of policy.

Interesting though I would claim these conclusions are, they must be treated with care. The model that produces them treats the price level as an exogenous constant, and it does not contain an accelerator relationship. These are serious omissions, and the only excuse for them can be that the model is complicated enough as it is, and that in work of this type it is best to build up the analysis one step at a time; the model dealt with here does, after all, encompass more phenomena than its predecessors.[5] Nevertheless, until it can be explicitly established that the results this model yields arise independently of assumptions whose only defence is analytic simplicity, they must necessarily be viewed with some scepticism.

II

The model to be analysed is, in essence, an orthodox post-Keynesian real income determination model. The usual assumption of price rigidity is combined with that of the existence of a stock of freely available productive resources which permit any level of aggregate demand to be matched by aggregate supply. Thus the extremely difficult issues surrounding the interaction of the price level and the level of real income are by-passed by making the price level an exogenous constant. As is customary in such models, government expenditure is assumed to be financed by sales of bonds in amounts small enough relative to the total amount outstanding that there are no monetary repercussions from the operation. Thus the problem of the existence of a government budget constraint (*cf.* Christ, 1968) is assumed away.

The model differs from the usual post-Keynesian static construction in that time lags appear in the behaviour relationships embodied in it. Both planned private expenditure on goods and services and planned holdings of real balances are made to depend upon expected rather than current income, while actual expenditure and money holdings are thought of as adjusting to their planned values with a time lag. For analytic convenience, time is divided into discrete intervals. The model may be set out as follows. Y is real national income, Y^e is real expected national income, E is real private expenditure, G is real government expenditure, M is real money balances, and R is the rate of interest. The symbol * attached to a variable indicates its planned, as opposed to its actual, value, while a bar over a variable indicates that it is exogenous. The subscript $t = -1, -2, \ldots$ indicates time lags of one, two or more discrete periods, while all parameters are positive. In addition $k < 1$, $b < 1$, $g < 1$ and $d < 1$.[6]

$$E^* = \overline{A} + kY^e - aR \tag{1}$$

$$E = gE^* + (1 - g)E_{-1} \tag{2}$$

$$G = \overline{G} \tag{3}$$

$$Y = E + G \tag{4}$$

$$M^* = mY^e - lR \tag{5}$$

$$M = dM^* + (1 - d)M_{-1} \tag{6}$$

$$M = \overline{M} \tag{7}$$

$$Y^e = bY + (1-b)Y^e_{-1} \tag{8}$$

If we substitute 8 into 1, 1 into 2, and 2 and 3 into 4 and solve for R, and then proceed to substitute 8 into 5, 5 into 6, 6 into 7, and again solve for R, this variable may be eliminated and the resulting equations solved for Y. Application of the Koyck transformation eliminates Y^e_{-1} from the resulting expression, and where

$$z \equiv k - \frac{a}{l}m \tag{9}$$

we get

$$Y = \frac{1}{1 - bgz}\overline{G} - \frac{2 - b - g}{1 - bgz}\overline{G}_{-1} + \frac{(1-b)(1-g)}{1 - bgz}\overline{G}_{-2}$$

$$+ \frac{g}{1 - bgz}\overline{A} - \frac{(1-b)g}{1 - bgz}\overline{A}_{-1}$$

$$+ \frac{1}{\frac{l}{a}\frac{d}{g}(1 - bgz)}\overline{M} - \frac{2 - b - d}{\frac{l}{a}\frac{d}{g}(1 - bgz)}\overline{M}_{-1}$$

$$+ \frac{(1-b)(1-d)}{\frac{l}{a}\frac{d}{g}(1 - bgz)}\overline{M}_{-2} + \frac{2 - b - g}{1 - bgz}Y_{-1}$$

$$- \frac{(1-b)(1-g)}{1 - bgz}Y_{-2} \tag{10}$$

The model yields a second order difference equation to describe the time path of income, and its properties are easily analysed by conventional methods. As I shall now show, equation 10 is quite capable of generating a cyclical time path for income in response to a disturbance, although it does not necessarily do so; at the same time the tendency is always for income to return to a steady state equilibrium level; equation 10 cannot produce explosive behaviour.

If $\hat{Y}$ is the stationary equilibrium value of income, and if we consider the consequences of a single disturbance arising either from a once-and-for-all shift in the quantity of money, or in government expenditure, so that after the passage of three time periods $\overline{M} = \overline{M}_{-1} = \overline{M}_{-2}, \overline{A} = \overline{A}_{-1}$ and $\overline{G} = \overline{G}_{-1} = \overline{G}_{-2}$, then substituting $\hat{Y}$ for Y, Y_{-1} and Y_{-2} in equation 12 and subtracting the resulting expression from equation 10 yields the following expression for the deviation of income from its steady state value, where y is the deviation in question

$$y = \frac{2-b-g}{1-bgz} y_{-1} - \frac{(1-b)(1-g)}{1-bgz} y_{-2} \tag{11}$$

Now the roots of this equation—call them χ_1, χ_2—are given by

$$\chi_1, \chi_2 = \frac{1}{2} \left[\frac{2-b-g}{1-bgz} \pm \sqrt{\left(\frac{2-b-g}{1-bgz}\right)^2 - \frac{4(1-b)(1-g)}{1-bgz}} \right] \tag{12}$$

If there are parameter values for which

$$\left(\frac{2-b-g}{1-bgz}\right)^2 - \frac{4(1-b)(1-g)}{1-bgz} < 0 \tag{13}$$

then equation 11 will produce a cyclical time path for y when the parameters take those values. Since

$$\left(\frac{2-b-g}{1-bgz}\right)^2 - \frac{4(1-b)(1-g)}{1-bgz} =$$

$$\frac{(b-g)^2 + 4(1-b)(1-g)bgz}{(1-bgz)^2} \tag{14}$$

and since

$$0 \leqslant (b-g)^2 < 1 \tag{15}$$

$$0 < (1-b)(1-g)bg < 1 \tag{16}$$

$$(1-bgz)^2 > 0 \tag{17}$$

whether or not the model yields cyclical behaviour depends upon the value taken by z.

It will be recalled that

$$z \equiv k - \frac{a}{l}m \tag{9}$$

Now by assumption, $0 < k < 1$, but all that can be said about the ratio a/l is that it lies between zero and infinity.

Whatever value the other terms on the right hand side of equation 16 might take, the possibility of z being a sufficiently large negative number to make the whole expression negative cannot be ruled out *a priori*. Thus the model may yield either cyclical or monotonic behaviour.[7]

That the time path of income always converges on a steady state solution, that there is no possibility of explosive behaviour, is not immediately obvious from inspection of equation 12. However, in general a second order difference equation of the form

$$y - \alpha_1 y_{-1} + \alpha_2 y_{-2} = 0 \tag{18}$$

is stable if

$$\alpha_1 - \alpha_2 - 1 < 0 \tag{19}$$

$$-\alpha_1 - \alpha_2 - 1 < 0 \tag{20}$$

and

$$\alpha_2 < 1 \tag{21}$$

For the particular model under analysis we have

$$\alpha_1 = \frac{2 - b - g}{1 - bgz} \tag{22}$$

and

$$\alpha_2 = \frac{(1 - b)(1 - g)}{1 - bgz} \tag{23}$$

It is clear that inequality 20 is satisfied. Since $0 < b, g < 1$ and $z < 1$, it is also clear that inequality 21 is satisfied. Furthermore

$$\alpha_1 - \alpha_2 - 1 = \frac{2 - b - g}{1 - bgz} - \frac{(1 - b)(1 - g)}{1 - bgz} - 1 =$$

$$\frac{bgz - bg}{1 - bgz} < 0. \tag{24}$$

Thus the transient component of income always tends to vanish as time passes.

It is clear from the foregoing analysis that the dynamic properties of this model depend critically upon the composite parameter z. The smaller z the more damped is the model, and, as we have seen from lines 14-17, there is a critical negative value for z at which the model begins to generate cycles. Thus if the model generates cycles at all we would expect them to be relatively strongly damped ones, and indeed the smaller z becomes (i.e. the larger a negative value it takes) the more damped would they become. The duration of the cycles will also fall with z. Their duration is given approximately by $2\pi/\theta$ periods, where

$$\tan \theta = \frac{\sqrt{-4\alpha - \alpha_1^2}}{\alpha_1} = \frac{\sqrt{-4(1 - b)(1 - g)bgz - (b - g)^2}}{2 - b - g} \tag{25}$$

Clearly $\tan \theta$ and therefore θ itself rise as z falls, the latter approaching an upper value $\pi/2$.

Clearly analysis of the behaviour of the rate of interest may be carried out. Equations 1-8, solved for R, yield

$$R = \frac{b}{\frac{l}{m}(1-bgz)}\overline{G} - \frac{b(1-g)}{\frac{l}{m}(1-bgz)}\overline{G}_{-1} + \frac{bg}{\frac{l}{m}(1-bgz)}\overline{A}$$

$$- \frac{1-gbk}{dl(1-bgz)}\overline{M} + \frac{(1-d)(1-gkb)-(b-g)}{dl(1-bgz)}\overline{M}_{-1}$$

$$- \frac{(2-b-d)(1-g)+(1-b)(1-d)}{dl(1-bgz)}\overline{M}_{-2}$$

$$+ \frac{(1-b)(1-d)(1-g)}{dl(1-bgz)}\overline{M}_{-3} + \frac{2-b-g}{1-bgz}R_{-1}$$

$$- \frac{(1-b)(1-g)}{1-bgz}R_{-2} \tag{26}$$

The expression for the transitory component of the rate of interest is

$$r = \frac{2-b-g}{1-bgz}r_{-1} - \frac{(1-b)(1-g)}{1-bgz}r_{-2} \tag{27}$$

The coefficients of this equation are identical with those of 11 for the transitory component of income. Thus whatever is true of the behaviour of income's transitory component over time is also true of the behaviour of that of the interest rate, and we need to carry the current line of analysis no further, except to note that the demand for money function ensures that the interest rate and permanent income will always move in the same direction when the money supply is held constant. Thus if there are cycles in the interest rate they may be led by or conform to the related cycle in measured income, but can never lead it.

So far the analysis has dealt with the time paths of income and the rate of interest after the impact effects of exogenous shocks have taken place. A good deal of work on somewhat simpler models than this has concerned itself directly with the analysis of these impact effects. In particular, attention has been paid to the tendency, under certain circumstances, of both income and interest rates to change more in the short run than in the long run in response to exogenous shocks.

The easiest way to see that the model currently being analysed behaves similarly is to compare what are usually called the 'impact multipliers' of policy variables—the coefficients of $\overline{G}$ and $\overline{M}$ in equations 10 and 26—with the steady state multipliers of these same variables. The latter coefficients are simple to obtain, for in the steady state all variables must have the same value in successive periods. This property of the steady state permits us to reduce our model to the simple, not to say familiar, form, where the symbol ^ over a variable indicates its steady state equilibrium value.

$$\hat{E} = A + k\hat{Y} - a\hat{R} \tag{i}$$

$$\overline{G} = \overline{G} \tag{iii}$$

$$\hat{Y} = \hat{E} + \overline{G} \tag{iv}$$

$$\hat{M} = m\hat{Y} - l\hat{R} \tag{v}$$

$$\hat{M} = \overline{M} \tag{vii}$$

As a reduced form expression for steady state income we have

$$\hat{Y} = \frac{1}{1-z}\,[\overline{G} + \overline{A}] + \frac{1}{\dfrac{l}{a}\,(1-z)}\,\overline{M} \tag{x}$$

and for the interest rate we have

$$\hat{R} = \frac{1}{\dfrac{l}{m}\,(1-z)}\,[\overline{G} + \overline{A}] - \frac{1-k}{l\,(1-z)}\,\overline{M} \tag{vi}$$

where the coefficients of the exogenous variables are the steady state multipliers we require.

It is convenient to compare the impact and steady state multipliers by computing the ratio of the latter to the former. If such a ratio is less than one in value, then the initial effect of a policy change is to cause income (or the interest rate) immediately to overshoot its ultimate equilibrium value. Denoting the relevant ratios L_G^Y and L_G^R for government expenditure and L_M^Y and L_M^R for the quantity of money, we get

$$L_G^Y = \frac{1 - bgz}{1 - z} \tag{28}$$

$$L_M^Y = \frac{\dfrac{d}{g}\,(1 - bgz)}{1 - z} \tag{29}$$

$$L_G^R = \frac{1 - bgz}{b\,(1 - z)} \tag{30}$$

$$L_M^R = \frac{d(1 - k)(1 - bgz)}{(1 - z)(1 - bgk)} \tag{31}$$

Dealing first with the income multipliers, it is clear from inspection of equations 28 and 29 that it is quite possible for either ratio to be less than one. A negative value for z is obviously a necessary and sufficient condition for the impact multiplier on government expenditure to exceed the steady state multiplier. Analysis of the relative sizes of the two money multipliers is more complicated. Even for a positive value of z, a sufficiently small value for d/g (i.e. a sufficiently long adjustment lag in the money market relative to that in the goods market) can reduce the value of equation 29 to less than one. Moreover for any given negative value of z, and any given value of b, there exists a sufficiently large value of d/g to maintain equation 29 at a value greater than one. Thus a negative value for z is neither necessary nor sufficient for the impact multiplier of a change in the quantity of money to exceed the steady state value, though, for given values of the other parameters, the smaller is z the smaller is the ratio denoted by equation 29.

The interest rate multipliers are more straightforward to analyse. If z is positive, then equation 30 always takes a value greater than unity, but a sufficiently large negative value can make it fall below unity. On the other hand, since $z \leqslant k$, equation 31 is always less than unity. Thus the rate of interest always overshoots its steady state value in response to a change in the money supply, but may either undershoot or overshoot in response to a change in government expenditure. These results, like those for the income multipliers, accord in the main with the properties of the simpler models alluded to above.[8]

Now there is virtually no limit to the analytic games that can be played with a model such as the one we have here, but the last few pages bring out the most important characteristics of this model's behaviour.[9] However, there still remains the matter of giving some economic interpretation to the analysis that has been developed, and it is to this task that I now turn.

III

The capacity of the model analysed above to generate cycles, and its ability to produce multipliers for income, both exogenous expenditure and money multipliers, that exceed in value the relevant long run multipliers are important characteristics from two points of view.

First, a fair amount of the literature on the lag effects of economic policy has concerned itself with trying to develop scalar measures of these effects. Attempts have been made to identify turning points in cycles in the level of economic activity with specific preceding turning points in the time path of the money supply (or its rate of change) and to estimate 'the lag effect' by

measuring the time elapsed between the two turning points. If
the time path of income can exhibit turning points that are independent of any cycle in a policy variable, it is hard to know what to
make of the results of such an exercise. The alternative procedure
of trying to measure these lag effects in terms of the length of
time it takes for income to move a given proportion of the way towards a new equilibrium presupposes that, after some disturbance,
income moves towards its new steady state value along a monotonic time path. The possible existence of cycles and overshoots
just as surely undermines this approach to the problem of lag
effects.[10] The lesson here would appear to be that the time path
of income's response to exogenous shocks must be analysed with
explicit attention to the structure of the economic model that generates the response, since this structure may well produce a time
path that is too complex to be characterised by scalar measures
of something called 'the lag effect'.[11]

These same characteristics of the model have considerable
bearing upon the matter of the design of discretionary stabilisation
policies. It is often said that the aim of these policies is to
'lean against the wind', but it is only when income responds to
exogenous shocks by moving off towards a new equilibrium along
a monotonic path that one can take the wind's current direction
as an indicator of its prevailing tendency. For example, in the
presence of overshoot effects and cycles, the fact that income is
observed to be rising at a particular moment gives no guarantee
that it will continue to do so—such an observation does not even
guarantee that the equilibrium towards which income is moving is
above its currently observed value. A world with overshoots and
cycles is a difficult one for which to design discretionary policies.[12]
Their existence would strengthen the case for replacing discretionary policy with rules.

Now a necessary condition for cycles is that the conglomerate parameter z be negative, and this is also a necessary and
sufficient condition for overshoots to occur in response to exogenous changes in either private autonomous expenditure or government expenditure. However, we have also seen that the more
negative is z the more heavily damped and the shorter are the
cycles the model generates. Moreover the more negative is z
the smaller are the exogenous expenditure multipliers. Thus the
very same factors that make discretionary policy more difficult
to design, and that tend to diminish the effectiveness of government expenditure as a policy variable, also make the need for
discretionary policy less pressing.

As the difficulty of pushing the economy in the right direction
with discretionary policy increases, so also does the speed with
which income, after being disturbed, converges of its own accord
on a steady state. At the same time, the sensitivity of income to

variations in exogenous private expenditure and government
expenditure decreases, leaving the quantity of money as the predominant determinant of the steady state equilibrium level of
income. The more negative z, the more strongly do all these conclusions follow, and the larger a positive number is z the stronger
becomes the case for their converse. Now it will be recalled that

$$z \equiv k - \frac{a}{l} m \tag{10}$$

The critical determinant of the sign and magnitude of z is the
ratio a/l. The more sensitive one believes expenditure to be to
the rate of interest, and the less sensitive the demand for money,
the more will one emphasise the inherent stability of the economy,
the more highly will one regard the quantity of money as an influence on economic activity and the more strongly will one favour
its behaviour being governed by a rule.[13] Conversely, the smaller
one's assessment of the likely value of a/l, the less confidence
will one have in the built-in stability of the economy and the more
strongly will one favour discretionary fiscal policy. That the
relative strengths of monetary and fiscal policies, when analysed
in terms of a static Hicks-Hansen model, depend upon the ratio
a/l is, of course, a commonplace, though an important one, but I
believe that there is some novelty in the conclusion that the value
of this ratio also has an important role to play in the 'rules versus
authorities' debate when a dynamic version of the same model is
applied to the analysis of policy lag effects.

Dubious though the direct empirical relevance of the model
analysed in this essay may be, it would, I think, be surprising if at
least some of its conclusions did not also emerge from more
complex models which, for example, made room for price level
variations or an accelerator relationship. One would hardly
expect such modifications to make the time path of the economy's
response to exogenous shocks simpler, or to render the economy's
dynamic properties independent of the static parameters of behaviour relationships. Whether the critical importance of the
relative sensitivity of expenditure and the demand for money to
the interest rate for the design of economic policy would also
carry over into a more complex model is more difficult to forecast. Only further analysis can settle this question, and such
analysis would be well worth having.

APPENDIX. TWO SIMPLER MODELS

The model presented in this paper has some properties in common with simpler constructions that are already to be found in

the literature; earlier papers by both Tucker (1966) and Laidler (1968) dealt with models whose properties included the possibility of impact multipliers being greater than steady state multipliers, though neither model produced a cyclical time path for income. Tucker's model relied solely upon adjustment lags, while my own earlier construction contained nothing but expectation lags. Thus a model similar in essence to Tucker's may be derived from equations 1-8 simply by setting the parameter b equal to unity so that measured income and expected income become equal; my own earlier effort is derived from the same set of equations by setting d and g equal to unity so that there is no divergence between planned and realised values of either private expenditure or real money balances. As an 'adjustment lag only' model we have

$$E^* = \overline{A} + kY - aR \tag{1'}$$

$$E = gE^* + (1-g)E_{-1} \tag{2}$$

$$G = \overline{G} \tag{3}$$

$$Y = E + G \tag{4}$$

$$M^* = mY - lR \tag{5'}$$

$$M^* = dM^* + (1-d)M_{-1} \tag{6}$$

$$M = \overline{M} \tag{7}$$

The 'expectations lag only' model is

$$E = \overline{A} + kY^e - aR \tag{1''}$$

$$G = \overline{G} \tag{3}$$

$$Y = E + G \tag{4}$$

$$M = mY^e - lR \tag{5''}$$

$$M = \overline{M} \tag{7}$$

$$Y^e = bY + (1-b)Y^e_{-1} \tag{8}$$

The first of these variants of the basic model yields

$$Y = \frac{1}{1-gz}\overline{G} + \frac{g}{1-gz}\overline{A} + \frac{1}{\dfrac{l}{a}\left(\dfrac{d}{g} - dz\right)}\overline{M} - \frac{1-g}{1-gz}\overline{G}_{-1}$$

$$- \frac{(1-d)}{\dfrac{l}{a}\left(\dfrac{d}{g} - dz\right)}\overline{M}_{-1} + \frac{1-g}{1-gz}Y_{-1} \tag{10'}$$

and

$$R = \frac{1}{\frac{l}{m}(1-gz)}\,\overline{G} + \frac{g}{\frac{l}{m}(1-gz)}\,\overline{A} - \frac{1-g}{\frac{l}{m}(1-gz)}\,\overline{G}_{-1}$$

$$- \frac{1-gk}{dl\,(1-gz)}\,\overline{M} + \frac{(1-d)(1-gk)-(1-g)}{dl\,(1-gz)}\,\overline{M}_{-1}$$

$$- \frac{(1-d)(1-g)}{dl\,(1-gz)}\,\overline{M}_{-2} + \frac{1-g}{1-gz}\,R_{-1} \tag{26'}$$

The transient component of income follows a time path determined by

$$y = \frac{1-g}{1-gz}\,y_{-1} \tag{11'}$$

and that of the rate of interest by

$$r = \frac{1-g}{1-gz}\,r_{-1} \tag{27'}$$

The corresponding equations for the second model are

$$Y = \frac{1}{1-bz}\,[\overline{G} + \overline{A}] - \frac{1-b}{1-bz}\,[\overline{G}_{-1} + \overline{A}_{-1}]$$

$$+ \frac{1}{\frac{l}{a}(1-bz)}\,\overline{M} - \frac{1-b}{\frac{l}{a}(1-bz)}\,\overline{M}_{-1} + \frac{1-b}{1-bz}\,Y_{-1} \tag{10'}$$

$$R = \frac{b}{\frac{l}{m}(1-bz)}\,[\overline{G} + \overline{A}] - \frac{1-bk}{l\,(1-bz}\,\overline{M} + \frac{(1-b)}{l\,(1-bz)}\,\overline{M}_{-1}$$

$$+ \frac{1-b}{1-bz}\,R_{-1} \tag{26''}$$

$$y = \frac{1-b}{1-bz}\,y_{-1} \tag{11''}$$

$$r = \frac{1-b}{1-bz}\,r_{-1} \tag{27''}$$

Both models exhibit dynamic behaviour that may be characterised by a stable first order difference equation.

However, if neither of them is capable of generating a cycle in either income or the interest rate, there is still scope in both for impact multipliers to exceed steady state multipliers. The steady state solution to these models is, of course, identical to that of the more complicated framework dealt with in the previous section so that the ratios of the steady state multipliers to the impact multipliers are given by

$$L_G^Y = \frac{1 - gz}{1 - z} \tag{28'}$$

$$L_M^Y = \frac{\frac{d}{g}(1 - gz)}{1 - z} \tag{29'}$$

$$L_G^R = \frac{1 - gz}{1 - z} \tag{30'}$$

$$L_M^R = \frac{d(1 - k)(1 - gz)}{(1 - z)(1 - gk)} \tag{31'}$$

for the first model, and for the second by

$$L_G^Y = L_M^Y = \frac{1 - bz}{1 - z} \tag{28''}$$

$$L_G^R = \frac{1 - bz}{b(1 - z)} \tag{30''}$$

$$L_M^R = \frac{(1 - k)(1 - bz)}{(1 - z)(1 - bk)} \tag{31''}$$

The sign of the conglomerate parameter z is a critical determinant of the magnitude of these ratios for income just as it is in the more complicated model. Interest rates always overshoot in response to changes in the quantity of money, just as they do in the more complicated model, but, in the expectations-lag-only framework, the interest rate always undershoots in response to changes in government expenditure. In the adjustment-lag-only model, as in the more complicated one, things are less straightforward; whether or not the interest rate undershoots or overshoots when government expenditure changes depends upon the sign of z. Models like these have been fully analysed elsewhere, and there is no need to go into their properties in any great detail here. However, it is at least worth noting that in the present context, because their dynamic properties may be characterised by a stable first order difference equation, it does make more sense to talk of a 'lag effect' being present in these models than in the more complex one dealt with earlier, so long as those who do so are willing to include cases in which the impact effect of a policy change overshoots the steady state solution of the model. If it does not do too much violence to ordinary usage or characterise such time paths as displaying 'very short' lag effects, the ratios defined in equations 28'-31' and 28"-31" may be regarded as providing scalar measures of these lag effects, and questions about both the length of lag effects and their variability may clearly be seen to be questions about the size and stability of the basic parameters of the model which enter into these ratios. This matter is analysed in some detail in Laidler (1971a), part IV.

NOTES

1   Reprinted from the *Journal of Money, Credit and Banking*, V, February 1973, part I, pp. 157-72; copyright © 1973 by the Ohio State University Press; all rights reserved.

2   Though it deals with a model in which the price level is rigid, this paper forms part of a more extensive study of macro-economic dynamics being carried out under the auspices of the SSRC-financed University of Manchester research programme in the economics of inflation. It has greatly benefited from comments on earlier drafts by John Black, to whom I am particularly indebted for having checked much tedious algebra as well as for help on several matters of substance, Roger Bowden, Dennis Coppock, Herschel Grossman, Michael Parkin, David Rose and an anonymous referee. The author accepts responsibility for all remaining errors and omissions.

3   Relevant papers include Walters (1965), Tucker (1966), Laidler (1968, 1971a), Tanner (1969) and Grossman and Dolde (1970). The simulation exercises reported in Brainard and Tobin (1968) were also prompted by a recognition of the interdependence of these two sets of time lags.

4   To faciliate comparisons, versions of two of the models (Tucker, 1966 and Laidler, 1968) that have already appeared in the literature are set out and analysed briefly in the appendix to this paper.

5   Preliminary attempts to build more complicated models, depending upon the precise formulation chosen, have resulted in anything between third and fifth order difference equations to describe the time path of income. Such equations are not very amenable to the analytic methods used in this paper, and it appears that further work along these lines will involve simulation exercises.

6   The assumption that $k < 1$ plays a not unimportant role in much of the following analysis; it is in this context that the absence of an accelerator relationship from the model makes itself felt.

7   It is worth stressing that this cyclical property of income's time path is not just a trivial consequence of our model's having generated a second order system. There are economically

meaningful second order systems that *never* generate cycles.
The reader may easily satisfy himself that equations 1-4, with
the interest rate treated as an exogenous variable, would, if
solved for income, produce just such a system.

8   *Cf.* the analysis carried out in the appendix to this essay.

9   For example, I have here analysed only the first-period impact
effects of a change in an exogenous variable. As should be clear
from equation 10 such effects spread over three periods for monetary changes and two periods for changes in fiscal policy. To deal
with these subsequent effects involves even more tedious algebra
than this paper already contains and does not seem to add much of
consequence to the analysis. Suffice it to note that if the initial
impact effect of a change in M or G undershoots final equilibrium,
income in subsequent periods remains below its equilibrium
value. An overshoot is followed by an immediate reversal of
direction which may or may not involve income's time path again
passing through its steady state value. In the former case, for a
change in M there is yet another change in direction in the third
period; in the latter case there is not. As the reader might expect,
the more negative is z the more prone to oscillation and complexity is income's behaviour. The reader should also note that
my analysis of 'overshoots' and 'undershoots' is carried out on
the assumption that all shocks occur when the model is in full
equilibrium. For example, if income is already below its steady
state value, then an expansionary shock may not cause it to overshoot its new steady state value even though the relevant impact
multiplier is greater than its steady state counterpart. Again,
detailed analysis is tedious and not productive of fresh insights
and I have chosen not to pursue this matter further in this paper.

10   The work of Friedman (1958) and Friedman and Schwartz
(1963b) are good examples of the first approach to the problem,
while that of Kareken and Solow (1963) adopts the second method.
Cf. Mayer (1968), especially chapter 8, for a survey of this and
much other relevant work.

11   Note that the work of Phillips (e.g. 1954), did take such an
explicitly analytical approach to the lag effect problem and the
problem of designing stabilisation policies.

12   Though the reader ought not to infer that the capacity of this
model to generate cycles implies that, to maintain income at a
given value, the money supply would have to follow a cyclical time
path for given values of G and A. The appropriate time path for
the money supply may be derived by solving equation 10 for M,
and though this yields a second order equation, it is one that is
incapable of generating cycles (as opposed to oscillations when
'impact effects' are analysed). The problem of choosing a time
path for the money stock to achieve and maintain a given level of
income is dealt with by Tanner (1969), using a second order model

that differs in some detail from the one used here, but which yields results sufficiently similar to make further analysis of this problem in the present paper unnecessary.

13   It is important to note that it is the relative sensitivities of these relationships and not the absolute sensitivity of either of them taken by itself that is important here. Brunner and Meltzer (1970), working with a somewhat different model, reach a similar conclusion on this matter, but their model does encompass a more complex and rich pattern of interaction between the goods and money markets than does the simple Hicks-Hansen framework used in this paper. The reader might note that although my argument is cast in terms of the magnitudes of slope coefficients of a linear model it may easily be recast in terms of elasticites. Write m as $\partial M/\partial Y$, a as $\partial Y/\partial R$ and l as $\partial M/\partial R$ and multiply $m\,a/l$ by $1 = MYR/MYR$. Evidently $k - m\,a/l = k - \eta_{MY}\,\eta_{YR}/\eta_{MR}$ where η_{MY} is the income elasticity of demand for money, η_{YR} the interest elasticity of expenditure and η_{MR} the interest elasticity of the demand for money. I am grateful to Michael Parkin for this formulation.

4   The Phillips curve, expectations and incomes policy[1]

I

The 'Phillips curve' made its first widely noted appearance in the literature only thirteen years ago and has ever since played a central role in the analysis of inflationary situations.[2] Even though the basic concept is extremely familar, it is worth discussing it briefly at the outset, for such a discussion will make it much easier to set out the way in which recent work on the role of price expectations in inflationary situations and on incomes policies fits in with the basic analysis.

    Figure 4.1 depicts a 'Phillips curve'. On the vertical axis is measured the percentage rate of change of money wages per

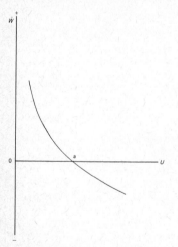

Figure 4.1 The Phillips curve

unit of time ($\dot{W}$), and on the horizontal axis the percentage of the labour force unemployed (U). The curve itself depicts a smooth negative relationship between two variables and cuts the horizontal axis at a positive level of unemployment. Now there are three questions (at least) to be asked about the relationship depicted in figure 4.1. What economic theory predicts that it should exist? Does empirical evidence confirm that it does? Finally, what does the existence of such a relationship imply for the design of economic policy in the face of inflation?

A textbook of scientific method would suggest that these questions should be answered in the order they are posed above. However, the world is not so tidy, and in early work on the relationship it was the last two questions that received most attention. In his original paper Phillips (1958) paid only slight attention to questions of theory and concentrated on presenting a formidable body of evidence that, at least as far as the United Kingdom was concerned, a relationship such as the one depicted in figure 4.1 did exist and indeed had existed unchanged since 1861. The methods that Phillips used to estimate the form and slope of the relationship were unorthodox, but details of those methods need not in any case concern us here. The important thing to note is that in estimating his curve he applied those methods only to data drawn from before the first world war. He then showed that post-first world war data lay along the very same curve, with the post-second world war data apparently lying closest of all.[3]

Such stability as this in a relationship between two variables over such a long time period is rare indeed in empirical economics, and taken by itself is sufficient to explain a great deal about the rapidity with which economists accepted the Phillips curve. However, there are two other attractive features to the analysis. First there is the matter of its policy implications. Up till the late 1950s the basic problem for macro-economic policy was thought of as being the simultaneous attainment of price stability and a high level of employment. Though early post-war pessimism about attaining high employment was not justified by events, price stability proved much more elusive.[4] The Phillips curve provided a ready made explanation for the 'failure' of policy. It suggested that high employment and price stability were incompatible, and that the British economy could have more of one only at the expense of less of the other. To the positive question 'How can one have price stability and high employment?' the Phillips curve seemed to give the answer 'One can't'. It also suggested that it would be more to the point to ask the normative question 'Which combination of unemployment and inflation of those attainable is the most desirable?'. Given that economists had been unable to answer the positive question, it is not surprising that they were (and are) attracted by a concept that suggested they were asking the wrong question in the first place.[5]

The final, but not necessarily the least important, attraction of simple Phillips curve analysis lies in the theoretical justification advanced for it. As it stands figure 4.1 merely portrays a relationship between two variables; it is clearly impossible to carry out any analysis of that relationship unless one has an explanation of why it exists. Lipsey (1960) provided such an explanation. He argued that wages tend to fall in conditions of excess supply of labour and to rise in conditions of excess demand and he also argued that unemployment varies systematically and inversely with the level of excess demand for labour. Clearly, when labour is in excess supply that excess supply will manifest itself in unemployed people seeking jobs. However, Lipsey also noted that a national labour market is far from frictionless: even when overall the supply of labour equals the demand for labour there will exist positive 'frictional' unemployment. Since supply and demand being in balance results in a steady wage rate, Lipsey argued that this frictional unemployment was indicated by point a in figure 4.1, where the Phillips curve cuts the horizontal axis. He then argued further that he would expect the pressure of positive excess demand for labour to result in frictional unemployment falling below a because jobs become easier to find as the job vacancy rate increases along with the demand for labour.[6]

Excess demand for labour can be produced by shifts in either the supply curve of labour or the demand curve, and is quite independent of the sources of those shifts. Thus Lipsey's theoretical explanation of the Phillips curve makes that analysis neutral as between 'demand pull' and 'cost push' theories of the inflationary process. One economist may regard inflation as being completely the result of bad monetary policy and another can argue that it is solely the consequence of the activity of monopolistic trade unions, but either position leaves room for its proponent to accept the Phillips curve analysis as elaborated by Lipsey. In short, the Phillips curve and its policy implications seemed to provide an insight into the nature of the inflationary process about whose importance economists on all sides of debates about the likely causes and appropriate cures for inflation could agree.[7]

II

The simple theory of the Phillips curve described above, and its apparent policy implications, were absorbed with remarkable speed into the generally accepted corpus of macro-economics, and though the early and mid-1960s generated a large enough literature on the topic, in my judgement at least, nothing of basic importance was added by this literature to the fundamental contributions of Phillips and Lipsey.[8]

It was not until the late 1960s that two circumstances were to produce both new academic interest in the Phillips curve and genuine intellectual advance in our understanding of it. In Britain the attempt by the Labour government to influence the rate of inflation by way of a prices and incomes policy, whether or not it was prompted by a conscious effort to by-pass the inflation-unemployment trade-off implicit in the Phillips curve, was certainly amenable to interpretation and analysis as such. Incomes policy seemed an important subject for study and the Phillips curve a natural tool to use in the course of that study.[9] In the United States an important role in the resurgence of interest in monetary economics was played by the analysis, both positive and normative, of the relationships between expectations about the rate of inflation and the behaviour over time of the velocity of circulation of money. The variable proved particularly powerful in dealing with data drawn from inflationary situations. It was again a natural, not to say fruitful, extension of the analysis of price expectations to look at their role in the determination of the rate of money wage inflation.[10]

Now in empirically analysing recent British experience Parkin (1970b) has shown that it is helpful to deal simultaneously with the effects of incomes policy and inflationary expectations; both seem to have played a role in generating the relevant data, so that the effects of both have had to be allowed for when the data are analysed. However, the two phenomena are analytically distinct, and it will be convenient initially to treat them separately here.

There is, as I noted earlier, an element of ambiguity in Lipsey's analysis of the labour market behaviour that produces the Phillips curve.[11] It starts from two propositions: that the supply and demand for labour determine the equilibrium wage level, and that the rate of change of the wage level in disequilibrium will depend upon the extent of the disequilibrium as measured by the excess demand for labour. Now the Phillips curve is a hypothesis about the behaviour of *money* wages, while orthodox supply and demand analysis of the labour market is about the behaviour of *real* wages, and the two concepts are interchangeable only in conditions of price level stability. If the excess demand for labour is inversely related to the level of unemployment and positively related to the rate of change of the *real* wage, then we may predict that there will exist a stable inverse relationship between the rate of change of *real* wages and the level of unemployment. However, this relationship is not the Phillips curve; to get from it to the Phillips curve we must introduce the expected rate of price inflation into our model.

We need the expected rate of inflation and not its actual current rate because individual wage bargains are stuck at discrete intervals and, for any particular bargain, it is not the current price level that matters in determining the real wage that is being aimed at but the level of prices that is expected to rule over the period for which the bargain is being struck. Thus the rate at which the money wage rate will change between any two bargains will be influenced by how price expectations have changed between the times at which the two bargains are struck, and not *directly* by how the price level itself has changed over the same interval; though in practice one would expect expectations to be based at least to some extent upon actual recent experience. In any case, merely to keep the real wage constant when prices are rising will result in money wages rising at the expected rate of price inflation, and attempts to increase real wages will result in money wages rising faster than the expected rate of price inflation.

Once we insist that the supply and demand for labour determine the real wage, and once we note that wage bargains get struck at discrete intervals so that it is expected and not current prices that enter into the determination of the relevant

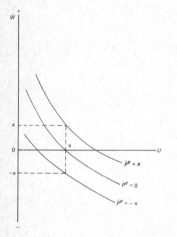

Figure 4.2 A family of Phillips curves

real wage, we find that, in terms of figure 1, there is a different Phillips curve for every expected rate of price inflation ($\dot{P}^e$) Representatives of a family of such curves are drawn in figure 4.2, and they have the characteristic implied by the above analysis that each level of unemployment corresponds to a unique rate of change of the *real* wage rate.

Now the foregoing argument implies much more than that there exists a variable changes in whose value can shift the Phillips curve. Causation does not run only one way from the

expected rate of price inflation to the rate of wage inflation. This
becomes clear the moment one considers the way in which these
variables are likely to interact over time, and, as we shall now
see, the nature of their interaction is such as to lead to the conclusion that the trade-off between wage inflation and the level of
unemployment implied by the Phillips curve is mainly a short-run
phenomenon. Indeed, the strict logic of the argument that follows
implies that the trade-off is *solely* a short-run phenomenon — that
the 'long-run' Phillips curve is vertical; but this latter proposition,
though it is the most contentious one in current academic debates
about the role of price expectations in the Phillips curve, is not in
my judgement fundamental to any of the implications of the
analysis for short-run anti-inflationary policy. The fact that the
trade-off becomes steeper with the passage of time is what is
important from this point of view, and everyone involved in these
debates seems to agree that it does so.[12]

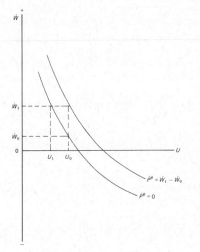

Figure 4.3 Short- and long-run response of unemployment to
the rate of wage inflation

Why the inflation-unemployment trade-off should become
steeper as time passes is best seen in terms of an example. Let
figure 4.3 depict the situation in an economy in which there is
price stability—and expected price stability—and in which U_0
yields a rate of wage inflation W_0 which is just compensated
for by rising labour productivity. Now if the authorities in this
economy were to decide that U_0 was too high a level of unemployment, that U_1 was preferable, they could initially achieve this

level of unemployment by policies which would also lead to the
rate of wage inflation of $\dot{W}_1$. However, with no change in productivity growth, prices would begin to rise at a rate equal to
$\dot{W}_1 - \dot{W}_0$. Now so long as people form their expectations about
inflation on the basis of current and past behaviour of prices
the price inflation thus induced would begin to become anticipated.
It would continue at the same rate as long as the authorities pursued policies to maintain wage inflation at a rate of $\dot{W}_1$, and the
longer it continued at that rate the closer to the actual rate of
inflation would the expected rate move. Thus the closer to its
ultimate location (at $\dot{P}e = \dot{W}_1 - \dot{W}_0$) would the short-run Phillips
curve shift and the closer to U_0 would the level of unemployment
compatible with the rate of wage inflation $\dot{W}_1$ become.

There have been a number of empirical investigations of the
kind of wage-price spiral implied in the above example, and there
seems to be abundant evidence that wage inflation which proceeds sufficiently fast to involve price inflation does lead the
public to form expectations about price inflation that shift the
traditional (what I am now calling the 'short-run') Phillips curve
upwards. In the long run the trade-off between inflation and unemployment vanishes completely only if actual inflation becomes
perfectly anticipated, and there does seem to be doubt as to whether
the mechanism involved works quite as perfectly in practice as it
does in the foregoing fairly abstract piece of economic analysis;
nevertheless there is no disagreement that the trade-off becomes
considerably less acute as time passes and people permit current
inflation to influence their expectations.[13] This is an extremely
important discovery from the point of view of the design of anti-
inflationary policy, as we shall now see.

The Phillips curve as orginally conceived presented policy-
makers with a simple trade-off indeed: more unemployment for
less inflation. The introduction of expectations into the analysis
complicates the trade-off. Again an example is the best way to
see this. Suppose the 'long-run' Phillips curve is such as is
depicted in figure 4.4—and I have drawn it with a slope to emphasise the independence of what I have to say of extreme assumptions about perfect learning mechanisms being embodied in the
model—and suppose we begin at point X on that curve with a given
rate of inflation and a given level of unemployment. Suppose the
government of the day finds point X uncongenial and prefers point
Y; how is it to get there? There are many routes, but a comparison of two of them will suffice to illustrate the nature of the
policy trade-off involved in choosing a route.

First, suppose the government attempts to attain at once the
rate of inflation compatible with Y. This would involve taking policy
steps to contract the excess demand for labour to such an extent
that initially the economy would move to Y' on the short-run

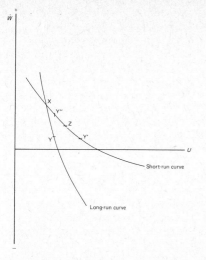

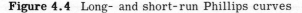

Figure 4.4 Long- and short-run Phillips curves

Phillips curve that passes through X. Clearly, the actual rate of inflation would then be below that expected on the short-run Phillips curve passing through X, and as expectations were revised downward this short-run Phillips curve would shift to the left until point Y was reached.

Alternatively the authorities could choose to move immediately to the level of unemployment compatible with ultimate equilibrium at Y. This would involve shifting the economy to point Y″ on the short-run Phillips curve. Again, the actual inflation rate would fall below the expected one, and again the constant revision of expectations in the light of experience would eventually result in the economy reaching Y. However, in as much as people learn about the likely future rate of inflation from current experience, the bigger is the discrepency between experience and expectations the faster are expectations likely to be revised. This is a well tested proposition and in the present context it implies that the first route from X to Y considered will be a more rapid one than the second. [An important question begged here, of course, is what policy actions the authorities might take in order to select one route or the other.]

The decision to start the foregoing analytic example from a point of equilibrium on the long-run Phillips curve was a matter of expositional convenience only. In Britain at the moment (February 1971) both the rate of inflation and the level of unemployment are high by standards of recent history. Phillips's original analysis suggested that a level of unemployment of just under

$2\frac{1}{2}$ per cent combined with productivity growth in the region of
2-3 per cent per annum would lead to virtual price stability!
This fact suggests that the current British situation is best
represented by a point on a short-run Phillips curve to the right
of the long-run one, a point such as Z. Indeed, if inflation expectations are still catching up with experience the point Z, far from
being static, might actually be moving upwards. However, this
does not mean that the foregoing analysis is irrelevant. If the
basic mechanism sketched out above is a good model of the effects
of inflation in the labour market, it is still true that we may expect
to reduce the rate of inflation only slowly if we maintain unemployment at its present level, and that if we seek a rapid end to
inflation this must involve a higher level of unemployment than
we have at present.

    This comparison of routes whereby inflation may be ended
is, of course, merely illustrative of a general proposition about
the trade-offs implied by the introduction of inflation expectations
into the Phillips curve, and that proposition is as follows. The
more rapidly the rate of inflation is reduced, the higher will be
the average level of unemployment while it is being reduced. One
can bring inflation to a halt quickly by having more unemployment
for a relatively short time, or slowly by having less unemployment
for a longer time. This is the qualitative nature of the policy
trade-off. I do not think we can yet say anything very precise
about its quantitative nature other than to note that the experience
of both Britain and the United States over the last few years suggests that, if unemployment rates are to be kept from rising
any higher than they are at present, then the timetable for significantly reducing the rate of inflation must be conceived of in
terms of years rather than months.

    Indeed, we need not confine ourselves to the evidence of the
last few years on this matter. The analysis we have been discussing leads to the conclusion that any attempt to reduce the current rate of inflation below its expected rate will lead to an increase in the unemployment rate which though 'transitory' may
nevertheless endure for an uncomfortably lengthy period. There
is no reason to suppose that this conclusion applied only to situations in which the relevant inflation rates are positive, and once
this is grasped the events of the later 1920's and 1930's in Britain and those of the 1930s in the United States may also be regarded as evidence of the consequences of rapid reductions in
the rate of inflation relative to its expected level. One might
also note than when viewed in this broader perspective modern
theories of the Phillips curve come to look like more general
versions of Keynes's hypothesis about the downward rigidity of
money wages. They predict, after all, that the rate of change of
money wages is rigid downwards relative to the expected rate of

price inflation, and a special case of this is downward rigidity in
the level of money wages when the expected rate of inflation is
zero.

Now the analysis of the last few paragraphs assumes that
price level expectations are influenced only by data generated
within a 'wage-price spiral', and that the workings of the labour
market are not interfered with so as to alter the manner in
which wages respond to market forces. Some form of incomes
policy is frequently put forward as a means of breaking into the
mechanism described above in such a way as to enable the
economy to by-pass the sacrifices of output inherent in the unemployment generated by reducing the rate of inflation by conventional methods.[14]

There are two distinct ways in which incomes policy might
break into this spiral. It might influence the way in which real
wages respond to shifts in the supply and demand for labour, or
it may influence expectations about inflation independently of the
current behaviour of prices. As we shall see in a moment, incomes policy as practised in the past seems to have been
effective in interfering with the supply and demand mechanism
in the labour market — not always with the results anticipated —
but I must confess to having doubts about according any unique
role to incomes policy as a means of influencing expectations;
since I know of no study either published or unpublished on this
particular issue, however, these doubts are not as firmly based
as they might be.[15]

There is no question that it would be highly desirable to have
a tool with which expectations about inflation could be damped
independently of a fall in the actual rate of inflation. In terms of
figure 4.4 such a tool would shift the 'short-run' Phillips curve
downward and to the left independently of the wage-price mechanism described above and hence enable the rate of inflation to
be reduced at a lower cost in unemployment than otherwise.

This shift of the short-run Phillips curve would not, in and
of itself, reduce the rate of inflation, of course. There is nothing
in the foregoing analysis to suggest that changing expectations
alone will have any influence on the rate of inflation; it simply
suggests that if expectations about inflation can be changed
independently of the influence of information transmitted by
market forces, then a given rate of inflation will be attainable at
a lower cost in transitory unemployment than otherwise. The
Phillips curve analysis is, as I noted at the outset, silent and
neutral on the appropriate policies with which to achieve a given
rate of inflation.

Even so, a policy with the ability to change expectations would
be a useful part of any anti-inflationary package, and incomes
policy is often portrayed as being peculiarly suited to that role.

However, I cannot see why. The key to breaking the expectations link in the wage-price spiral involves convincing those involved in wage bargaining that past evidence on price increases is not a reliable indicator of which is going to happen in the future. If the government announces its intention of influencing the future rate of inflation by way of an incomes policy, this will change expectations if incomes policy is expected to work. Equally, however, an announced intention to reduce the rate of inflation by reducing the rate of growth of the money supply will influence expectations if the policy proposal is credible. What is important is that the government's willingness and ability to reduce the rate of inflation should be believed in, and not the means by which this end is to be achieved. Since there is no reason to suppose that the public has more faith in the anti-inflationary powers of incomes policy than in those of more traditional policy tools, there is no reason why the recognition of the importance of the role played by expectations in the inflationary process should imply that incomes policies are peculiarly effective anti-inflationary devices.

There is another side to the case for using incomes policy to affect expectations, however, though it seems no better grounded. It can be argued that by actually imposing restraints on prices and incomes for a period the actual rate of inflation will be reduced, the expected rate of inflation reduced, and the spiral broken. However, to have anything more than a temporary effect such a policy would have to convince the public that the course of prices while it was in force was a good indicator of the likely course of prices when the policy was removed.

As I have already noted, there is a good deal of evidence to support the view that price expectations are on the whole largely based on past experience, but it is probably a mistake to apply this evidence to the very special circumstances of the transition from a period of prices and incomes control to one in which such controls are relaxed. It is at least a plausible hypothesis that this is the very time at which the public would regard past experience as a particularly bad guide to the future. If this hypothesis is true, incomes policy can at best interrupt the wage-price spiral only for so long as it is imposed. If the act of imposing the policy leads to a downward revision of expectations about inflation, then the act of removing it is as likely to lead to those expectations being revised upwards again; unless, of course, the end of incomes policy is accompanied by the introduction of other anti-inflationary measures which the public expects to hold down the rate of change of prices. In that case, though, it is the public's belief in the efficiency of the new policies rather than the legacy of an incomes policy that holds down expectations of inflation. One cannot help but wonder if the so-called 'wage-price explosion' that followed the relaxation of incomes policy by the Wilson government may not be explained by the government's failure to replace that policy with some other credible (and visible) anti-inflationary measures.

Be that as it may, if incomes policy has no special virtue as a means of influencing expectations about the rate of change of prices, this does not imply that it is a generally ineffective anti-inflation weapon. Casual analysis might suggest—and indeed the view was quite widely held among economists until recently—that incomes policy would hold back the rate of wage inflation which might be experienced at any particular level of excess demand for labour; this because the imposition of incomes policy somehow involved introducing extra friction that forces tending to make money wages rise would have to overcome. Incomes policy could be though of as shifting the Phillips curve (presumably long-run and short-run, though the distinction was not current at the time this view of incomes policy was at its most popular) and lessening the seriousness of the inflation-unemployment trade-off implied by it.

Early attempts to investigate the degree to which incomes policies had shifted the Phillips curve in post-war Britain suggested that they had some success. There did seem to be evidence that some systematic shifting of the relationship had taken place upon the introduction of incomes policy.[16] However, this evidence rested on the assumption that the only effect of incomes policy was to shift the Phillips curve parallel to itself; Lipsey and Parkin (1970) found no difficulty at all in demonstrating that careful analysis of the theory underlying the curve did not in fact lead to the prediction that incomes policy would shift the curve parallel to itself.[17] Rather they argued that an effective incomes policy would both shift and alter the slope of the relationship. Hence the evidence alluded to above was produced by misconceived tests and implied nothing at all about the effectiveness of otherwise of incomes policy.

Not only were Lipsey and Parkin able to show that incomes policies had shifted the Phillips curve in post-war Britain in principle, they were able to show (using statistical methods that have, admittedly, been much criticised) that it had apparently done so in practice, that the use of incomes policy seemed to have pivoted the curve until it became virtually horizontal, in the man - ner illustrated in figure 4.5. Their original work did not allow for the likely influence of inflationary expectations — surely the reason why their so-called 'policy off' results do not extrapolate well to present experience - but subsequent work by Parkin showed that to make explicit allowance for expectations did not in any way affect the conclusion that in the presence of incomes policy the rate of wage inflation is independent of the level of unemployment, and indeed of the level of excess demand for labour.

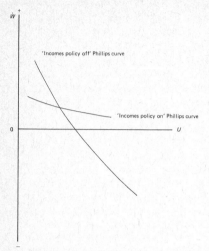
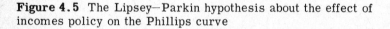

Figure 4.5 The Lipsey—Parkin hypothesis about the effect of incomes policy on the Phillips curve

Now this suggests that incomes policy is a double-edged weapon. Applied at a low level of unemployment it decreases the rate of wage inflation, but applied at high level it increases it. Moreover - with the single exception of the period 1947-50, in which price and wage controls were only part of a much larger array of restrictions imposed on market behaviour - Lipsey and Parkin found that incomes policy had been applied at times of relatively high unemployment, so that it had, if anything, worsened rather than improved the situations with which it was supposed to deal.

The interesting question about these results is what it is that determines the rate of wage inflation when it is not responding to the market forces of supply and demand for labour. The answer advanced by Lipsey and Parkin, which has not been subjected to any independent testing and hence must not be regarded as anything more than a tentative hypothesis, is that, although enough of the national labour market is competitive to ensure that the market as a whole works approximately 'as if' it were competitive throughout in normal (policy off) times, there are important segments of the market—notably the public sector—where competitive theory is far from obviously applicable. Incomes policy affects the Phillips curve by disrupting the competitive sectors of the labour market. This leaves the other, non-competitive sectors to set a 'norm' for wage increases that then tends to be widely adopted.[18]

This is not to say that non-competitive sectors of the labour market are unaffected by incomes policy, but since we have little idea about how they work in its absence there is no way of knowing whether or how they are in fact influenced. This is unfortunate, because the implications of the Lipsey and Parkin results are clear enough. Either incomes policy is applied at periods of below average unemployment or it will make matters worse rather than better. This conclusion can be escaped only if some way can be found of ensuring that wage increases in non-competitive sectors of the labour market are brought down to below what competitive forces would allow at times of above-average unemployment. Since we know so little about wage bargaining in non-competitive conditions it is hard to see how such policies can be devised other than by a process of trial and error. Moreover this presupposes that the trouble does stem from non-competitive sectors of the labour market in the first place; it is worth reiterating this this proposition is an as yet untested hypothesis.

One final *caveat* is in order before this discussion of incomes policy is brought to a close. Even if it did prove possible to devise an incomes policy that could be seen unambiguously to shift the Phillips curve downwards and to the left so that the rates of wage and price inflation could be reduced at a smaller cost in unemployment than in the absence of such policy, it would not follow that it was desirable to implement it. We regard unemployment as a 'cost' of reducing the rate of inflation mainly because unemployment involves loss of output. Output can be lost by misusing resources as well as by not using them. Fluctuations in relative wages in competitive labour markets are, in principle at least, the means whereby labour gets reallocated towards more productive uses. If incomes policy interferes with this mechanism, it is at least possible that it will produce, as a by-product, sufficient misallocation of the employed labour force to impose losses that more than offset the gains that arise from having more of the labour force employed. In judging the effectiveness of incomes policy in reducing the costs of bring down the rate of inflation these potential allocative effects are just as important as the more obvious impact of the policy on the overall level of employment. However, since there seems to be no evidence that we know even how to use incomes policy in such a way as to reduce consistently the rate of inflation associated with a given level of unemployment, the lack of any work on the allocative effects of incomes policy does not perhaps represent such a serious gap in the literature as it otherwise might.

III

The conclusions that have been drawn in the foregoing discussion are easily summarised. The Phillips curve represents a hypothesis about the way in which the labour market behaves during inflationary situations. Neither in its original form nor in the more sophisticated versions that have been produced recently does it have anything to say about the causes of or cures for inflation. The Phillips hypothesis states that, if a lower rate of inflation is desired, then a higher rate of unemployment must be tolerated. Originally it appeared that the rate at which one variable was traded off against the other was independent of the time horizon over which policy was being designed, and of the past inflationary experience of the economy. More sophisticated analysis, both theoretical and empirical, has shown that the trade-off is more complex.

The amount of unemployment that will be associated with a given rate of inflation at any moment in time will be higher the more rapid inflation has been in the recent past, at least so long as past experience affects expectations about the future. Given that past experience has been of higher rates of inflation, the longer a given rate of inflation is sustained the lower will be the level of unemployment associated with it. This is because expectations adjust to current experience and what we have termed the 'short-run' Phillips curve shifts so that unemployment and inflation rates approach equilibrium on a steep - in the ideal limiting case, vertical - 'long-run' Phillips curve. Thus the policy trade-off when seeking to reduce the rate of inflation is between a rapid reduction associated with a relatively short period of 'high' unemployment and a slow reduction associated with the existence of 'low' unemployment, over a longer period.

It would undoubtedly be desirable to find a way round this trade-off if possible, and one method of softening it would be to influence expectations independently of the market information that normally goes into their formation. It would appear that incomes policy is neither better nor worse conceived to break into the wages-price spiral in this way than any other policy. An announced intention of bringing down the rate of inflation can persuade the public to discount past experience in forming expectations so long as it is believed that the announcement will be followed by effective action. There is no reason to suppose that an announced intention to use incomes policy will be any more credible than an announced intention to use any other policy tool. Moreover we know so little about the factors determining expectations that we cannot rule out as implausible the possibility that the removal of even a successful policy of incomes restraint might not itself lead to an increase in inflationary expectations and a worsening of the terms of the inflation-unemployment trade-off.

Incomes policy can influence the inflationary spiral at
another point by breaking the excess demand for labour-rate of
change of (real) wage link in the causative chain. However,
available evidence suggests that this has only been done once in
the post-war period in such a way as to lower the rate of inflation;
in all the other instances incomes policy seems to have increased
the rate of inflation above what it otherwise would have been. We
have no well tested explanation of why the policy has worked this
way, and hence can have little confidence in our ability to design
an incomes policy that will not have a similar effect on the future.
Moreover nothing is known about the effects of such policies on
the allocative efficienty of the labour market.

All in all, I would conclude that we know so little about how
to design a successful incomes policy that it would probably be
better to forget about it altogether, face up to the difficult policy
choice inherent in modern versions of the Phillips curve, and,
recognising that the time horizon for noticably reducing the rate
of inflation without further significant increases in unemployment
is a matter of years and not months, set about designing a long-
term strategy for dealing with the problem, using more conventional tools of monetary and fiscal policy. Given the current state
of the balance of payments, and, given that Britain is far from
being the only country facing inflation, it may even be the case
that a policy of reducing the rate of inflation only very slowly can
be carried through without exchange rate depreciation. If it
cannot, then the policy choice becomes more complicated still.
To discuss this issue in any detail would take me far beyond the
scope of this paper; for this reason, and not because I regard
policy towards the exchange rate as an unimportant element in
the control of inflation, I shall not pursue this aspect of the problem any further.

NOTES

1   This paper was prepared for a conference on inflation held at
the London School of Economics, 22 February 1971, and is reprinted from H. G. Johnson and A. R. Nobay (eds.), *The Current
Inflation,* London, Macmillan, 1971. I am grateful to Michael
Parkin for his help at all stages of its preparation, and to George
Zis for drawing my attention to a number of errors in the first
draft. Remaining errors and omissions are, of course, my own
property.
2   In Phillips (1958). Note, however, that the relationship was
implicit in the model used in Phillips (1954).
3   Cf. Phillips (1958), fig. 1 (1861-1913), fig. 9 (1913-48), fig. 10
(1949-57).

4   Hutchinson (1968, particularly chapter 1) provides a ready source of quotations from the pronouncements of economists on this problem in the immediate post-war period.

5   It has often been remarked that the Radcliffe committee was unfortunate in that the period over which its report (1959) was prepared saw a revival of interest and faith in traditional monetary policy among academic economists, so that the report was out of fashion by the time it appeared. It is also true that the idea of trade-offs between policy goals came to the forefront over the same period and the Radcliffe report was totally uninfluenced by this concept. I suspect that this omission contributed just as much to the cool reception of the report among academic economists as did its failure to note the 'monetarist revolution'.

6   The reader will note that there is an ambiguity about the term 'wages' here. The Phillips curve has to do with money wages and orthodox analysis of the supply and demand for labour with real wages. As we shall see below, it was precisely this ambiguity, and the desire to clarify it, that led economists to introduce expectations about inflation into the analysis of the Phillips curve. However, in 1961 the problem apparently went unremarked. We may, in retrospect, regard Lipsey as having produced a theory of the Phillips curve for the special case in which the expected rate of inflation is zero.

7   This argument presupposes that the 'cost push-demand pull' distinction is synonymous with the distinction between demand-side and supply-side disturbances. Matters are not quite so clear-cut, for, as Michael Parkin has pointed out to me, the term 'cost push' when applied to wage inflation has sometimes been used to characterise circumstances in which wages rise independently of the concurrent existence of excess demand for labour. As we shall see below, expectations of inflation shared by both demanders and suppliers of labour can cause money wages to increase without any excess demand for labour ever arising. Thus recent Phillips curve analysis incorporating expectations about inflation can comprehend this other 'cost push' concept in a manner that earlier analysis could not.

8   A good deal of the 1960s literature had to do with the fact that, for the United States, a simple two-variable Phillips curve was far from stable over a long period. A glance at fig. 1 of Samuelson and Solow (1960) will confirm the extent of this problem. The United States experience need not concern us here, but two aspects of British work ought to be noted.

First Hines (1964) showed that the rate of change of trade union membership as a proportion of the labour force was a statistically significant variable, additional to the unemployment rate—indeed, virtually swamping the unemployment rate—in explaining the rate of change of money wages. He argued that this variable was a proxy for union aggressiveness and that his result was evidence for the existence of 'cost push' inflationary pressures. However, he failed to explain why this aggressiveness did not operate through shifts in the supply curve of labour and hence have its influence taken account of, along with the many other factors that presumably influence the excess demand for labour, in the unemployment rate. Thus Hines's statistical relationship is difficult (if not impossible) to interpret in terms of Lipsey's rationalisation of the Phillips curve. At the same time Hines did not present clear alternative specifications of labour market behaviour, so it is hard to know whether the interpretation he offers of the apparent importance of the rate of change of unionisation is reasonable.

Second, the point at which the Phillips curve cuts the horizontal axis (if we ignore inflationary expectations) is supposed to measure 'frictional' unemployment. Phillips's original curve implies a frictional unemployment rate of between 6 and 7 per cent. Lipsey argued that frictional unemployment was likely to be particularly high when there were large inter-regional discrepencies in the excess demand for labour - even though these cancelled out in the aggregate. This is because it is more difficult for the unemployed to move inter-regionally than intra-regionally to find work. This argument of Lipsey's thus suggests that the Phillips curve would tend to shift leftward as inter-regional discrepencies in unemployment rates become smaller, and vice versa. Work by Archibald (1969) has tended to confirm this hypothesis and has potentially interesting implications for regional policy.

9   Principal contributions here are Smith (1968), Lipsey and Parkin (1970) and Parkin (1970b)
10   Though the idea of an expected rate of inflation goes back at leat as far as Irving Fisher (1896), it made its first explicit appearance in modern monetary economics in the work of Friedman (1956), Cagan (1956) and Bailey (1956). It was introduced into the Phillips curve literature by Phelps (1967), who has also used the concept in work on monetary problems (1965), and Friedman (1968). The only study of which I am aware that uses the concept when dealing solely or even mainly with UK data on wage inflation is Parkin (1970b). Cagan (1968) does, however, present some preliminary results for Britain.
11   *Cf.* note 6. This is not to say that the analysis which follows is free of ambiguities. To a demander of labour, the real wage is given by the ratio of the money wage rate to some index of the price of his output, while to a supplier it is given by the ratio of the money wage rate to some index of the price of the bundle of goods he typically consumes. In a closed economy in which relative prices were not changing these two different price indices would

necessarily move together, but not otherwise. I know of no work
on this particular point, and hence cannot judge the extent to which
the following analysis might be vitiated by ignoring the problems
raised by it.

12   [In the long run matters are a little different, for here, if the
long-run Phillips curve is vertical, then the relevant trade-off
is between unemployment and *accelerating* inflation rather than
between unemployment and a higher rate of inflation.]

13   On this matter see, for example, work by Cagan (1968) and
Solow (1968) for the US and, as already noted, Cagan (1968) and
Parkin (1970b) for the UK. Of these only Cagan's results might
imply that the Phillips curve becomes vertical in the long run,
though this writer has severe doubts about the methods by which
Solow produced results implying that it did not (*cf.* Laidler, 1970).

14   Much in what follows hinges on what is meant by 'incomes
policy'. I take it to mean direct intervention to control prices and
money incomes, either by legal restraints or moral suasion, and
would not term the mere setting of a target rate of growth of
prices and money incomes an 'incomes policy'. Thus it is the
choice of policy instruments that defines an incomes policy, not
the choice of policy targets.

15   [Subsequent work by Carlson and Parkin suggests that in
Britain incomes policies have had no impact on inflationary
expectations. *Cf.* J. A. Carlson and J. M. Parkin, 'Inflationary
expectations', *Economica* (forthcoming).]

16   Smith (1968) is a typical example of such studies, which hinge
on the inclusion in regression equations of an intercept shift
dummy variable for 'incomes policy on' periods. This method is
an adequate device for investigating shifts in functional relationships only if there is good *a priori* reason to suppose that the
shift being investigated would be a parallel one if it occurred.

17   The Lipsey-Parkin paper and much of the relevant literature
which it subsequently generated are to be found in J. M. Parkin and
M. T. Sumner (eds.) *Incomes Policy and Inflation,* Manchester
University Press, 1972)

18   This explanation is set out by Lipsey and Parkin (1970), pp.
120-2. There is less emphasis there on the public-private sector
division, and on the distinction between competitive and non-competitive segments of the labour market, than there is in my interpretation of the Lipsey-Parkin hypothesis. I am indebted to
Michael Parkin for clarifying the original analysis along these
lines.

5 On Wicksell's theory of price level dynamics[1]

I

Recent contributors to monetary theory, notably Clower (1965) and Leijonhufvud (1968), have argued that the mainstream of post-Keynesian macro-economics has failed to capture the fundamental contribution made by Keynes in the *General Theory*.[2] According to these contributors, the 'economics of Keynes' is based upon a view of the workings of the market economy that may be summarised, at some risk of oversimplification, in the following three propositions:

1 In a money economy, Say's law of markets (that the excess demand for goods must always sum to zero) holds true only in full employment equilibrium.

2 Unemployment (and presumably unanticipated inflation as well, though this is not made explicit) is a disequilibrium phenomenon to which the conclusions of classical general equilibrium analysis do not necessarily apply. In particular the characteristic of demand and supply functions for goods and factors of production that they contain only prices is a property of such functions in markets where prices are formed by a tâtonnement with recontract process in which no trading takes place until full general equilibrium is reached. Hence these properties are incompatible with the analysis of unemployment situations. Trading at non-equilibrium prices is of the essence in such circumstances, and as a consequence, quantities as well as prices enter the budget constraints of traders and influence their behaviour.

3 A property of the dynamics of markets in which such disequilibrium trading takes place is that, because of imperfections in the knowledge of traders, prices adjust slowly, particularly when the required movement is a downward one, and quantities adjust instead. Because quantities influence behaviour, such variations may produce cumulative forces that tend to move income and employment further away from full employment equilibrium rather than back towards it.

Now the analysis of disequilibrium in a money economy in terms of a cumulative process is not original to Keynes. The Wicksellian element in his work has long been recognised. This element is most obvious in the *Treatise* but Leijonhufvud has argued that there is far more continuity between the *Treatise* and *General Theory* than is commonly supposed and that, as a consequence, the Wicksellian flavour of the latter is greatly under-rated.[3] This paper is intended to provide support for this view. It attempts to show that, of the three foregoing propositions which are claimed to form the basis of 'the economics of Keynes', the first two play an explicit and central role in Wicksell's analysis. It will be argued that it is the third of them, concerning the role of expectations in the generation of price rigidities, that is missing from Wicksell's work, and that its absence ensures that Wicksell's dynamics involve the price level rather than real output even in deflationary situations. By implication, then, the analysis of the role of expectations in the economic process is seen to form the core of the 'Keynesian revolution'.[4]

II

Wicksell seems to have given five accounts of his 'cumulative process', and only the earliest of these is unavailable in English.[5] The latest of them is also the briefest, being a summary printed in the *Economic Journal* for 1907 of a lecture given to the British Association at Leicester in 1906. It seems reasonable to suppose that this short paper contains what Wicksell regarded as the essence of his views on price level fluctuations.

The outlines of his doctrine are well enough known. Nevertheless it will be convenient to set out the model implicit in this 1907 paper in order to show that, despite its overall 'modern' quality, there are elements missing from it that a post-Keynesian economist would as a matter of course build in to any macro dynamic model.

The fundamental thesis argued in the 1907 paper is as follows:

> If, other things remaining the same, the leading banks of the world were to lower their rate of interest, say 1 per cent below its ordinary level, and keep it so for some years, then the prices of all commodities would rise and rise and rise without any limit whatsoever; on the contrary, if the leading banks were to *raise* their rate of interest, say 1 per cent, above its normal level, and keep it so for some years, then all prices would *fall* and fall and fall without any limit except zero. [1907, p. 213]

He noted that

> According to the general opinion among economists, the interest on money is regulated in the long run by the profit

on capital, which in its turn is determined by the productivity
and relative abundance of real capital, or in the terms of
modern political economy, by its *marginal productivity*.
[1907, p. 214]

but asserted that in an economy with a well developed banking
system there is no link between the rate of interest and the rate of
profit 'except precisely the *effect on prices,* which would be
caused by their difference' (1907, p. 215).

The mechanics of this link are simple enough.

> When interest is low in proportion to the existing rate of
> profit, and if, as I take it, *the prices thereby rise,* then ...
> trade will require more sovereigns and banknotes, ... the
> bank reserves will melt away while the amount of their lia-
> bilities very likely has increased, which will force them to
> raise their rate of interest.' [1907, p. 215]

How rapid would be the adjustment of the rate of interest to a
level compatible with price stability depends on how widespread
the initial disequilibrium might be. Of course, a single bank has
no power to create price movements by varying its interest rate,
since it must carry on its business at rates prescribed by the
market.

> Not even all the banks united of a single country could do it in
> the long run; a too high or too low rate would influence its
> balance of trade, and thereby cause an influx or reflux of gold
> in the well known way, so as to force the banks to apply their
> rates to the state of the universal money market.
>   But supposing ... all the leading banks of the commercial
> world were to follow the same course, then ... the action
> exercised on prices would have its sway without any hindrance
> from the international movement of money. Still, even then
> it would ... have its obvious limits.... so long as ... gold
> itself remains the standard of value, this factor evidently will
> take the lead in the long run [as a determinant of prices] ...
> the ever growing demand for gold for industrial purposes
> would gradually reduce the bank stores, and could only be
> checked by raising the price of gold—that is, by lowering the
> average money prices. [1907, pp. 217-18].

However, none of this means that we should expect to observe
low interest rates when prices are rising and high rates when they
are falling.

> The rate of interest is never high or low in itself, but only in
> relation to the profit which people can make ... and this, of
> course, varies.... The rate of interest on money follows, no
> doubt, the same course, but not at once, not of itself; it is, as

it were, dragged after the rate of profit by the movement in prices and the consequent changes in the state of bank reserve, caused by the difference between the two rates ... this difference acts on prices in just the same way as would be the case ... if profit on capital were to remain constant, and interest on money were to rise or fall spontaneously. In one word, the interest on money is, in reality, very often low when it seems to be high, and high when it seems to be low. [1907, p. 217][6]

A modern counterpart of the model implicit here is easily set out in a four-quadrant diagram. In figure 5.1 we plot a negative relationship between aggregate demand and the rate of interest in the north-east quadrant. For the particular relationship drawn, R^* is the value of the rate of interest that equates aggregate demand to an exogenously given level of full employment aggregate

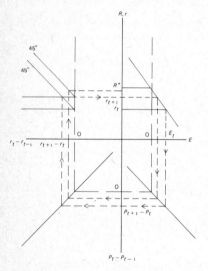

Figure 5.1 The Wicksellian inflation model. E is excess demand, p the log. of the price level, R the natural rate of interest and r the money rate of interest

supply. In the south-east quadrant we relate the pace of price inflation to the level of excess demand, while we may capture Wicksell's proposition that a higher price level leads to a higher rate of interest with a relationship between the rate of inflation and the rate of change of the rate of interest plotted in the south-east quadrant. A suitably located 45° line in the north-west quadrant permits us to add any change in the rate of interest to the rate of interest itself. This diagram is easily used to portray the mechanisms of Wicksell's cumulative process.

If we suppose that, with the money rate of interest at r_t, the aggregate demand-rate of interest relationship has shifted upward so that the latter variable's value would have to be R^* to equate aggregate supply and demand, we may trace out the time path whereby equilibrium is restored. The initial discrepancy between the rate of interest and the rate of profit sets up excess demand of E_t, which starts prices rising at $p_{t+1} - p_t$. The drain on banks' reserves brought about by this rise in the price level causes them to raise their rate of interest by $r_{t+1} - r_t$, so that at the beginning of the next time period the money rate of interest is at r_{t+1}. The diagram then enables us to trace out subsequent price increases with the rate of interest coverging on R^* and prices rising continuously while it does so.[7]

The same diagram can equally well be used to portray Wicksell's treatment of falling prices, as the reader may easily satisfy himself by setting a rate of interest above R^* and tracing out the course of the subsequent deflation.

However, as soon as the diagram is put through its paces for the deflationary case discrepancies between Wicksellian analysis and post-Keynesian macro-economics become very apparent. The notion that prices are as flexible in a downward direction as upward is quite alien to modern theory, of course, while the idea that aggregate demand could be perpetually below full employment aggregate supply without output contracting and setting up a downward multiplier effect on real income is very hard to grasp. Moreover even in the inflationary case the model seems to be missing a common ingredient of modern work, namely an explicit treatment of inflationary expectations. The 'modern' element in the model lies in its explicitly analysing the behaviour of an economy in disequilibrium, and hence in its implicit abandonment of what I termed above 'Say's law'. I shall now go on to argue that in his earlier, more detailed expositions of the cumulative process Wicksell showed that he was well aware of abandoning Say's law but that an inadequate treatment of the role of price level expectations in determining market behaviour in disequilibrium was responsible for his failure to develop the theory of output fluctuations.

The institutional background of the cumulative process as Wicksell set it out for the *Economic Journal* is that of an economy in which the means of payment are the liabilities of a well developed commercial banking system. In common with all his contemporaries, Wicksell did not normally use the word 'money' to describe these liabilities. Thus to a modern reader of this 1907 paper the link between Wicksell's work on the cumulative process and the classical quantity theory of money tradition is not immediately obvious. Nevertheless the link is strong.[8] Wicksell did not regard the quantity theory as perfect by any means, but he termed it 'the most competent of all the methods of interpretation that have so far been advanced of the oscillation of the general price level' (1898a, p. 50). He believed the main fault in the classical tradition to lie in the unsatisfactory treatment his predecessors had given to what we would now call the real balance effect.

> A general rise in prices is … only conceivable on the supposition that the general demand has for some reason become, or is expected to become, greater than the supply. This may sound paradoxical, because we have accustomed ourselves, with J. B. Say, to regard goods themselves as reciprocally constituting and limiting the demand for each other. And indeed *ultimately* they do so; here, however, we are concerned with precisely what occurs, *in the first place,* with the middle link in the final exchange of one good against another, which is formed by the demand of money for goods and the supply of goods against money. Any theory of money worthy of the name must be able to show how and why the monetary or pecuniary demand for goods exceeds or falls short of the supply of goods in given conditions.
>
> The advocates of the Quantity Theory have perhaps not sufficiently considered this point. They usually make the mistake of postulating their assumptions instead of clearly proving them. That a large and a small quantity of money can serve the same purposes of turnover if commodity prices rise or fall proportionately to the quantity is one thing. It is another thing to show why such a change of price must always follow a change in the quantity of money and to describe what happens. [1905, pp. 159-60]

The main stimulus to Wicksell's work on prices seems to have been his desire to fill this gap in his predecessors' analysis. In the pages of the *Lectures* following the passage quoted he shows in considerable detail how it is that the increase in prices that is observed to result from new gold discoveries, or indeed from government issues of inconvertible paper, is brought about by a mechanism very much akin to the modern 'wealth effect'; an excess supply of money at going prices results directly in an excess demand for goods. In these circumstances the price level is bid up without the intervention of interest rate fluctuations. However, he then turns to consider a world with a banking system and well developed credit markets, and the emphasis shifts away from a direct wealth effect to the interest rate effects on prices that are central to the cumulative process. To Wicksell this represents only a shift of emphasis, introduced to deal with a particular institutional framework, and not a radical break with the quantity theory tradition.

> ... it [the analysis of the cumulative process] is in full agreement with what would occur if prices rose in consequence of an actual superfluity of gold, if the new gold came into the hands of the public in the form of loans from the banks. This is certainly not usually the case, for gold flows into the country from abroad to some extent directly in payment for goods. In such a case it should immediately give rise to an increase in commodity prices, and this increase may even precede the arrival of the gold, so that in relation to the continually rising price level there may be no excess of gold and consequently no reason for lowering the rate of interest. But to some extent also the new gold enters the country and finds its way to the banks as 'capital', i.e. the owner of the gold ... wishes to lend the money out at interest ... the banks, in order to put it—or an equal amount of notes—in circulation must inevitably lower their loan rate, and ... all commodity prices will rise and business will thus require more media of exchange. As soon as that happens there will be an end to the relative excess of money, the banks will again raise their rates to the normal, i.e. to correspond with the real rate, and at that rate the prices already raised will be maintained.... The condition on which the banks could maintain a rate of interest permanently below the real rate would ... be an incessant flow to them of new gold, and under such circumstances commodity prices would also rise continuously. If this be admitted there can scarcely be any difference if for gold we substitute banknotes, fictitious deposits, or other bank credit. The *causa efficiens,* the direct and active cause, is in both cases the same, namely a rate of loan interest below the normal, and in both cases the consequences must be the same. [1905, pp. 197-98]

The cumulative process, then, does not represent a radical break with the analysis of Wicksell's classical predecessors; it supplements that analysis. But in doing so it shifts the emphasis of monetary economics away from the comparative statics of an economy in full equilibrium situations and towards the dynamics of the process whereby such an economy moves from one full equilibrium situation to another. For Wicksell, Say's law holds true in the equilibria between which the economy is moving, as does the quantity theory of money (if we make due allowance for the semantics of what is and is not money), but neither has much relevance in the periods of disequilibrium when the cumulative process is at work.

Thus the first of what I have termed the three essential propositions of Keynes's economics is clearly a vital part of Wicksell's economics as well. What is strikingly different, however, is that for Wicksell disequilibrium meant price level fluctuations whether demand was excessive or deficient. If we look more closely at his analysis of the cumulative process we shall easily see (with the benefit of hindsight) how he came to overlook the capacity of an economy to generate output fluctuations in response to shifts in aggregate demand. However, it ought to be acknowledged first of all that, to some degree at least, the reason for this, to us, crucial deficiency may be no more subtle than that Wicksell was primarily concerned with the analysis of inflation. A reading of any one of his accounts of the cumulative process reveals that, having dealt with the case of rising prices in some detail, he is usually content to assert that the deflationary situation is the same as the inflationary one with the appropriate signs reserved.[9]

Nevertheless the market behaviour that Wicksell postulated as underlying the formation of prices in disequilibrium did not leave room for output fluctuations, even though it involved another very Keynesian concept, an income constrained aggregate demand function.

In the account given earlier of the cumulative process it was taken for granted that prices rose with excess demand; indeed, my geometric reconstruction of the analysis postulated that the rate of price increase was proportional to excess demand. This is so common an assumption about the behaviour of prices in disequilibrium that it is easy to forget that it is completely arbitrary. The assumption in question perhaps has its origins in descriptions of the behaviour of the Walrasian 'auctioneer' who, during the tâtonnement process, raises the prices of those goods in excess demand and lowers the prices of those in excess supply; it seems a short and harmless step to apply this analysis to the behaviour of the general price level in a situation of overall excess demand (or excess supply) for goods, nor is the assumption that price adjustments are proportional to the excess demand in question particularly hard to swallow.

However, the important thing about the Walrasian tâtonnement process is that no contracts are binding except that set of contracts by which all markets are cleared. There is no trading except that at equilibrium prices. In any actual inflation, or deflation, trading goes on while prices change, and if inflation is to be explained as a disequilibrium phenomenon, the assumption—albeit usually a tacit one—that prices are formed by something akin to a tâtonnement with recontracting process must be given up.[10]

Wicksell dealt explicitly with the price formation mechanism in disequilibrium and did indeed abandon Walrasian tâtonnement with recontracting. The process with which he replaced it, however, still left prices to do all the adjusting necessary in disequilibrium.

Chapter 9 of *Interest and Prices* bears the title 'Systematic exposition of the theory'. The model there set out is based upon a period of production idea. The stock of fixed capital is inherited from the past, does not depreciate and is not to be added to. Variable capital is raised by enterpreneurs by selling bonds to banks at the beginning of the period. Labour and land are hired with the proceeds of the bond sales, which proceeds in turn are then used to purchase from the capitalists who have just bought them the consumption goods to maintain labourers and landlords during the period of production. The capitalists, who in this model are also traders, buying from entrepreneurs and selling to final consumers, thus finance output by holding the liabilities of the banks during the period of production. The stock of consumption goods available for sale is equal to the previous period's output less the interest income of capitalists and the wages of management that accrue to entrepreneurs.

Production thus begins with the labour force and landlords holding the stock of circulating capital and capitalists holding bank deposits equal in value to entrepreneurs' debts to the banking system. At the end of the period output is (by assumption) the same as in the previous period: it is sold by entrepreneurs to capitalists in exchange for the latter's holdings of money, including their interest receipts from the banks, which in turn goes to pay off entrepreneurs' debts to the banks. The system is now ready to begin another cycle as entrepreneurs renew their bank loans in order to finance the next period's production.[11]

Now Wicksell did not, of course, take this model literally. It obviously contains many simplifying assumptions 'made purely for the sake of simplicity and clarity' (p. 136); in particular, towards the end of this chapter he relaxes the assumption that there is no accumulation of fixed capital, accompanies it with the postulate that technical progress exists to prevent the natural rate of interest (i.e. the marginal productivity of capital) falling to zero, and argues that these complications do not alter the basic nature of his analysis or the conclusions to be drawn from it (*cf*. 1898a, pp. 150 *et seq*.).

Again, the rather curious social arrangement whereby capitalists are also engaged in dealing in commodities at no profit is defended only for the sake of producing an analytically simple model (*cf*. 1898a, p. 138), as is the notion that the period of production is of the same length and begins and ends at the same time in all branches of production (*cf*. 1898a, pp. 137, 146-7, 148).

This latter assumption, however, is not so harmless as it might seem, for it permits a sequential price formation mechanism of a type that ensures the maintenance of full employment.

Entrepreneurs, expecting the price of goods to be as it was in the previous period, take their loans from the banks, and bid for labour and land with the proceeds of these loans. The relevant markets clear, and labourers and landlords, given their incomes, buy the previous period's output from the capitalists. Production then takes place and the output (equal to that of the previous period) is sold at the end of the period to the capitalists in exchange for the money they received, and hence at the price set, at the beginning of the period. Now this is not a full Walrasian tâtonnement with recontracting market mechanism. The labour market clears before the goods market, and the outcome of bargains struck in the labour market constrain the demand for goods. Thus a simple prototype of the income-constrained process which, according to Clower, is central to the economics of the *General Theory* is explicitly present as an integral part of Wicksell's cumulative process, without producing the Keynesian conclusions when the bargains struck by this mechanism produce different prices to those that would arise if goods and labour (not to mention bond) markets were permitted to clear simultaneously with recontracting.[12]

As usual, Wicksell analyses the matter in detail for the inflationary case. He assumes an exogenous increase in the natural rate of interest of 1 per cent, and, dismissing as unimportant the tendency of the associated increase in output to lower prices both because 'the fall that could on such grounds be expected would be a very small one' and, more important, because it would 'occur only *once and for all*', notes that the main consequence of such a change would be to set up 'a tendency for an expansion of their activities' on the part of the entrepreneurs, which in turn

> ... brings about an increase in the demand for labour and other factors of production.... Money wages and money rents are forced up, and although there is no general expansion in production, entrepreneurs are obliged to borrow more capital from the banks for the production of the current year. It is impossible to tell directly how much wages will go up.... But ... it is possible to fix a limit. If entrepreneurs are not reckoning for the moment on any rise in future prices, the upper limit to the possible rise in wages is the fall of the rate of interest.[13]

> It might ... be thought that the rise in wages must deprive the entrepreneurs of the whole of the surplus profit for which they are hoping in respect to the current year. But ... if the workers and landlords raise their demands for goods for the consumption of the current year to the extent that money wages and money rents have gone up, this increased demand is met by the same amount of commodity capital as

before. It necessarily results in *a rise in all prices*—a rise which it is simplest to regard as *proportional* to the increase in demand.... The dealers receive this increased sum in the form of money (bank drafts) ... but this sum represents only the same amount of real capital as before.

The total amount of consumption goods produced in the course of the year is no more than it was at the end of the previous year... if the entrepreneurs exchange among themselves 1 per cent of the total amount of goods ... they can sell the remainder to the capitalists ... and they are then able to repay their bank loans.... It can easily be seen that the entrepreneurs have earned as a surplus profit over and above their 'wage' an amount equal to 1 per cent of the capital—precisely that amount per cent by which the natural rate exceeded the contractual rate. [1898a, pp. 144-5].

In the following year this process repeats itself and continues to do so until the banks raise their lending rate, and the rate which they pay to capitalists on their deposits, to equality with the natural rate of interest.

Having analysed the inflationary process in some detail, Wicksell devotes less than a page to the deflation that results from the lending rate of the banks remaining above the natural rate of interest.

Not only will the entrepreneurs now fail to obtain any surplus profit, but they will suffer losses.... To prevent this, they will *desire* to confine their activities to the more profitable channels, and there will be a corresponding contraction in their demand for labour and land. But workers and landlords will respond by scaling down their claims for wages and rents, and on the whole activity will be maintained at its former level...

These diminished wages and rents have to be set against an unaltered amount of consumption goods (real capital). The result is a corresponding fall in the prices of commodities, and entrepreneurs are unable to avoid a loss, which is expressed by the difference between the two rates of interest.... There ensues a further fall in money wages etc., which results in turn in a fresh fall in prices. And so the movement continues. [1898a, pp. 149-50]

Thus in Wicksell we have explicit acknowledgment that inflation and deflation involve trading at disequilibrium prices, that the wages paid to workers constrain their demand for goods, and that their demand for goods thus constrained in turn influences the demands of entrepreneurs for land and labour. This is quite close to a fully developed Keynesian circular flow model of income determination in disequilibrium. There is only one ingredient missing and that is the Keynesian analysis of expectations both as they effect the supply price of goods and as they affect the supply side of the wage bargain. Wicksell was aware of the importance of expectations only in as much as they determined entrepreneurial behaviour with regard to the demand side of the wage bargain.

Entrepreneurs in Wicksell's model have to form expectations about the price at which their output can be sold before they can fix a limit to their bids for land and labour at the beginning of the production period. He usually assumed that the price level determined in the previous period formed the basis of entrepreneurs' calculations, but the very fact that the assumption was almost invariably made explicit attests to the fact that Wicksell realised how important expectations were as a determinant of extrepreneurial behaviour. He did consider certain complications here as well, for he recognised that in an inflation

> The upward movement in prices will in some measure 'create its own draught'. When prices have been rising for some time, extrepreneurs will begin to reckon on the basis not merely of the prices already attained, but of a further rise in prices. The effect on supply and demand is clearly the same as that of a corresponding easing of credit [1898a, p. 96]

Clearly, we have here a version of the analysis of the effects of anticipated inflation on the real value of the rate of interest, given a nominal value and of its subsequent influence on aggregate demand. Such analysis plays an important role in modern work on inflation, but Wicksell never stressed the matter, partly perhaps because it was not necessary to produce his cumulative rise in prices, its effect being only to make 'that actual rise more and more rapid' (p. 148) but partly one suspects he did not produce any explicit theory as to the way in which expectations about inflation were generated that fitted easily into his model.[14] For whatever reason, however, the idea in question gets but two mentions, amounting to about one page, in *Interest and Prices* (cf. 1898a, pp. 96-7, 148), is accorded a single sentence in the *Lectures* (1905, p. 207) and is not mentioned at all in the *Economic Journal* article. We can hardly regard it as central to Wicksell's thought on this issue.

Nevertheless, the idea that the formation of expectations about future prospects is an essential task of the entrepreneur is a well developed and integral part of Wicksell's thought. The insight that forms the basis of chapter 5 and hence of much else of the *General Theory,* namely that

> Time usually elapses ... between the incurring of costs by the producer (with the consumer in view) and the purchase of

> the output by the ultimate consumer. Meanwhile the entre-
> preneur ... has to form the best expectations he can as to
> what the consumers will be prepared to pay when he is ready
> to supply them .. he has no choice but to be guided by these
> expectations, if he is to produce at all by processes which
> occupy time. [1936, p. 46]

certainly underlies Wicksell's view of the entrepreneur's role in
the formation of prices.

However, only entrepreneurial expectations play an explicit
role in Wicksell's model. The price level expectations of the
labour force, which are crucial to the Keynesian analysis of unemployment, are totally absent from his work.

It will be recalled that in Wicksell's model the labour market
clears at a moment in time at the beginning of the production
period. Moreover it clears at whatever money wage rate ensures
that all variable capital is spent and all labour employed; nothing
at all is said of the attitude of labour force members towards that
money wage rate. The tacit assumption is simply that they will
accept it whatever its level rather than be unemployed. For
Keynes the fact that in any actual market economy there was no
mechanism whereby the money wages of all members of the
labour force could be changed uniformly and simultaneously was
a matter of basic importance.

> Except in a socialised community where wage policy is
> settled by decree, there is no means of securing uniform
> wage reductions for every class of labour. The result can only
> be brought about by a series of gradual, irregular changes...
> [1936, p. 267]

Because it is impossible to bring out a synchronous fall in
money wages,

> any individual or group of individuals, who consent to a re-
> duction of money wages relatively to others, will suffer a
> *relative* reduction in real wages, which is a sufficient justifi-
> cation for them to resist it [1936, p. 14]

Indeed, even if it were possible to get money wages to fall
across the board simultaneously, if members of the labour force
did not expect prices also to fall they would again see a cut in
real wages as the consequence, and resist the cut (*cf.* 1936, p. 264)

Throughout Wicksell's analysis the real wage rate in fact
remains constant. That (for Keynes) special set of circumstances
called full employment at which the real wage rate represents
both the marginal product of labour and the marginal disutility
of work is always maintained. But it is maintained in the deflationary case only because money wage cuts are accepted simultaneously and without question by the whole labour force.

If we drop this assumption (and it will be recalled that Wicksell's main reason for having a model in which the labour market clears at one moment in time was no more than simplicity of exposition), and replace it with the Keynesian one of downward rigidity of the money wage, we immediately generate unemployment in the Wicksellian model; whether the unemployment in question is of the Keynesian type or not, however, is another question.

If rigidity of the wage rate is the only assumption we introduce, then Wicksell's model produces no analogue to the multiplier. The prices of goods in Wicksell's model are determined by a tatonnement that takes place at a different time to the striking of the wage bargain, and influenced by the wage bargain only in as much as the demand for goods is constrained by the wage bill. The capitalists selling the goods take whatever prices will rid them of their entire stock. Thus, if we follow Wicksell's logic through, it will be clear that, when full employment equilibrium is initially disturbed by the discrepancy arising between the natural and the market rates of interest, the sum of money available to buy the previous period's output from the capitalists will be the same regardless of the level of money wages that is fixed. Only the number of labourers bidding for goods will be different. Thus, even if the wage rate is rigid, at the end of the production period the capitalists will have the same sum to spend on output as they would have under conditions of completely flexible wages. However, with rigid wages, and hence unemployment, there will be fewer goods to spend it on. Indeed, the reduced output will sell for exactly the price initially expected by entrepreneurs, their subsequent borrowings will be the same, and, with money wages rigid, the level of employment and output will be the same in the next and all subsequent periods. This is a very 'classical' type of unemployment indeed, and yet we get it in a model with rigid wages and an income-constrained aggregate demand function.

The extra assumption we need to get to a Wicksellian analogue to the multiplier is a reluctance on the part of capitalists to lower the price of goods in the face of excess supply. For Keynes, whose model is one of continuous production, the demand side of the goods market is constrained by incomes, but the supply side is also influenced as to price by marginal production costs, which he associated mainly with wage payments (*cf.* 1936, p. 12). As with wage rigidity, an obvious rationale for downward price rigidity is not so easy to come by within the structure Wicksell's period model, but if we do arbitrarily introduce this further assumption then we find that the reduced wage bill will not buy the full stock of goods held by capitalists. Unwanted inventories will be left, and, if capitalists expect their future sales to be the same as those of the current period, their purchases from entrepreneurs will

not take up all output. In effect the unwanted inventories will be
shifted to entrepreneurs. Upon finding that the volume of their
sales to capitalists is lower than expected, entrepreneurs would
presumably cut back their borrowing further, and another round
similar to the one just described would then take place but with
a lower level of output. In Wicksell's model, where the marginal
propensity of the labour force to consume is unity, output would
contract without limit. If the model was modified to include a
fractional marginal propensity to consume we would have a
Keynesian dynamic multiplier process with a finite limit to the
fall in output.[15]

III

The main argument of this paper has been that a number of ideas
nowadays associated with the Keynesian revolution were in fact
central to Wicksell's dynamic analysis. That there is a strong
Wicksellian flavour to Keynes's contribution has long been a
commonplace and I would not claim to have done any more than
document this a little more fully than has been done in the past.
In particular Leijonhufvud's attribution of Wicksellian characteristics to the analysis of the *General Theory* is, I believe,
amply borne out by the evidence I have presented here. However,
this ought in no way to detract from our assessment of the
fundamental nature of Keynes's contribution.

Though Wicksell did step away from the prevailing orthodoxy
in his abandonment of Say's law, and in his explicit analysis of
a process of price formation without complete recontracting,
neither of these innovations led him to question the basic
'classical' proposition about the price system—a proposition that
is still enshrined in most of our textbooks to this day, Keynesian
revolution or not. This proposition is that the role of prices, a
role they successfully perform, is to transmit information about
changes in tastes, technology and available resources in such a
way that scarce resources are continuously reallocated to be
fully utilised in some optimal fashion. The tacit assumption of
classical competitive theory is that prices are called by an all-
seeing auctioneer and that participants in the market respond to
those prices with bids and offers that do not become binding till
complete harmony has been achieved. Keynes saw that, in the
absence of the auctioneer (or of freely available and complete
information which amounts to the same thing), participants in the
market would themselves have to adjust prices. Thus, instead of
exogenously given price changes being the signal for quantity
adjustments, quantity changes are required to signal the need for
price changes which in turn bring about further quantity changes.
While this process continues over time, binding contracts are

entered into at disequilibrium prices on the basis of false and inconsistent expectations, and dynamic forces that may or may not
lead the economic system towards something resembling the competitive solution are set in motion.

Keynes himself applied this insight only to the analysis of
what we would now term unanticipated deflation, and showed that
a capacity to generate unemployment in the face of contractions
in aggregate demand was an inherent characteristic of a market
economy whose members were forced to act on the basis of
incomplete information about the consequences of their actions.
It was his explicitly stated view that inflationary situations were
adequately analysed in terms of classical theory. However,
recent extensions of Phillips curve analysis that focus on the
influence of price level expectations on the unemployment—inflation trade-off show that the basic Keynesian insight has considerable relevance to the problem of inflation. If we look upon Keynes
as having provided the basis of what is usually termed 'the new
micro-economics' it is immediately apparent that the force of the
Keynesian revolution is far from spent.[16] Thus to recognise
Wicksell's contribution to the development of macro-economics as
considerable, and to find strong links between his work and that
of Keynes, in no way requires that we downgrade Keynes.

Indeed, one of the main benefits from reading Wicksell (but
only one of them, for Wicksell clearly has much to offer us in his
own right) is that we gain a clearer perspective on the nature of
Keynes's contribution to economics.

NOTES

[1]   This paper, reprinted from *The Manchester School*, June 1972,
is part of a broader study of inflation theory carried out under the
auspices of the SSRC-financed Manchester Inflation Programme. I
am grateful to members of that programme for their helpful comments. In particular I have benefitted greatly from discussions with
Malcom Gray and Michael Parkin. Comments by Michael Kenndey
and Professor Thomas Wilson on an unpublished essay written
jointly with Michael Parkin and entitled 'Wicksell's cumulative
process; a pedagogic note' were also most useful in the preparation of this essay. Special thanks are due to John Hargreaves, who
checked the quotations and references for accuracy.

[2]   It is worth noting that Don Patinkin's *Money, Interest and
Prices* is now coming to be regarded as a vital book in transmit-
ting the 'true' Keynesian message (*cf.* for example, Barro and
Grossman, 1971). This is somewhat ironic given the fact that at
its first appearance book was widely regarded as an attempt to
reinstate so-called classical (i.e. anti-Keynesian) economics.

[3]   *Cf.* Leijonhufvud (1968), pp. 321-2.

4   That the analysis of expectations lies at the core of the Keynesian revolution is, of course, the view of Shackle (1967).

5   The accounts available in English are Wicksell (1898a and b, 1905, 1907). However, on p. 97 of (1898a) is a reference to a paper entitled 'Der Bankzins als Regulator der Warenpreise' that appeared in the *Jährbücher für Nationalökomie and Statistik,* LXVIII, 1897.

6   The last sentence of this quotation sounds very much like Milton Friedman! However, it is important to note that for Friedman inflationary expectations are a major reason for 'High' interest rates seeming 'low' and vice versa. Thus he is able to reconcile the positive correlation between interest rates and economic activity with a monetary explanation of the business cycle. Wicksell did not fully incorporate such a theory of expectations into his analysis (*cf.* p. 112 below) and hence was forced to regard shifts in the real rate of interest as the driving force behind economic fluctuations.

7   A stable approach to equilibrium in this model does, of course, require certain assumptions about the slopes of curves. Algebraically the model is

$$E_t = a(R^* - r_t)$$

$$p_t - p_{t-1} = dE_{t-1}$$

$$r_t = r_{t-1} + b(p_t - p_{t-1})$$

It yields

$$p_t - p_{t-1} = [1 - \text{dab}] (p_{t-1} - p_{t-2})$$

and hence the price level smoothly approaches an equilibrium value if $0 < \text{dab} < 1$.

8   The link is fully and carefully analysed in Patinkin (1965), note E, pp. 581-97, and hence is treated somewhat sketchily here.

9   There is some faint recognition in *Interest and Prices* that unemployment might accompany deflation, for, having asserted that during a deflation '. . . on the whole activity will be maintained at its former level', Wicksell adds in parentheses, '(It is not, however, to be denied that there may be a more or less permanent, though not progressive, loss of employment by some of the workers—the industrial reserve)' (p. 149). However, this is a parallel to the possibility that, in an inflationary situation '. . . as a result . . . of longer working hours, there is a certain non-cumulative increase in production . . .' Particularly in view of the denial of a cumulative property to these output and employment changes, this passage can in no sense be regarded as foreshadowing Keynesian analysis.

10   Not all inflation models are disequilibrium ones. Once we have a notion of inflationary expectations, a model in which actual and

expected inflation are equal to one another can be in full equilibrium while prices rise. Cagan (1956) analyses such a model and
indeed also applies it to situations in which realised inflation
differs from what was expected.
[11]   This model is surely eloquent testimony to the classical
roots of Wicksell's analysis. Its basis is, after all, the Ricardian
model of the stationary state, transmitted to Wicksell, as Klaus
Hennings has pointed out to me, through the work of Böhm-
Bawerk.
[12]   If one could have recontracting, of course, there could be no
trading until the bank rate of interest equalled the natural rate.
In short, there would be no cumulative process.
[13]   I think we are safe to interpret this rather clumsy phrase as
meaning that the wage bill can increase by the same *percentage*
as the interest rate has fallen in *percentage points*.
[14]   Wicksell's analysis of expectations is most fully set out in
a passage in small type on p. 97 of *Interest and Prices*. I find this
passage very confusing and can make some sense of it only by
assuming that he had at the back of his mind some model in which
entrepreneurs try to assess the effect on prices of their current
wage policy and then adjust their wage policy in the light of these
expectations, form new expectations, etc. The wage bill then at
any moment emerges as the limit to some sort of iterative process—a limit which would not exist short of infinity if the effect
on prices of current wage policy was correctly foreseen and acted
on (*cf.* also p. 148). This latter case is equivalent to tâtonnement
with recontracting and is, as we have seen, incompatible with the
cumulative process (*cf.* note 10 above).
[15]   Presumably one could carry the analysis of a 'Wicksellian'
multiplier process much further, but this seems a rather fruitless
exercise, given that it is the one thing missing from Wicksell's
own analysis! However, two points might be made.
   First, to get a 'Wicksellian' multiplier, it has been seen that
entrepreneurs must be 'pushed off' the demand for labour curves
that rule in the initial full employment situation, for the inability
to sell all the output that they expect to sell, and hence produce, is
an essential ingredient in the process whereby the fall in output
cumulates. Patinkin (1965, chapter 13) argues that this is also
an important property of the Keynesian model of unemployment,
properly understood. Whether or not this idea is to be found in
the *General Theory* is a moot point. Much of the argument of
chapter 2 is directed to defending the idea that the marginal productivity of labour does determine the demand for it, and hence
may be used as evidence that Keynes did not have this idea.
Certainly this is Grossman's view (1972). On the other hand a
charitable reading between the lines of chapter 5 might be used to
provide evidence to the contrary.

Second, the mechanism I have described in the text will only work so simply if capitalists are willing to accumulate indefinitely large amounts of bank liabilities at a given rate of interest. The 'Wicksellian multiplier', just like the Keynesian one, requires a liquidity trap to permit it to work itself out fully.

16   The 'new micro-economics' is, of course, associated with the name of Phelps (*cf.* 1970 in particular). However, Friedman (1968) has also made an important contribution here. As in the case of Patinkin, there is a certain irony that recent reinterpretations of Keynes should make Friedman appear to be an important contributor to the Keynesian tradition.

6 Simultaneous fluctuations in prices and output: a business cycle approach[1]

I

The coexistence in recent years of high rates of inflation and high levels of unemployment has focused attention on the problem of what the factors are that determine the manner in which variations in money income are divided up between variations in real income and employment on the one hand and in prices on the other. The hypothesis of a negative rate of trade-off between wage inflation (and hence presumably price inflation) and unemployment, embodied in the simple Phillips curve, has fallen into widespread disrepute in the face of this recent evidence.[2] At the same time, more elaborate versions of the Phillips curve that allow for the influence of inflationary expectations, though they are compatible with this evidence, have commanded much less than universal acceptance.

This paper first argues that there are a number of quite central questions about inflationary situations on which even sophisticated Phillips curve analysis is silent. Second, it attempts to bring together orthodox post-Keynesian macro-economics and a species of Phillips curve analysis in an extremely simple model of price and output fluctuations in terms of which the above-mentioned questions may be analysed; moreover the model's predictions about the interaction of these variables appear to be of some empirical interest.

II

The Phillips relationship is based upon the proposition that the rate of change of wages is positively related to the excess demand for labour, and that the unemployment rate is inversely related to the same variable.[3] Inflationary expectations enter the picture once it is recognised that, although the Phillips curve deals with the rate of change of *money* wages, the supply and demand for labour determine the *real* wage. Since the rate of change of money wages that is bargained for at any moment in time is equal to the desired rate of change of real wages plus the expected rate of

change of prices, there is a different (short-run) Phillips curve
for every expected rate of price inflation. In the long run, and in
the ideal case, the Phillips curve becomes vertical.

This sophisticated Phillips curve analysis surely represents
an interesting approach to understanding the disequilibrium behaviour of the labour market, but it is far from satisfactory if
treated, as it sometimes is, as a model of the determination of
inflation and unemployment rates in the macro-economy. Changes
in the level of aggregate demand (and perhaps there are also
shifts on the supply side of the labour market) that cause unemployment and wage inflation rates to vary are completely exogenous
to the analysis. The whole of that branch of economic theory that
is concerned with aggregate demand determination is left to one
side.

Inflationary expectations impinge upon the analysis only as
they affect the wage bargain. In traditional macro theory, at least
since Irving Fisher (1896), the central role of inflationary expectations has been to cause the nominal and real interest rates to
diverge from one another in such a way that aggregate demand is
affected. This particular linkage in the inflationary process is
completely ignored by the Phillips curve.

Another symptom of the same general problem is encountered
in empirical work on prices and incomes policies.[4] The effects of
such policies have typically been investigated using the Philips
curve and asking questions about whether, and the extent to which,
such policies shift and change the slope of the curve. However,
prices and incomes policies typically are part of a broader
package that includes the use of orthodox demand management
techniques as well. There are surely questions worth asking
about the interaction of these policy tools but, because it is not
a model of the macro-economy in which aggregate demand is
endogenous, it is impossible to frame such questions using the
Phillips curve.[5]

In short, the Phillips curve is not a complete model of a
macro-economic system and should not, therefore, be expected
to provide a complete analysis of price and output dynamics in
an inflationary situation. At best it can be one component of such
a model, albeit perhaps an important one. The analysis that
follows is an attempt to build a simple macro-model that incorporates a type of Phillips curve relationship, produces simultaneous, endogenously determined fluctuations in prices and output, and hence is capable of dealing with the type of question
raised in the last few paragraphs. Whether the reader will find
the model congenial and helpful must depend very much upon the
criteria by which he judges economic models. If 'realism' and
'descriptive accuracy' of assumptions are given any significant
weight, the model will be found extremely unappealing; for it was

constructed with the express aim of being as simple as possible while still being capable of producing predictions that appear to conform to reality. If predictions rather than assumptions are the main criteria by which a model is judged, then this model will perhaps be found to be of some interest.

III

The basis of the model with which this section of the paper deals is the Hicks trade cycle model of 1950. This Hicks model is cast in terms of discrete time, and divides expenditure into three categories. There is an autonomous component, A; a component that depends upon lagged income, Y—usually but not out of any logical necessity referred to as consumption, C; and a component that depends upon the lagged rate of change of income. The latter is usually referred to as induced investment, I.

The model dealt with here retains autonomous expenditure and a consumption function of the form

$$C = (1 - s)Y_{-1} \tag{1}$$

but it modifies the induced investment equation. The latter, in Hicks, is based upon a relationship between the desired level of the capital stock, K^*, and the previous period's income, and upon the assumption that so long as desired investment is positive sufficient investment may always be carried out to achieve the desired capital stock. Thus, from the demand for capital relationship,

$$K^* = vY_{-1} \tag{2}$$

and, ignoring depreciation for simplicity, we get the investment relationship

$$I = K^* - K^*_{-1} = v(Y_{-1} - Y_{-2}) > 0 \text{ or } I = 0. \tag{3}$$

If we add the lagged value of the real rate of interest, R, as a determinant of the desired capital stock, the induced investment equation becomes

$$I = v(Y_{-1} - Y_{-2}) - a(R_{-1} - R_{-2}) > 0 \text{ or } I = 0 \tag{4}$$

This investment function is extremely simple, and some might think it over-simple. If, as so much empirical work suggests we should do, we made the demand for capital depend upon the expected level of income and interest rates, measuring these as some sort of weighted averages of past values of the variables, and then had less than complete adjustment of the capital stock within each time period, investment would emerge as a potentially quite complicated function of current and past levels of income and interest rates. This procedure would certainly add something to the realism of the model under discussion; but it would have the unfortunate consequence of making the model sufficiently complicated to ensure that we would not produce any readily interpretable predictions from it by analytic methods. The sacrifice of realism in assumptions to simplicity and clarity in prediction implicit in the use of equation 4 surely needs no defence.

It is the real rate of interest that appears in our investment equation. This variable is equal to the nominal rate, r, minus the expected rate of price inflation, Δp^e. Thus we have

$$R = \bar{r} - \Delta p^e \tag{5}$$

with the bar over r indicating that it is treated as an exogenous variable.

The choice of the nominal interest rate rather than the money stock as an exogenous variable is mainly the result of a desire to keep the model as simple as possible, though there are, of course, quite enough episodes in recent economic history in which this variable has been the one manipulated by the authorities to justify the potential empirical relevance of the choice.[6] I shall in any event sketch out below some of the model's properties when the money stock is treated as exogenous, in order to show that the most interesting results that emerge from the current analysis do not depend critically upon the choice of the exogenous monetary variable. For the moment the important point to note is that treating the nominal rate of interest as exogenous does not imply that the quantity of money is an unimportant variable in this model —even when it does not explicitly appear in it. Monetary authorities can, after all, control the nominal interest rate only by standing ready to buy and sell bonds at a given price, hence permitting the quantity of money to take on whatever value is necessary, given the level of real income and prices, to maintain the value of that interest rate. Thus the quantity of money plays an extremely important permissive role in the analysis that follows.

Two more equations complete the model. First, the expected rate of inflation is defined as follows:

$$\Delta p^e = d\Delta p + (1 - d)\Delta p^e_{-1} \tag{6}$$

This is a completely conventional characterisation of a process whereby expectations are formed on the basis of experience, having first appeared in a continuous time formulation in the work of Cagan (1956).

The final equation of the model concerns the determination of the actual rate of change of prices, and it is here that we introduce a relationship that is a very near relative of the sophisticated Phillips curve. The basis of the so-called 'new microeconomics' is that market participants have less than perfect information about the prices and quantities at which markets will

clear. In such circumstances it is necessary for them to form
the best expectations they can, call out their own prices on the
basis of these expectations, and then, in response to the quantities
bought and sold at these prices, revise their expectations and
hence the prices they call. The final equation of the model applies
these ideas to the determination of the rate of change of prices in
general. It is assumed that at the beginning of each period firms
have expectations about the amount by which prices in general
will change from the previous period, and initially change their
own individual prices by the same amount. It is then assumed that
a discrepancy between aggregate demand and full employment
output during the period causes them to revise their prices up or
down, so that within each period there is simultaneously determined an actual rate of inflation from the previous period and a
level of aggregate demand which, if it falls short of full employment output, Y^*, is also the level of realised output. In short, we
have as the final equation

$$E > Y^*, \Delta p = \Delta p^e{}_{-1} + c(E - Y^*) \tag{7}$$

$$E = Y \leqslant Y^*, \Delta p = \Delta p^e{}_{-1} + g(Y - Y^*) \tag{7a}$$

I have used different symbols for the coefficients linking the
rate of inflation of a positive and negative discrepancy between
aggregate demand and full employment output in these equations
because I can think of no particular reason why there should be
symmetry of response to these two states of the world. An excess
of aggregate demand manifests itself initially in terms of depleted
stocks and then queues of unsatisfied customers, while a shortfall
of aggregate demand produces a build-up of stocks and queues of
people unsuccessfully seeking employment. It would be wise to
leave the matter of stocks to one side, for they do not appear within the formal structure of the model under analysis; but though
queues of unsatisfied customers would presumably lead to an
increase in prices above their planned level, and queues of people
seeking employment a decrease, I can see no reason why the
amounts of the changes involved need to be related to one another.

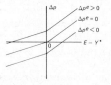

Figure 6.1

Equations 7a and 7b are plotted in figure 1, with a different
relationship between Δp and $(E - Y^*)$ for every expected inflation
rate, in order to illustrate the close relationship between this

function and the sophisticated Phillips curve. If one re-labelled the horizontal axis of figure 1 'Excess demand for labour' and the vertical 'Rate of change of money wages', one would have exactly the kind of relationship which Lipsey (1960) postulated as under-lying the Phillips curve, adjusted for the role of expected inflation in the manner that the Phelps (1967)-Friedman (1968) analysis requires. In a model which follows the tradition set by at least the simpler version of post-Keynesian macro-economics, and which takes no explicit note of the labour market but rather implicity assumes that there is an inverse monotonic relationship between the level of aggregate demand and the unemployment rate (at least up to 'full employment', where the latter variable becomes a constant), equation 7 seems to be as close as one can get to a Phillips curve.

Before putting the model through its paces two difficulties ought to be drawn to the reader's attention. First, we are going to assume that Y^*, full employment output—or 'ceiling output' in the Hicksian vocabulary—is exogenously given and constant. As a matter of strict logic this is incompatible with the model's capacity to generate positive investment, particularly since the introduction of the real rate of interest into the demand for capital relationship must reflect the existence of a variable proportions production function. Though it would be of some interest to in-troduce explicitly a production function into the model and incor-porate the effects of capital accumulation upon full employment output, I have as yet been unable to find a way of doing this that preserves any semblance of the model's simplicity.[7] The simplest way out of the dilemma, and a stratagem that is commonly adopted in short-run macro-economic model building, is to assume that the capital stock already in existence is sufficiently large relative to current accumulation to render harmless the treatment of full employment output as approximately an exogenous constant.

The second problem arises from the relationship between 6 and 7. From these equations it follows that

$$\Delta p^e = d\Delta p + (1 - d)\Delta p^e_{-1} = dg(E - Y^*) + \Delta p^e_{-1} \qquad (8)$$

But when we put matters this way it is apparent that the orthodox error-learning model of the formation of expectations [will not necessarily provide a forecast of the rate of inflation that is con-sistent with the behaviour of the model of which it forms a part.] Indeed, as we shall see, the model is quite capable of generating a perpetually increasing level of excess demand, and in such circum-stances equation 6 will consistently under-predict the rate of inflation by an increasing amount.[8] To find a forecasting scheme that is both optimal and consistent with the structure of the model into which it is to be embedded is an analytic problem with which I am not going to deal in this paper. However, equation 6 does represent a weak point in the model under discussion; and the observation that we are concerned with how people actually behave rather than how they would behave if they did everything optimally, so that the simple error-learning mechanism may still be a useful component of models such as this one, still does not leave one completely happy with its use.

Be that as it may, one object of the model building exercise in question is to use components that are already well established in the literature and combine them in as simple a way as possible in order to produce a model in which prices and output fluctuate simultaneously. There are certainly shortcomings in the model; but they are shortcomings in the conventional pieces of analysis that make up its components rather than in the way in which they are put together. Thus it is perhaps reasonable to ask the reader to suspend final judgement until the behaviour of the model as a whole has been set out.

It will be convenient initially to describe this behaviour without comment, beginning by analysing the model's characteristics at full employment. In this case we are concerned only with price fluctuations. With Y set equal to Y^* for every time period, we get the following expression for the rate of inflation:

$$\Delta P = dc(A - sY^*) + (1 - cad)\Delta P_{-1} - cad\Delta P_{-2} \qquad (9)$$

This may be written instead as a first order equation in the rate of acceleration of the rate of inflation:

$$\Delta P - \Delta P_{-1} = dc(A - sY^*) + cad(\Delta P_{-1} - \Delta P_{-2}) \qquad (10)$$

Thus the rate of acceleration of inflation either increases without limit if cad exceeds one or converges towards a negative (since $A - sY^*$ is negative by assumption) steady state value.[9] However, it is, after all, the influence of the rate of acceleration of inflation on investment that maintains aggregate demand at a greater than full employment level in this model. Thus, if the convergent case holds, it must be true that before this steady state is reached —indeed, while the rate of acceleration of expected inflation is still positive—aggregate demand will fall below its full-employment level, and equation 10 will cease to be relevant to the model's behaviour.

When aggregate demand falls below the full employment level the assumption that income is given by Y^* becomes inappropriate. With falling income, and a falling anticipated inflation rate, investment goes to zero, and thus only the multiplier mechanism governs the behaviour of real income on the downswing. At less than full employment we have

$$Y = A + (1 - s)Y_{-1} \qquad (11)$$

while the behaviour of the inflation rate is given by

$$\Delta P - \Delta P_{-1} = g(Y - Y_{-1}) + dg(Y_{-1} - Y^*) \tag{12}$$

If income is falling, this expression must be negative (which of course is *not* the same thing as saying that the rate of inflation must be negative). Real income thus approaches its floor monotonically, but there is no steady state solution for the rate of inflation in this case; instead, the rate of *acceleration* of inflation goes to a constant value given by

$$\Delta P - \Delta P_{-1} = dg[(1/s)A - Y^*] \tag{13}$$

This is worth noting; even with positive depreciation this model would imply no inevitability about the eventual expansion of real income. The constant rate of deceleration of inflation can, in principle, reduce the demand for capital faster than depreciation wears it out.[10] However, on the assumption that it does get going, perhaps in response to an expansionary policy change, we may now consider the characteristics of the upswing.

The time path of prices is again given by

$$\Delta P - \Delta P_{-1} = g(Y - Y_{-1}) + dg(Y_{-1} - Y^*) \tag{12}$$

but, with income rising, the first term of this expression is positive. $(Y - Y_{-1})$ must always be absolutely smaller than $(Y_{-1} - Y^*)$, but the latter becomes smaller as time passes and full employment is approached, while its coefficients dg is necessarily smaller than g. Thus the rate of inflation is likely to begin accelerating before full employment is reached.[11] The time path of income is given by

$$Y = A + (1 - s + v)Y_{-1} - vY_{-2} + a(\Delta \dot{p}^e{}_{-1} - \Delta \dot{p}^e{}_{-2}) \tag{14}$$

This equation is indeed similar to that generated by the simple Hicks model. It differs from it only by including a term in the rate of acceleration of the expected inflation rate. The latter variable will always be negative, since the actual rate of inflation will be below the expected rate so long as aggregate demand is deficient, so that the accelerator must provide a stronger expansionary force for this modified model to reach full employment than is required in the Hicks model.

Should there be a downturn before full employment is reached, equations 11 and 12 take over again. However, if the ceiling is reached, the multiplier-accelerator mechanism cuts out. It is still possible, though, for the expansion to continue, with rising real income being replaced by an accelerating rate of inflation. One would expect there to be positive excess demand at the point at which the ceiling is reached; at that point the expected rate of inflation will begin to increase. Thus, though one term in the

investment equation goes to zero, the other changes sign from
positive to negative, and, provided investment is sensitive enough
to the real rate of interest, this will so influence aggregate demand that full employment and an accelerating rate of inflation,
rather than a downturn in real income, follow the reaching of the:
ceiling.

The model can clearly generate a wide variety of results. For
example, there is nothing inevitable about a repeating cycle in
economic activity. The economy can remain stuck at the floor,
while the achievement of full employment can as well lead on to
perpetual accelerating inflation as it can to a subsequent fall in
the level of real income. However, turning points may easily
enough be generated by policy changes. A cut in the money rate
of interest in sufficient amount can clearly start an upswing either
from the floor or even before the floor is reached, while a sufficient increase in the same variable can reverse an accelerating
inflation and turn it into a downswing in real income with a declin-
ing rate of inflation.

One may nevertheless derive certain general propositions
about the interaction of prices and real income from the model.
Falling real income is always associated with a falling rate of
inflation, as inspection of equations 11 and 12 will confirm. It
also follows from equation 12 that rising real income will typically
be associated first with a falling then with a rising rate of inflation as income continues to expand and full employment is
approached. The achievement of full employment will initially
be accompanied by accelerating inflation and, as equation 10
shows, this tendency may be reinforced by the passage of time or
tend to die out, with the rate of acceleration of inflation dying
down and perhaps becoming negative of its own accord, a downturn in real income and hence a definite deceleration of inflation
ensuing.

Now the foregoing paragraph tells us nothing at all about the
level of the inflation rate, only about its rate of change; and it is
this that perhaps constitutes the most interesting and general
implication of the model. Either rising prices or falling prices
could well persist throughout a complete cycle, depending upon the
expectations about inflation held by economic agents at its
beginning, and within any particular phase of the cycle the level
of the inflation rate is determined in part by what happened in
the previous phase. Thus a long period of accelerating inflation
which is interrupted by policy will be succeeded by a downswing
in real income accompanied by prices still rising, albeit at a
decelerating rate; while a prolonged depression in which prices
have been falling can easily be a prelude to a period of full employment and excess demand in which prices nevertheless continue to
fall. On the other hand, the tendency of the inflation rate to accele-

rate on the upswing may result in prices beginning to rise before
full employment is reached if the preceding trough has been
shallow and short-lived and has followed in the wake of a prolonged period of rising prices. We should expect to find no obvious
relationship between the level of the rate of inflation and that of
output according to this model. It predicts instead that the rate
of change of the inflation rate should be systematically related to
output.

Now it was mentioned earlier that to treat the money supply
as an exogenous variable does not significantly alter the results
that this model generates. It still produces fluctuations in prices
and output—albeit more damped ones; nor does this change in the
exogenous monetary variable produce the possibility that the
model generates a steady state solution with aggregate demand at
any save its 'floor' level. At the same time, the emphasis on the
rate of change of the rate of inflation as a key variable is maintained. The following brief sketch of the model's properties when
money is exogenous ought to convince the reader of the truth of
these assertions and render a complete analysis unnecessary.

If we write a demand for money function as follows:[12]

$$M = mY - lr + p \tag{15}$$

where M is the natural log. of the nominal money supply, and we
postulate that the money supply grows at a constant percentage
rate, $\Delta \overline{M}$, our model yields, as a solution for the rate of inflation
at full employment:

$$\Delta p = dc(\overline{A} - sY^*) + \frac{dca}{l} \Delta \overline{M} + \left[1 + \left(d - \frac{1}{l} \right) ca \right] \Delta p_{-1}$$
$$- \left(d - \frac{1-d}{l} \right) ca \Delta p_{-2} \tag{16}$$

...[Application of the stability conditions for a second order
difference equation set out above (chapter 3, p. 70) will reveal that
equation 16 is more likely to be stable than equation 10.]

The exogeneity of the money supply tends to make it more
likely that the rate of inflation will converge towards a steady
state. The steady state in question is given by

$$\Delta p = (l/a)(A - sY^*) + \Delta \overline{M} \tag{17}$$

and clearly the equilibrium rate of inflation will equal the rate of
change of the money supply only if

$$A - sY^* = 0 \tag{18}$$

However, this is the only condition upon which this equilibrium
will be attained in the first place. If we rely upon induced investment to fill the gap between autonomous expenditure and full

employment saving, then the expected rate of inflation must
accelerate. As the rate of inflation approaches a steady state, so
does the expected rate, aggregate demand falls short of full
employment output, and the downswing phase begins.

At less then full employment the behaviour of prices is still
governed by equation 12. On the downswing the behaviour of
output may still be given by equation 11, i.e. a simple dynamic
multiplier; for, though falling real income puts downward pressure
on the nominal interest rate through the demand for money function,
there is no logical necessity that the nominal rate falls fast
enough to maintain a positive value for induced investment. However, should the latter turn out to be the case, then the behaviour
of income on both downswing and upswing would be given by

$$Y = \left(1 - s + v - \frac{ma}{l}\right)Y_{-1} - \left(v - \frac{ma}{l}\right) Y_{-2} + A$$

$$+ \frac{a}{l}\Delta M - \frac{a}{l}\Delta P + a(\Delta p^e_{-1} - \Delta p^e_{-2}) \tag{19}$$

The role played by the coefficient v in equation 14 is here given to
the expression $(v - ma/l)$. The exogeneity of the money supply
produces a tendency towards damped behaviour.

Finally, it might be noted that there is normally no steady
state solution to equation 19. Its existence would require the
simultaneous constancy of A, ΔM, ΔP and $(\Delta p^e_{-1} - \Delta p^e_{-2})$; but,
given equations 6 and 7, Δp and $(\Delta p^e_{-1} - \Delta p^e_{-2})$ can simultaneously
be constant at full employment only when the latter expression is
zero. As we have already seen, we obtain full employment equilibrium only if $A = sY^*$.[13]

The picture that emerges from this analysis, then, is of a
model in which output fluctuates (albeit in a manner that is more
likely to be damped than when the nominal interest rate is exogenous), and in which the rate of inflation fluctuates around the
rate of change of the money supply, but in which the relationship
between the time path of the inflation rate and that of output is the
same as in the simpler model which this paper has analysed in
more detail.

IV

The results generated by the foregoing analysis are easy enough to
summarise. First, the model in question does not necessarily
generate a repeating cycle. As we have seen, it can become stuck
at either the floor or the ceiling and require exogenous changes in
the nominal rate of interest, or autonomous expenditure, to move
it off in some direction or other. Thus it is perhaps best to re-

gard the foregoing results as telling us what might be observed in various phases of the cycle rather than as providing in and of itself a comprehensive explanation of the generation of the cycle.

Viewed in this light, the results nevertheless are surely of interest. The pricing equation 7 implies that, so long as expectations of the rate of inflation are generated solely from observations on the actual rate, inflation, once established, can be reduced below its anticipated rate and be eliminated only by generating excess supply. This proposition is perhaps obvious enough, and certainly does not need a model to generate it; but it does account for the coexistence of inflation and unemployment in the wake of a period of full employment and inflation.

However, a much less obvious implication of the model is that, after inflation has ceased or even become negative, expanding real income can lead to it starting up again before full employment is reached. This result, which is implicit in equation 12, arises from the fact that a zero or a negative actual rate of inflation can coexist for a time with expectations of a positive rate of inflation, if these expectations have become deeply embedded in the economy as a result of past experience. A falling level of excess supply in such circumstances can be sufficient for the expectations component of the pricing equation to dominate and produce positive inflation. There is, I believe, some novelty in a model in which the only 'cost push' element is expectations of inflation and which makes no allowance for 'bottlenecks' but which nevertheless is able to generate a rate of inflation that becomes positive and actually accelerates in the presence of positive, albeit falling, unemployment. It does, after all, imply that there are circumstances in which 'demand pull' forces can set inflation going without having first to generate positive excess demand.

More generally, the model I have constructed does succeed in embedding a Phillips-type relationship in a complete macromodel so that a framework is provided in which the effects of fiscal policy (working through A or s), monetary policy (working through r or M) and prices and incomes policies (presumably working on c, g, d or perhaps introducing additional exogenous variables into the expectations-determining equation) may be analysed simultaneously. Such a framework is surely worth having.

Having said all this, the model presented here is certainly not the only one that can be constructed to deal with such problems, nor can there be any presumption that it is the best. Although I hope that the reader is satisfied that the exercises carried out here are worth doing, I also hope that he will not regard them as anything more then exploratory investigations of one potentially fruitful line of thought.

NOTES

[1]   Reprinted from *Economica,* n.s., XL, February 1973, an issue in honour of Sir John Hicks, this paper was originally prepared for and given at the second Dauphine conference on Monetary Economics held at the University of Paris (IX) Dauphine in the spring of 1972. I am grateful to members of the Manchester Inflation Workshop, and in particular to John Carlson, Herschel Grossman and Michael Parkin, for comments on earlier drafts.

[2]   But recent observations have not in fact strayed further from the simple Phillips curve than did those in a number of earlier periods (*cf.* Parkin 1971). Note also that Walters (1969) found it difficult to explain the time paths of prices and real income. Thus there is nothing particularly novel about recent experience, though this, or course, does not mean that it does not need explaining.

[3]   I have set out a fuller analysis of the Phillips curve and the role that inflationary expectations play in it elsewhere (*cf.* Laidler 1971b). The original work on this problem is, of course, that of Phelps (1967) and Friedman (1968).

[4]   For such work on the United Kingdom economy, see Parkin and Sumner (1972).

[5]   Hines (1971) suggests that prices and incomes policies are more effective when demand management policies are expansionary; but in the absence of any model it is hard to know whether this suggestion is or is not well grounded.

[6]   The Bank of England certainly pursued such a policy until 1971, and it is not clear yet how far it has changed its practices more recently. The United States authorities pursued an interest rate pegging policy in the immediate post-war years, and even after the 'Accord' did not move to a policy of attempting to control the money supply.

[7]   Note that the introduction of a production function would also make possible an explicit analysis of the interrelationship between the goods market and the labour market.

[8]   I am indebted to Malcolm Gray and David Rose for discussion on this point.

[9]   Note that the investment function which underlies equation 10 may be derived from the desired capital stock relationship only if we assume that firms *always* obtain all the resources they want. Thus forced saving is very much a characteristic of the inflationary process described here. It is interesting to note that Wicksell's (1898a) inflation model is one in which firms *never* obtain the additional resources they want, so that their unsatisfied demand spills over from period to period. The model set out here does, of course, imply that, if an inflationary process explodes, investment demand will eventually exceed output. At this point the model obviously becomes internally inconsistent; but this need

not trouble us if we regard the linear nature of the investment function as being adopted for no other reason than analytic simplicity.

10 It is because depreciation has no central contribution to make to the behaviour of this model that I have ignored it in describing the behaviour of income on the downswing. Because Hicks's primary aim was to explain cyclical turning points, and because depreciation was central to his explanation of the lower turning point, he had to analyse its role in other phases of the cycle.

11 The smaller is d, i.e. the slower do expectations adjust to current experience, the sooner will the rate of inflation begin to accelerate. This is a particular case of a general characteristic of this model which many would regard as reflecting an important empirical phenomenon, namely that the longer it takes for inflationary expectations to become established the longer it takes (and the more unemployment it takes) to rid the economy of their influence.

12 Note that this is a model which derives the impetus to a changing rate of inflation from the existence of a discrepancy between the 'natural' rate of interest—that which would equate aggregate demand to full employment output—and the 'real' rate of interest—the nominal rate minus the expected rate of inflation. Thus there is no unique measure of the opportunity cost of holding money in this model. The selection of the nominal rate to appear in the demand for money function is somewhat arbitrary, and is based on the supposition that bonds are easier to substitute for money than is real capital.

13 I would conjecture that the explicit introduction of a production function, depreciation of capital, and hence replacement investment into this model would produce a steady state solution for income at full employment, with the rate of inflation equal to the rate of change of the money supply.

7 The influence of money on real income and inflation: a simple model with some empirical tests for the United States, 1953-72[1]

I

Orthodox short-run macro-economics has been severely under-mined in the last few years by the so-called 'new micro-economics'. The widely used LM-IS model deals with conditions of static equilibrium and treats the price level either as exogenously given when the level of income (and hence of employment) is to be determined or as the only variable to be determined if the model is cast in a 'full employment' form. The new micro-economics, by way of contrast, is concerned with the dynamics of disequilibrium situations in which the value of economic variables evolves and interacts over time. It deals with the determinants not of an equilibrium level of prices but of the rate of inflation. It is particularly concerned with the way in which the inflation rate interacts with the level of income and employment. However, it does not treat these subjects in the context of a complete macro-model, and the need for a new and explicitly dynamic macro-economics is widely recognised. However, it has proved far easier to diagnose this need than to meet it, and for two inter-linked reasons.

First, it is notoriously easy in dynamic economics to build models of sufficient complexity that they become incomprehensible to all but specialised research workers, to say nothing of requiring simulation exercises rather than analytic methods to reveal any of their properties. Second, the interaction of the inflation rate and the level of income and employment is only one of several relationships which can form part of a macro-model. Lags in behaviour relationships linking real variables abound in empirical work. The permanent income hypothesis, various forms of the accelerator relationship, to give but two examples, are well supported by evidence and are strong candidates for inclusion in any attempt to construct a dynamic macro-model.

To include every lagged relationship at once in a model is impossible because of the analytic complexity that would result, but if we are to be selective in order to keep the analysis manageable we must have clear criteria upon which to base our selection.

Without such criteria the number of *a priori* plausible and simple but nevertheless contradictory dynamic models that could be built would be enormous. Two guiding principles immediately come to mind. First, it is desirable to build models with specific and quite narrowly defined purposes in mind, so as to minimise the number of variables that they must contain. This seems preferable to attempting to build immediately a general model that is capable of dealing with a wide variety of problems. A satisfactory general model is more likely to emerge as an end product of the piecemeal construction of a series of small specific-purpose models than as the consequence of a conscious effort to achieve generality from the very outset. Second, even when trying to deal with narrowly defined problems there are many alternative tacks to be taken, and only the application of the test of empirical relevance seems to offer much hope of enabling us to recognise the more promising lines of investigation.

This paper presents the results of one model-building exercise which attempts to conform to these two criteria. The problem with which the model is designed to deal is that of showing how variations in the rate of monetary expansion divide themselves up over time between variations in real income on the one hand and prices on the other. Moreover the model was explicitly constructed in order to deal with this problem in a manner analytically simple enough to be accessible even to undergraduate students of economics. To achieve accessibility of this order has, of course, required ruthless simplification, but it will be shown that even in its simplest form the model is not without empirical content. Moreover it will also be shown that slight extensions of the basic model which do complicate its analytical properties without, however, departing from its basic economic content considerably improve its empirical performance.

The model in question is of a closed economy and combines the quantity theory of money with a species of expectations-augmented Phillips curve. It is tested against United States data, rather than British, because *a priori* considerations as well as preliminary examination of the evidence suggest that a closed-economy model has little chance of dealing satisfactorily with British data.[2] The model is by no means the only one that could be built, and its empirical performance leaves some room for improvement. However, the work which is reported in the following pages seems to open up a potentially fruitful line for further research as well as establishing some sort of standard of empirical performance against which future empirical work with alternative simple models may be judged. For these reasons it seems worth taking seriously.

II

The basic model has three components: an hypothesis about money market behaviour, an hypothesis about the process of price formation, and an hypothesis about how those who set prices form their expectations about the rate of inflation.

Consider the money market first of all. The money supply is treated as an exogenous variable. This should not be taken as meaning that the present writer regards the money supply as being under the direct control of the monetary authorities. Rather it means that, in a model in which the interrelationships between prices, real income and the quantity of money are under study, and which is intended to be relevant to the United States economy, it is appropriate to postulate that causality runs predominantly from money to income and prices, and not in the opposite direction. Recent statistical work by Christopher Sims (1972) lends weight to this assumption, as do certain results repeated below.

The demand side of the money market is described by a relationship that makes the demand for nominal money balances proportional to the price level and a function of real income. This is a considerable simplification of what we know to be the best-fitting demand for money relationship for the United States or any other economy.[3] It contains no measure of the opportunity cost of holding money, nor does it allow for lags in the response of money holdings to changes in their determinants.[4]

However, a prime purpose of the current exercise is to construct as simple a model as possible of the interaction of money, real income and prices, and to introduce either of these factors into the demand for money function would complicate the analysis considerably. To allow for the permanent income hypothesis introduces extra lags into the system, making it difficult to analyse; to introduce a rate of interest variable would require us to expand the system to encompass explicitly the aggregate expenditure functions of the economy. Again, a more complicated and difficult to analyse model would result. Moreover there is no methodological presumption that the most precise—albeit complicated—version of a function should be the first choice for inclusion in any model. Analytic simplicity and empirical content must often be traded off against one another, and there is no way of finding out how serious are the empirical consequences of the approximations adopted in the demand for money function without looking at the model's performance.

The price formation behaviour hypothesised in this model is a version of the expectations-augmented Phillips curve, applied directly to the determination of the rate of price inflation, however, rather than to the determination of a rate of wage inflation from which the rate of price inflation might be derived by way of some mark-up-adjusted-for-productivity-change mechanism.[5] It is suggested that the rate at which firms will mark up their prices over time, when markets are in equilibrium and full employment prevails, is equal to the expected rate of inflation. In the presence of general excess supply firms raise their prices by less than the expected inflation rate and, faced by general excess demand, they raise their prices by more. It is further postulated that there exists at any moment a unique level of real income which grows exogenously over time and at which the supply and demand for labour are equal. At this income level the so-called 'natural' level of unemployment, caused by the inevitable frictions to be found in a less than perfect market, prevails. The degree to which actual national income exceeds or falls short of this level of income is presumed to be mono-tonically related to the level of excess demand or supply in the economy, so that the ratio of actual to full employment real income may be used as a proxy measure for excess demand.[6]

The foregoing hypotheses are far from uncontroversial. It is not difficult to construct alternative models of price formation that are equally plausible *a priori* and which lead to quite different predictions.[7] The defence of the choice made here rests on a combination of analytical simplicity and empirical content; the reader is asked to suspend judgement until these issues have been discussed.

I shall use the well known 'adaptive expectations' mechanism to deal with the expected inflation rate. The public is thought of as forming expectations about the inflation rate, observing it, and 'adapting' its expectation in proportion to the error that such observation reveals. Whatever the shortcomings of this scheme as an optimal predictor in the statistical sense, its simplicity makes it an attractive device to use in the present exercise, and in any event the extent of the problem caused by so doing can only be discovered by examining the empirical evidence.

In order to reduce the foregoing rather general discussion to a model capable of precise analysis certain extra assumptions need to be made. First, every relationship will be treated as linear in the logarithms: since the first difference of the natural logarithm of any variable measures its percentage rate of change, this is an extremely convenient functional form to use in the present context. Second, because we are interested in analysing the time paths of variables we must introduce explicit time lags into the system. To do so we first divide time into discrete intervals (years). It is then assumed that the money market adjusts sufficiently rapidly as to have its behaviour satisfactorily captured without lagged relationships. Inflation expectations are treated as if formed at annual intervals, and the price formation

equation to be used postulates the existence of a time lag between
the factors influencing the inflation rate and the rate itself.[8]
    The model may be written in three equations in the following
way. M is the log. of the money stock; Y is the log. of real income;
Y^* is the log. of full employment real income; y is $Y - Y^*$, and
P is the log. of the price level. Subscripts $-1, -2$ refers to lags
of one and two years; the prefix Δ indicates the first difference
and Δ^2 the second difference of a variable; the superscript e
indicates the expected value of a variable, and a bar over a
variable denotes that it is exogenous.

$$\Delta \overline{M} = b \Delta Y + \Delta P = b \Delta y + b \Delta \overline{Y}^* + \Delta P, \quad b > 0 \tag{1}$$

$$\Delta P = g y_{-1} + \Delta P^e_{-1} \qquad\qquad g > 0 \tag{2}$$

$$\Delta P^e = d \Delta P + (1 - d) \Delta P^e_{-1} \qquad 0 < d < 1 \tag{3}$$

    Consider the steady state properties of this model first of
all. For the rate of inflation ΔP, to be constant it must be equal
to the expected rate of inflation, ΔP^e, which itself must be constant.
Equation 2 tells us at once that this can occur only if y is equal to
zero: that is to say, if real income is on its (exogenously given
in terms of this model) full employment growth path.
    Setting y equal to zero, we may solve equation 1 for the
equilibrium inflation rate, and it yields

$$\Delta P = \Delta \overline{M} - b \Delta \overline{Y}^* \tag{4}$$

This tells us that, *in the long run*, any rate of monetary expansion
is compatible with full employment and that the rate of monetary
expansion affects only the rate of inflation.[9] Whether this is of
any interest or not depends upon whether the equilibrium in question is one that is likely to be reached. We may rephrase the
implicit question here as 'Are the dynamic properties of this system such as to ensure that y converges on a value of zero?'
    The general expression for y that equations 1–3 yield may be
written as follows:

$$y = \frac{1}{b} \Delta^2 \overline{M} - \Delta^2 \overline{Y}^* + \frac{2b - g}{b} y_{-1} - \frac{b - (1 - d)g}{b} y_{-2} \tag{5}$$

With an unchanging growth rate and rate of monetary expansion
the first two terms become zero. It is easy to show that only if
b is relatively 'small' or g is relatively 'large' is there any
danger that this second-order difference equation 5 will fail to
converge upon zero. It is also easy to show that there is a logical
possibility of this convergence following a cyclical pattern. Hence
the steady state solution to this model may be of some interest,
since it is a model whose dynamics are capable of taking it towards that steady state in the long run.[10]
    There is more to equation 5 than this, for the presence of
$\Delta^2 \overline{M}$ in that equation tells us that *changes in the rate of change* of

the money supply will disturb the system, and that, in the short run changes in the rate of monetary expansion affect real income as well as prices.

What about the inflation rate when the system is out of equilibrium? Equations 2 and 3 yield

$$\Delta^2 P = g\Delta y_{-1} + dgy_{-2} \tag{6}$$

This tells us that the rate of change of the inflation rate rather than the level of that variable will be related to both the level and the rate of change of excess demand in the economy. In as much as there might be a cycle of real income's time path about full employment, then the presence of the rate of change of income relative to full employment on the right hand side of equation 6 tells us that the cycle in the inflation rate will tend to conform to it. However, the presence of the lagged value of the level of this variable leads to a prediction that the inflation rate will lag real income at turning points.[11]

Now what is striking about this model is the way in which it encompasses among its predictions what many would regard as the salient features of the so-called 'monetarist' view of inflation. It characterises the economy as tending to full employment in the long run and predicts that, in that long run, monetary expansion affects *only* the inflation rate. However, it also predicts that variations in the rate of monetary expansion can have impact effects on the level of real income and employment in a short run that may well be long enough to be interesting to economic historians and policy-makers. It also predicts that there should be no simple inverse trade-off between unemployment and inflation rates, telling us rather that the interaction of these variables over time is subject to time lags brought about by the influence of expectations derived from past experience. No one who took equation 6 seriously would conclude that the recent coexistence of high inflation and unemployment rates indicates that the market mechanism has ceased to work. It would take a good deal more than casual inspection of the data in question to enable one to see whether or not they are compatible with some version of equation 6.

All this is very tantalising, then, but not very interesting unless the model described here has some empirical content. I shall now discuss evidence that suggests its content to be by no means negligible.

III

The model with which we are concerned here employs one exogenous variable, the rate of change of the money stock, and one exogenous constant, the growth rate of full employment income.

These determine the values of the actual rate of change of real
income and the actual inflation rate. In order to grasp the causative chain involved, equations 1-3 are best rearranged in the
following way:

$$\Delta y + \Delta \overline{Y}^* = \Delta Y = \frac{1}{b} \Delta M - \frac{1}{b} \Delta P \tag{7}$$

$$\Delta P = g y_{-1} - (1 - d) g y_{-2} + \Delta P_{-1} \tag{8}$$

The rate of inflation in any year is determined by the preceding
year's rate of inflation and the level of excess demand ruling in
the two preceding years. The current inflation rate interacts
with the rate of monetary expansion to determine the change in
real income that takes place in the current year. This year's
real income in turn becomes a determinant of the next period's
inflation rate, and so on.

The model's simple recursive structure thus makes it
amenable to estimation utilising ordinary least squares, albeit
with certain constraints imposed upon parameter values. It was
fitted to annual data for the United States economy for the period
1953-72, and also to the sub-period 1953-65 to check upon the
stability of parameter estimates over time, though it should go
without saying that the low number of observations available make
this a very tentative exercise indeed.[12]

In most cases the choice of data is straightforward. Thus real
income is measured by gross national product, while the price
level is measured by the GNP deflator. As far as the money supply
is concerned there does exist a choice between M_1, currency in
the hands of the public plus demand deposits at commercial banks,
and M_2, M_1 plus time deposits but excluding large certificates of
deposit. This writer has consistently, though not strongly, favoured
M_2 in the past, and this is the series used here.[13] Some estimation
was done using M_1, however, and produced rather unsatisfactory
results. We appear to have here an instance of the choice of
definition of money making a crucial difference to empirical
results, and indeed one might expect a broad definition of money
to perform better when rate of interest variables are not taken
into account in the demand for money function.

The only other variable that needs measuring is 'full employment income'. This appears as a trend variable in the model; in
order to stay as close to the theoretical model as possible the
trend value of income over the sample period was used to measure
it. The Council of Economic Advisers does, of course, calculate a
direct estimate of this variable year by year, and this series was
used to check on the desirability of utilising a simple trend.
Though the use of this variable produced satisfactory results,

there was no improvement over those obtained using a trend value.

Let us now consider the estimation of the model, beginning with the demand for money function. The direction of causation in the model makes it clear that real income ought to be the dependent variable here, and the estimates made were variations on the theme:

$$Y = \beta_0 + \beta_1 M + \beta_2 P + e \tag{9}$$

Our model tells us that, in this relationship,

$$\frac{1}{b} = \beta_1 = -\beta_2$$

and so the simplest way to estimate $1/b$ is from the regression

$$Y = \beta_0 + \beta_1(M - P) + e \tag{10}$$

For the period 1953-72 this regression yielded the following results:

$$\beta_1 = 1\cdot125 \qquad t = 26\cdot585 \qquad R^2 = 0\cdot974 \qquad dw = 0\cdot571$$

In order to ascertain whether or not the constraint $\beta_1 = -\beta_2$ was indeed satisfied, equation 9 was estimated, with the following result:

$$\beta_1 = 0\cdot914 \; t = 6\cdot473; \beta_2 = -0\cdot628 \; t = 1\cdot946; R^2 = 0\cdot976$$
$$dw = 0\cdot576$$

There is no reason, on the basis of this result, to conclude that the constraint in question is not satisfied, though β_2 is sufficiently badly determined that we cannot take too much comfort from this conclusion.

Both of these regressions display an extremely low Durbin-Watson statistic. Though auto-correlated residuals do not involve bias in the estimates of coefficients they do lead to a systematic overstatement of the statistical significance of these estimates. Thus the t value of 26·6 attached to the estimate of β_1 in equation 10 is spuriously high. The degree of auto-correlation indicated here is so high that first differencing might be expected to take care of the bulk of the problem, and a first difference version of equation 10 with the intercept constrained to zero yields

$$\beta_1 = 0\cdot914 \qquad t = 6\cdot381 \qquad R^2 = 0\cdot107 \qquad dw = 2\cdot265$$

The much more modest t value here probably gives a better indication of the significance of the relationship whose estimation has been under discussion.[14]

Now one cannot claim much for these results. One could certainly produce more satisfactory demand for money functions than the one implicit in these estimates. For example, one could introduce interest rates into the relationship and make allowances for permanent income effects. It is precisely because there are variables missing that our parameter estimates are not too well determined and tend to vary between different formulations of what should be the same relationship. But we knew that we were leaving out variables before we began to discuss estimation.

The purpose of the exercise is not to find the best-fitting demand for money function but to see whether an admittedly simplified theory of money market behaviour has empirical content in the context of particular macro-economic model. The results presented here suggest that it does have some content. Whether it has 'enough' content depends upon how the complete model behaves, and before we can discuss this issue we need to look at the estimation of the other behavioural relationship in the model, the price formation equation.

The basic form chosen for estimation here was

$$\Delta^2 P = \gamma_1 y_{-1} + \gamma_2 y_{-2} + u \tag{11}$$

where $\gamma_1 = g$ and $\gamma_2 = -(1 - d)g$. In this form it produced the following results.[15]

$$\gamma_1 = 0 \cdot 233 \qquad t = 3 \cdot 418$$

$$\gamma_2 = -0 \cdot 157 \qquad t = 2 \cdot 276$$

$$R^2 = 0 \cdot 381 \qquad dw = 1 \cdot 330$$

These estimates imply in turn that $g = 0 \cdot 233$ and $d = 0 \cdot 331$. As with the demand for money function, so here the form chosen for fitting imposed a constraint implied by our theory on the data, namely that in the relationship

$$\Delta P = \gamma_1 y_{-1} + \gamma_2 y_{-2} + \gamma_3 \Delta P_{-1} + u \tag{12}$$

γ_3 should be equal to unity. There is no reason to take it for granted that this constraint is satisfied, but estimation of equation 12 yields strong evidence that it is. We get:

$$\gamma_1 = 0 \cdot 233 \qquad t = 3 \cdot 418$$

$$\gamma_2 = -0 \cdot 156 \qquad t = 2 \cdot 447$$

$$\gamma_3 = 1 \cdot 003 \qquad t = 17 \cdot 536$$

$$R^2 = 0 \cdot 739 \qquad dw = 1 \cdot 336$$

This result is strongly consistent with the so-called 'natural unemployment rate' hypothesis and the proposition that, in the long run, there is no unemployment inflation trade-off. However, the presence of a lagged dependent variable in equation 12 does mean that biases may be present in the relevant parameter estimates, so that this evidence must not be regarded as conclusive.

Finally, it should be noticed that equations 11 and 12 contain no constant term. Again this is a constraint that our model tells us the data should satisfy. Fitting equation 12 allowing a constant to appear produced one that did not differ significantly from zero, and although the numerical estimates of γ_1, γ_2 and γ_3 changed a little, they did not change enough for it to be possible to conclude that they significantly differed from the value already reported. In fact the exercise in question yielded the following results:

$$\gamma_1 = 0\cdot217 \qquad t = 3\cdot301$$
$$\gamma_2 = -0\cdot103 \qquad t = 1\cdot402$$
$$\gamma_3 = 0\cdot799 \qquad t = 5\cdot885$$
$$\text{Constant} = 0\cdot604 \qquad t = 1\cdot641$$
$$R^2 = 0\cdot763 \qquad dw = 1\cdot263$$

All in all, I would judge these results to be more satisfactory than those for the demand for money function. The constraints that our model tells us the data ought to satisfy are on the whole more easily satisfied, and the parameter estimates obtained are not too sensitive to the precise functional form fitted to the data. However, the rather low Durbin-Watson statistics do suggest that there might be a variable missing from the equations, and this is further discussed below.

As I noted earlier, the model was fitted to the sub-period 1953-65 as well as to the whole period 1953-72, and the parameter values obtained for this sub-period differ little from those reported above. With so few observations involved, formal statistical tests of the stability of the relationships are out of the question, so the following results are presented for the reader's own informal assessment.

For the demand for money function fitted to the levels of the data with the constraint $\beta_1 = -\beta_2$ imposed, we get

$$\beta_1 = 1\cdot320 \qquad t = 12\cdot051$$
$$R^2 = 0\cdot923 \qquad dw = 0\cdot791$$

Relaxing the constraint yields

$$\beta_1 = 0\cdot836 \qquad t = 8\cdot327$$
$$\beta_2 = -0\cdot121 \qquad t = 0\cdot562$$
$$R^2 = 0\cdot980 \qquad dw = 2\cdot430$$

while first differencing produces the following estimates:

$$\beta_1 = 1\cdot013 \qquad t = 4\cdot303$$
$$R^2 = -0\cdot012 \qquad dw = 2\cdot334$$

Only when β_2 is free to be estimated do we get any sign that the sub-period is producing results that may differ from those obtained from the whole sample.

The price formation equation results look even better. With γ_3 constrained to be unity we have

$$\gamma_1 = 0\cdot200 \qquad t = 2\cdot64$$
$$\gamma_2 = -0\cdot169 \qquad t = 2\cdot312$$
$$R^2 = 0\cdot344 \qquad dw = 1\cdot363$$

Relaxing this constraint gives us

$$\gamma_1 = 0\cdot200 \qquad t = 2\cdot317$$
$$\gamma_2 = -0\cdot169 \qquad t = 2\cdot159$$
$$\gamma_3 = 1\cdot002 \qquad t = 9\cdot618$$
$$R^2 = 0\cdot327 \qquad dw = 1\cdot363$$

Adding an intercept produces

$$\gamma_1 = 0\cdot180 \qquad t = 2\cdot101$$
$$\gamma_2 = -0\cdot122 \qquad t = 1\cdot433$$
$$\gamma_3 = 0\cdot700 \qquad t = 2\cdot668$$
$$\text{Constant} = 0\cdot661 \qquad t = 1\cdot250$$
$$R^2 = 0\cdot323 \qquad dw = 1\cdot131$$

There is certainly no reason in these results to question the stability of the equation that determines the inflation rate in our model.

To summarise, then, empirical evidence does suggest that the model under discussion has more than purely theoretical content. For the period 1953-72 it appears that the model, written in the form given in equations 7 and 8, may be characterised as follows:[16]

$$\Delta y + \Delta \overline{Y}^* = \Delta Y = 0\cdot914 \, \Delta M - 0\cdot914 \Delta P \qquad (7')$$

$$\Delta P = 0\cdot233 y_{-1} - 0\cdot157 y_{-2} + \Delta P_{-1} \qquad (8')$$

These results imply that the structural parameters of the model are $b = 1\cdot094$, $g = 0\cdot233$ and $d = 0\cdot331$. An income elasticity of demand for real balances of $1\cdot094$ is reasonably enough, particularly when a broad definition of money is used, and this result certainly gives us no cause for thinking that the omission of variables from the demand for money function has resulted in a large bias in this parameter's estimate. An elasticity of the expected with respect to the actual inflation rate of $0\cdot331$ is also *a priori* plausible enough.

However, it is one thing to show that the separate components of a model have empirical content and another to make
the same claim for the model as a whole. The last paragraph or
two have taken it for granted that the model as a whole does indeed have content. This claim can be backed only by the results
of simulation exercises carried out with the complete model, and
I shall now turn to describing such exercises.

Two types of simulation were carried out. Coefficients
obtained from the whole sample period were used to generate the
values of the endogenous variables over the same sample period,
taking as data only the actual values of the exogenous variables
and starting values of lagged endogenous variables. The coefficients for 1953-65 were also used to generate values of the
endogenous variables for the whole sample period, 1953-72.
Since 1966 was precisely the year in which the time paths of the
inflation rate and real income began to behave in the manner that
has led some commentators to the view that the structure of the
United States economy has changed in recent years, the latter
test is a particularly stringent one. The results of the simulation
exercises are presented in a set of charts and tables, the tables
being given in the appendix. Figure 7.1 and table 7.1 deal with
results obtained using coefficients estimated for the entire sample period.

Figure 7.1(a) and table 7.1(a) deal with the growth rate of
real income, and here it is the 1955-58 period that produces the
most conspicuous errors. Thereafter the major swings in the
growth rate of real income are reasonably well tracked, though
turning points are not pinned down with great precision; one
would not expect them to be with an annual model. 1971 sees a
large over-prediction in the rate of change of real income, which
is followed by an under-prediction for 1972.

Figure 7.1(b) and table 7.1(b) show that the model deals with
the inflation rate with less success, but again it is the 1950s
rather than the late '60s where the main trouble arises. Having
completely missed the step up in the inflation rate that took
place in 1956-57, the model does not get back on track until 1966,
though it follows the *rate of change* of the inflation rate quite well
after 1957, as figure 7.1(c) and table 7.1(c) show. 1972 is a bad
prediction for both the level and the rate of change of the inflation
rate. Whether this is merely a matter of the model's being somewhat early in picking up the increase in the inflation rate that
1973 appears to be witnessing or whether the over-prediction
reflects effects of wage-price guidelines on the inflation rate must
remain to be seen.[17]

The results presented in figure 7.2 and table 7.2 were obtained using the coefficients estimated from the sub-period
1953-65. Here too the late 1950s produce the most striking errors

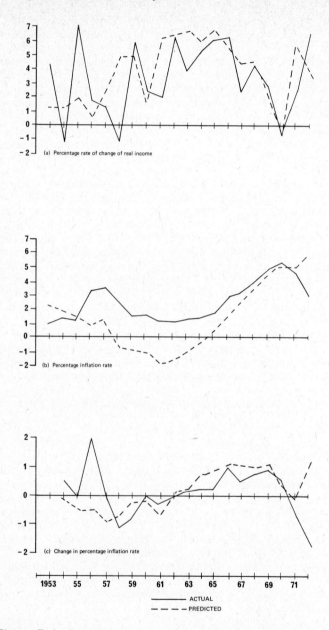

Figure 7.1 Original model, coefficients estimated 1953-72: actual *v.* simulated values of endogenous variables

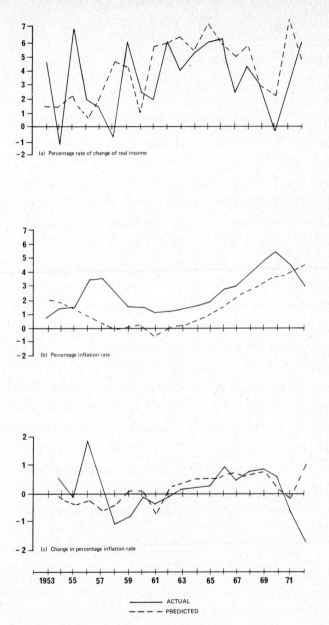

Figure 7.2 Original model, coefficients estimated 1953-65: actual *v*. simulated values of endogenous variables

for both the rate of change of real income and the rate of inflation, and again 1971 produces serious over-predictions of the rate of growth of real income, while 1972 sees a false prediction of an upturn in the inflation rate. Overall, though, the tracking of the variables here is slightly superior to that using the coefficients estimated over the whole period even for the period after 1965, whose data were not used in estimating the coefficients upon which these simulations are based. Even though there is a tendency for the rate of change of real income to be over-predicted after 1965 and for the inflation rate to be under-predicted, the model does not go seriously or increasingly awry in these years, and this is surely a point in its favour.

The results obtained with the simulation exercises just discussed give the impression of having been generated by a model that captures some important characteristics of the United States economy, but this impression is, of course, a subjective one. It would be pleasant to report that it is confirmed by an application of some simple and widely accepted criteria that are more objective in character. Unfortunately this is not entirely the case, as I shall now show.

A frequently employed test of an econometric model's performance is to compare it with a naive hypothesis. When we compare this model's performance with that of the hypothesis that the percentage rate of growth of real income and the percentage rate of inflation are simply random variables fluctuating about their mean values we find that, when coefficients estimated from the entire 1952-73 sample are used, the naive hypothesis wins. The root mean square error of the model in predicting the percentage rate of change of real income is 2·613, in predicting the percentage rate of inflation it is 2·035, and in predicting the rate of change of the inflation rate it is 0·955. The naive hypothesis yields root mean square errors for these three variables of 2·575 1·314, and 0·814 respectively. When this simple and quite orthodox test is applied the model's bad predictive performance in the 1950s and in 1972, already noted in discussing figure 7.1, turns out to swamp its relatively good performance in the 1960s.

But we also have coefficients estimated from the period 1953-65. Their predictive power over data for 1966-72 may be compared with that of the naive hypothesis that the mean percentage growth rate of real income and the mean percentage inflation rate over the years 1953-65 are good predictors of the values of these variables from 1966 onwards. Even here the model does not do too well. For the percentage rate of growth of real income the model's root mean square error is 2·266, for the inflation rate 1·221 and for the rate of change of the inflation rate 1·059. The naive hypothesis yields, for the same variables, errors of 2·232, 2·293 and 0·911 respectively. The model clearly performs better

on the inflation rate, while its failure to outshine the naive hypothesis on the rate of change of the inflation rate results solely from
from the bad prediction of 1972. Its inability to do better when
predicting the rate of change of real income is less easy to attribute to one particular observation, though a better prediction for
1971 would have tipped the balance in the model's favour.

Nevertheless we must be careful not to end up selecting
ex post the criterion on which the model performs best and then
claiming that it is, after all, satisfactory.[18] What we appear to have
is a model whose individual components perform well enough by
orthodox criteria but which, when put together, produce, to say the
least, very mixed results. This particular failure ought not to be
too surprising, for the model is extremely simple and has many
a priori constraints imposed upon its structure. These constraints
are of two types. First, we have those which are implications of
economic theory: a unit price level elasticity of demand for
nominal balances, a unit coefficient on the expected rate of inflation
in the equation determining the current inflation rate, zero inter-
cepts to exclude unexplained time trends from the model, and
so on. Second, we have constraints imposed to keep the model
analytically manageable but which have little if any grounding in
economic theory: in particular much of the lag structure of the
model is quite arbitrary. The question then arises as to whether it
is possible to relax one or more of these arbitrary constraints
while maintaining those which have an economic basis and thereby
to improve the model's performance. As we shall now see this
is indeed possible.

Two modifications were made to the model. The money
multiplier relationship which we have so far employed postulates
an instantaneous response of the growth rate of real income to
changes in the growth rate of real balances, despite the fact that
a relatively long lag is well known to characterise the first stage
of the time pattern of the response of economic activity to monetary stimuli. Moreover this formulation leaves open the question
of whether causation really does run from real balances to real
income and not in the opposite direction. All this suggests that
the one-year lagged value of the rate of change of real balances
might fruitfully be added to the money multiplier equation giving
it the form:

$$\Delta Y = \Delta y + \Delta \overline{Y^*} = \beta_1 (\Delta M - \Delta P) + \beta_2 (\Delta M_{-1} - \Delta P_{-1}) \qquad (13)$$

The excess demand proxy that appears in the equation determining
the rate of inflation is a measure of the amount by which income
deviates from full employment over a specific period. The rationale for expecting excess demand to influence the inflation rate is
that its appearance causes firms to revise their expectations of
the volume of output they can sell if they follow current pricing

policies. This suggests that perhaps a measure of the *expected* level of excess demand, rather than its *current* level, might be included in the price formation equation. It is not unreasonable to postulate that such a variable might be generated by applying the adaptive expectations hypothesis to our original excess demand proxy, so that we get

$$\Delta P = g y^e_{-1} + \Delta P^e_{-1} \tag{14}$$

and

$$y^e = hy + (1 - h)y^e_{-1} \quad 0 < h < 1 \tag{15}$$

with the effect that we slow down and smooth out the response of the current inflation rate to the current level of income.

If we recall that we have defined the expected inflation rate as

$$\Delta P^e = d \Delta P + (1 - d)\Delta P^e_{-1} \tag{3}$$

successive applications of the Koyck transformation yield an expression for the rate of inflation in terms of observable variables that may be written as

$$\Delta P = hg\, y_{-1} - (1 - d)\, hg\, y_{-2} + (2 - h)\Delta P_{-1}$$
$$- (1 - h)\Delta P_{-2} \tag{16}$$

or alternatively

$$\Delta^2 P = hg\, y_{-1} - (1 - d)\, hg\, y_{-2} + (1 - h)\Delta^2 P_{-1} \tag{16'}$$

Now these modifications to our model are well within the spirit of what may be termed monetarist analysis. They leave the basic causative chain to run from money to real output to inflation and thence back to real output as it did in the simple model discussed earlier and alter only certain aspects of the timing of the interaction of these variables. However, the empirical performance of the model is considerably enhanced by these modifications.

Consider first the behaviour of the money multiplier equation, which, it might be noted, cannot be directly related back to demand and supply for money relationships as could the unlagged version.[19] When the expression

$$\Delta Y = \beta_1(\Delta M - \Delta P) + \beta_2(\Delta M_{-1} - \Delta P_{-1}) + \epsilon$$

is fitted to data for 1953-72 it yields the following results:

$$\beta_1 = 0 \cdot 514 \qquad t = 2 \cdot 720$$
$$\beta_2 = 0 \cdot 559, \qquad t = 2 \cdot 778$$
$$R^2 = 0 \cdot 339 \qquad dw = 2 \cdot 483$$

while for 1953-65 we get

$$\beta_1 = 0\cdot493 \qquad t = 1\cdot495$$
$$\beta_2 = 0\cdot735 \qquad t = 2\cdot037$$
$$R^2 = 0\cdot198 \qquad dw = 2\cdot660$$

These results confirm the suspicion that our initial formulation was attributing too large an instantaneous effect to monetary changes, and show reasonable stability between the whole period and the sub-period. Moreover they give us some reason to believe the causation does indeed run from money to income and not in the opposite direction. If we replace the lagged value of the rate of change of the real money supply with a led value we would expect this variable to show up with a significant coefficient if causation was running income to money, but in fact when this was tried the variable in question took on an insignificant negative coefficient.[20]

For the price formation equation the following expression was initially estimated:

$$\Delta^2 P = \gamma_1 \, y_{-1} + \gamma_2 \, y_{-2} + \gamma_3 \, \Delta^2 P_{-1} + v$$

For 1965-72 the results were

$$\gamma_1 = 0\cdot228 \qquad t = 3\cdot924$$
$$\gamma_2 = -0\cdot159 \qquad t = 2\cdot806$$
$$\gamma_3 = 0\cdot249 \qquad t = 2\cdot353$$
$$R^2 = 0\cdot506 \qquad dw = 1\cdot637$$

and for 1953-65 they were

$$\gamma_1 = 0\cdot207 \qquad t = 3\cdot018$$
$$\gamma_2 = -0\cdot168 \qquad t = 2\cdot543$$
$$\gamma_3 = 0\cdot208 \qquad t = 1\cdot871$$
$$R^2 = 0\cdot465 \qquad dw = 1\cdot648$$

The lagged value of the rate of change of the inflation rate enters significantly but scarcely alters the value of the coefficients obtained in its absence. Again the sub-period results confirm that we are dealing with a stable relationship. Furthermore, if instead we run the regression

$$\Delta P = \gamma_1 y_{-1} + \gamma_2 \, y_{-2} + \gamma_4 \Delta P_{-1} + \gamma_5 \Delta P_{-2} + v$$

we should expect to find $\gamma_5 = -\gamma_3$ and $\gamma_4 = 1 + \gamma_3$ if the coefficient of the expected inflation rate of the actual rate is indeed unity. When we carry out this experiment we get, for 1953-72

$\gamma_1 = 0\cdot228 \qquad t = 3\cdot729$

$\gamma_2 = -0\cdot158 \qquad t = 2\cdot571$

$\gamma_4 = 1\cdot246 \qquad t = 10\cdot545$

$\gamma_5 = -0\cdot149 \qquad t = 2\cdot283$

$R^2 = 0\cdot791 \qquad dw = 1\cdot631$

and for 1953-65

$\gamma_1 = 0\cdot221 \qquad t = 2\cdot813$

$\gamma_2 = -0\cdot174 \qquad t = 2\cdot473$

$\gamma_4 = 1\cdot260 \qquad t = 7\cdot487$

$\gamma_5 = -0\cdot219 \qquad t = 1\cdot844,$

$R^2 = 0\cdot457 \qquad dw = 1\cdot822$

We have further strong evidence here in favour of the natural unemployment rate hypothesis.[21]

The results of carrying out simulation exercises with this version of the model are presented in figures 7.3-4 and tables 7.3-4, and largely speak for themselves. There is an overall improvement in the model's performance, with the mid-1950s, however, still proving a source of some difficulty. Moreover, the impression gained by casual observation of the relevant charts is confirmed by more formal tests. The model's root mean squared errors of prediction when coefficients obtained from the entire period are used are: for the percentage change in real income 2·111, for the inflation rate 1·791, and for the rate of change of the inflation rate 0·701. The reader will recall that the comparable errors yielded by the naive hypothesis were 2·575, 1·314 and 0·814. Only for the inflation rate does the model perform in an inferior fashion, and this problem clearly results from its missing, as done the simpler version, the step-up in the inflation rate that took place in 1956 and 1957. Given that the model's worst performance is for the 1950s, it should come as no surprise that when prediction beyond the sample sub-period 1953-65 is at issue the model now appears to be decisively better. The relevant root mean squared errors for the model are: for real income 1·095, for the inflation rate 1·611, and for the rate of change of the inflation rate 0·576; for the naive hypothesis the comparable errors are 2·232, 2·293 and 0·911.

Before concluding this account of the empirical performance of the model something should be said about its stability and

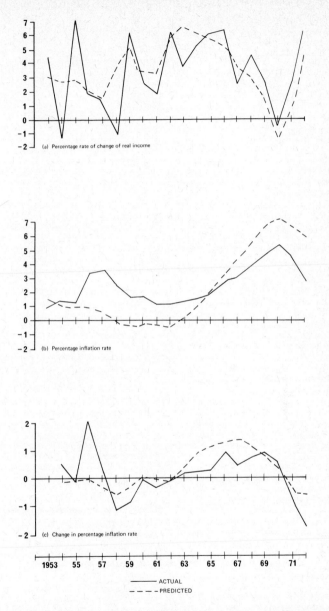

Figure 7.3 Model with extra lagged variables, coefficients estimated 1953-72: actual *v*. simulated values of endogenous variables

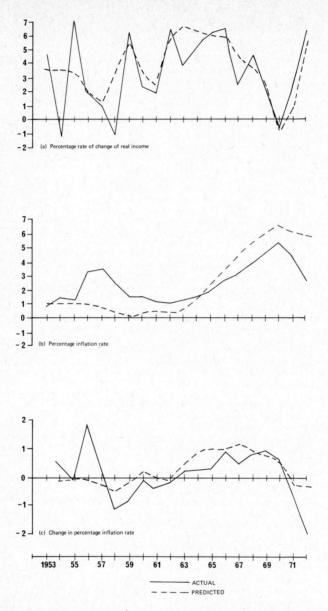

Figure 7.4 Model with extra lagged variables, coefficients estimated 1953-65: actual *v.* simulated values of endogenous variables

cyclical properties, for the analysis carried out earlier suggested
that these would depend upon the precise magnitudes of the model's
parameters. There are in fact four different versions of the model,
because we have two sets of parameters for both its simpler form
and that which incorporates extra lags. However, all four versions
are stable and all four show a marked tendency to approach the
steady state with long cyclical swings. Certain relevant information is tabulated in table 7.5 and was generated with a simulation
exercise in which the system was started out in equilibrium with
a rate of monetary expansion of 5 per cent, this rate then being
doubled once and for all to 10 per cent. The more complex version of the model shows more uniformity between the consequences of using different sets of parameter estimates, as one
might expect.

However, the precise quantities involved in the results set out
in table 7.5 are not so interesting as is their qualitative nature.[22]
We have here a macro-model that in its simplest form has a zero
elasticity of demand for money and exogenous money supply, properties that maximise the inherent stability of the system according to conventional LM-IS analysis; and yet this model shows a
marked ability to generate cycles of significant length and ampli-
tude as a result of a once-and-for-all change in the rate of monetary expansion. It has this ability because it permits prices and
output to fluctuate together, rather than, as is the case in orthodox
macro-economics, allowing only one or the other of these variables to fluctuate at a time. This suggests that further analysis
of explicitly dynamic macro-models which include some version
of a Phillips relationship would be well worth while, for even the
very simple model analysed in this paper seems to undermine
an important piece of conventional wisdom that is frequently
derived from more traditional analysis. It *is* possible for real
income and the price level to fluctuate when the money supply is
constant; a zero interest elasticity of demand for money is no
guarantee that all shocks will be absorbed by the interest rate.

IV

This paper has covered a good deal of ground, and it would be as
well now to summarise its content, paying particular attention to
the problems that it still leaves open. First, a dynamic macro-
model of the influence of money on the time path of real income
and prices has been constructed, and this model is simple enough
to be readily accessible even to undergraduates. In it the chain of
causation runs over time from the inflation rate and the rate of
growth of the nominal money supply to the level of real income,
thence back to the inflation rate and so on in a recursive process.
The model was subjected to empirical tests, and, whatever one's

judgement about its overall performance, two specific items in the empirical section of the paper are of interest in their own right.

First, the explanatory power of the money multiplier is enhanced by adding the lagged value of the rate of change of the money stock to the relationship. This is another small piece of evidence, to be added to the considerable amount already available, that, as far as the United States is concerned, causation runs from money to economic activity rather than vice versa, and that monetary changes take a considerable time to make even their impact effects felt. Second, we have generated evidence about the nature of the expectations-augmented Phillips curve. Not only are our empirical results consistent with the so-called natural unemployment rate hypothesis but they also suggest that expectations about the time path of aggregate demand, and not just its current level, affect the rate of inflation. These results open up a new and potentially interesting line of enquiry about the role of expectations in the macro-economic system.

I would also claim that the model's performance is reasonably satisfactory, though this point is perhaps more debatable. The model is, after all, driven by one, and only one, exogenous variable, the rate of change of the nominal money supply, and contains only three—or, in its slightly extended form, four—behaviour relationships. These are a money multiplier, a price setting equation, an equation relating the expected to the actual inflation rate, and one relating the expected to the actual amount by which real income deviates from its equilibrium level. Though a more complicated model would undoubtedly be capable of doing a better job of tracking output and the inflation rate over a twenty-year period than is this one, it would use a good deal more information in doing so. I know of no model as simple as this one that has been asked to do so much. To construct an alternative simple model that performs better ought to present an interesting challenge to someone.

However, none of this is to say that the model presented above has performed in a totally satisfactory fashion. The extreme simplicity imposed upon it for analytical reasons proved to be too much simplicity when it came to dealing with empirical evidence. In particular the analytic framework initially presented provided no account of the transmission mechanism between monetary changes and aggregate demand. This suppression of any explicit account of what we might term the *IS* side of the economy produced an enormous gain in analytic simplicity, as the reader will easily discover if he tries for himself to incorporate such material into the model I have presented, but unfortunately the model did not give a satisfactory empirical performance until a time lag was introduced into the money multiplier relationship. The modification converts the money multiplier from a relationship properly grounded in explicit, albeit simple, structural equations into a reduced form of some structure which is not specified. In short, the attempt to build a simple structural model which is both analytically simple and empirically satisfactory has not been totally successful. However, what was attempted was ambitious indeed, and failure was far from complete. At the very least I would argue that the work reported here represents a promising start in the building up of a new and *empirically relevant* body of short-run macro-economic dynamics upon which we may base both policy discussions and teaching.

APPENDIX

Table 7.1 Original model, coefficients estimated 1953-72: actual *v*. simulated values of endogenous variables

	(a) Percentage rate of change of real income		(b) Percentage inflation rate		(c) Change in percentage inflation rate	
Date	Actual	Simulated	Actual	Simulated	Actual	Simulated
1953	4·38	1·36	1·01	2·24		
1954	−1·41	1·34	1·47	1·96	0·46	−0·28
1955	7·34	1·93	1·36	1·51	−0·11	−0·45
1956	1·82	0·63	3·39	1·07	2·03	−0·48
1957	1·45	2·29	3·66	0·11	0·27	−0·91
1958	−1·15	4·91	2·50	−0·64	−1·16	−0·75
1959	6·21	4·97	1·68	−0·88	−0·82	−0·24
1960	2·44	1·81	1·61	−1·01	−0·07	−0·12
1061	1·91	6·27	1·26	−1·76	−0·34	−0·75
1962	6·35	6·62	1·11	−1·61	−0·15	0·15
1963	3·94	6·80	1·31	−1·17	0·20	0·44
1964	5·30	5·97	1·55	−0·45	0·25	0·72
1965	6·14	6·74	1·83	0·32	0·28	0·77
1966	6·32	5·50	2·74	1·46	0·91	1·14
1967	2·56	4·44	3·15	2·55	0·41	1·09
1968	4·56	4·57	3·92	3·54	0·77	0·99
1969	2·65	1·69	4·73	4·64	0·82	1·09
1970	−0·49	−0·78	5·33	5·14	0·60	0·50
1971	2·68	5·72	4·61	4·92	−0·72	−0·22
1972	6·25	3·54	2·97	5·88	−1·64	0·96

Table 7.2 Original model, coefficients estimated 1953-65: actual *v.* simulated values of endogenous variables

Date	(a) Percentage rate of change in real income		(b) Percentage inflation rate		(c) Change in percentage inflation rate	
	Actual	*Simulated*	*Actual*	*Simulated*	*Actual*	*Simulated*
1953	4·38	1·66	1·01	2·09		
1954	−1·41	1·64	1·45	1·80	0·46	−0·28
1955	7·34	2·19	1·36	1·46	−0·11	−0·35
1956	1·82	0·56	3·39	1·16	2·03	−0·30
1957	1·45	2·15	3·66	0·49	0·27	−0·66
1958	−1·15	4·74	2·50	0·05	−1·16	−0·44
1959	6·21	4·53	1·68	0·09	−0·82	0·03
1960	2·44	0·88	1·61	0·11	−0·07	0·03
1961	1·91	5·73	1·26	−0·56	−0·34	−0·67
1962	6·35	6·06	1·11	−0·35	−0·15	0·21
1963	3·94	6·35	1·31	−0·0007	0·20	0·35
1964	5·30	5·67	1·55	0·48	0·25	0·48
1965	6·14	6·88	1·83	0·91	0·28	0·43
1966	6·32	5·91	2·74	1·65	0·91	0·74
1967	2·56	5·18	3·15	2·29	0·41	0·64
1968	4·56	5·76	3·92	2·86	0·77	0·57
1969	2·65	2·93	4·73	3·60	0·82	0·74
1970	−0·49	0·45	5·33	3·84	0·60	0·24
1971	2·68	7·71	4·61	3·57	−0·72	−0·27
1972	6·25	5·17	2·97	4·65	−1·64	1·08

Table 7.3 Model with extra lagged variables, coefficients estimated 1953-72; actual *v.* simulated values of endogenous variables

Date	(a) Percentage rate of change in real income		(b) Percentage inflation rate		(d) Change in percentage inflation rate	
	Actual	Simulated	Actual	Simulated	Actual	Simulated
1953	4·38	3·15	1·01	1·07		
1954	−1·41	2·77	1·47	0·93	0·46	−0·14
1955	7·34	2·79	1·36	0·90	−0·11	−0·03
1956	1·82	1·97	3·39	0·85	2·03	−0·06
1957	1·45	1·55	3·66	0·54	0·27	−0·30
1958	−1·15	3·61	2·50	−0·03	−1·16	−0·57
1959	6·21	5·18	1·68	−0·33	−0·82	−0·31
1960	2·44	3·35	1·61	−0·21	−0·07	0·12
1961	1·91	3·44	1·26	−0·29	−0·34	−0·08
1962	6·35	6·13	1·11	−0·41	−0·15	−0·12
1963	3·94	6·58	1·31	0·06	0·20	0·47
1964	5·30	6·11	1·55	0·96	0·25	0·90
1965	6·14	5·76	1·83	2·06	0·28	1·11
1966	6·32	5·29	2·74	3·32	0·91	1·25
1967	2·56	3·75	3·15	4·65	0·41	1·33
1968	4·56	2·97	3·92	5·77	0·77	1·12
1969	2·65	1·46	4·73	6·67	0·82	0·90
1970	−0·49	−1·57	5·33	7·14	0·60	0·46
1971	2·68	0·74	4·61	6·65	−0·72	−0·48
1972	6·25	4·41	2·97	6·10	−1·64	−0·55

Table 7.4 Model with extra lagged variables, coefficients estimated 1953-65; actual *v.* simulated values of endogenous variables

Date	(a) Percentage rate of change in real income		(b) Percentage inflation rate		(c) Change in percentage inflation rate	
	Actual	Simulated	Actual	Simulated	Actual	Simulated
1953	4·38	3·61	1·01	1·16		
1954	−1·41	3·04	1·47	1·10	0·46	−0·06
1955	7·34	2·96	1·36	1·10	−0·11	−0·0003
1956	1·82	2·17	3·39	1·07	2·03	−0·02
1957	1·45	1·34	3·66	0·86	0·27	−0·22
1958	−1·15	3·44	2·50	0·37	−1·16	−0·48
1959	6·21	5·36	1·68	0·18	−0·82	−0·19
1960	2·44	3·47	1·61	0·45	−0·07	0·26
1961	1·91	2·68	1·26	0·48	−0·34	0·04
1962	6·35	6·03	1·11	0·30	−0·15	−0·18
1963	3·94	6·65	1·31	0·74	0·20	0·43
1964	5·30	6·31	1·55	1·52	0·25	0·79
1965	6·14	5·95	1·83	2·43	0·27	0·91
1966	6·32	5·88	2·74	3·40	0·91	0·97
1967	2·56	4·45	3·15	4·46	0·41	1·06
1968	4·56	3·75	3·92	5·34	0·77	0·87
1969	2·65	2·57	4·73	6·06	0·82	0·73
1970	−0·49	−0·79	5·33	6·52	0·60	0·46
1971	2·68	0·82	4·61	6·19	−0·72	−0·33
1972	6·25	5·59	2·97	5·86	−1·64	−0·33

Table 7.5 Certain characteristics of the model's response to an increase in the rate of monetary expansion from 5 per cent to 10 per cent

	Period of cycle (years approx.)	Years elapsed till rate of growth of income back to within		Maximum rate of growth of income (%)	Minimum rate of growth of income (%)	Maximum inflation rate (%)	Minimum inflation rate (%)
		0·5% of equilibrium rate	1% of equilibrium rate				
Original version of model							
Parameters estimated 1953–72	24	26	15	8·2	1·2	8·7	5·0
Parameters estimated 1953–65	36	22	19	8·6	1·9	8·1	6·2
Version of model with extra lags							
Parameters estimated 1953–72	18	29	20	8·6	0·0	10·3	4·8
Parameters estimated 1953–65	22	22	14	9·5	0·5	9·6	6·6

NOTES

[1]   Reprinted from the *Manchester School,* XLI, December 1973, this paper is part of a continuing study being carried out under the auspices of the University of Manchester—SSRC Inflation Programme. Much of the empirical work reported was carried out at the Federal Reserve Bank of St Louis, to whose research department I am extremely grateful for the magnificent facilities they provided. In particular I am grateful to Michael McCoy for programming and other assistance with empirical work. At the University of Manchester Linda Westle and Rodney Cross provided valuable help. An earlier version of this paper was read to the Manchester Inflation Workshop, where it received much useful criticism; Leonall Andersen, George Borts, Frank Brechling, Keith Carlson, Herschel Grossman, Thomas Mayer, Robert Rasche and Ronald Teigen all commented most helpfully on earlier drafts but are in no way responsible for any errors in the current version.

[2]   For a discussion of a theoretical model that deals with an open economy see Laidler (1972c). For evidence that open economy considerations are indeed relevant to the British economy see Laidler (1972b).

[3]   For a survey of most of the relevant evidence on this matter *cf.* Laidler (1969a).

[4]   [The reader who find the absence of an opportunity cost variable in the demand for money function particularly hard to swallow might recall that if money is the liability of a competitive banking system it will bear interest at a rate which will vary with that on other assets, though not necessarily in a one-to-one relationship; moreover changes in the expected rate of inflation will become incorporated in the rate of return on money just as they will in that on other nominal assets. In such a case the only scope for the opportunity cost of holding money to vary will arise from changes in the relative supplies of money and other assets, and, if we assume that the effect of such changes is negligible, it might be appropriate to omit the opportunity cost variable from our demand equation.

In any event, one can incorporate the expected rate of inflation as the opportunity cost of holding money into equation 1. This complicates the model's structure without, apparently, altering any important characteristics of its behaviour. Where c is the semi-log. coefficient of the demand for money with respect to the expected rate of inflation, and $\Delta^2 Y^*$ is assumed equal to zero, equation 5 below becomes a third-order equation of the form

$$y = \frac{1}{b} \Delta^2 \overline{M} - \frac{(1-d)}{b} \Delta^2 \overline{M}_{-1} + \frac{bcdg + 2b - g + (1-d)b}{b} y_{-1}$$

$$- \frac{b - (1-d)g + (1-d)(2b-g) + bcdg(1-d)}{b} y_{-2}$$

$$+ \frac{(1-d)(b - (1-d))g}{b} y_{-3}$$

where c is set equal to zero; the above equation reduces to equation 5.]

5   An account of the expectations augmented Phillips curve is given in Phelps (1972), part 1.

6   This ratio measure of excess demand has been used by Petersen *et. al.* (1971) and by McCallum (1973).

7   For example, *cf.* Tobin (1972) for an alternative view of the interaction of price and output fluctuations.

8   Expectations about the future inflation rate are formed at a particular moment on the basis of inflation rates experienced up to the moment, and form the basis for pricing decisions taken at that moment for the following year. The average level of excess demand—as proxied by the ratio of actual to 'full employment' output—over a one-year period centred at the moment at which pricing decisions are taken also affects the rate of inflation. There is, in affect, a six-month lag between the average level of excess demand and the inflation rate. An earlier version of this model, constructed entirely for heuristic purposes, used a measure of excess demand centred at the end of the period for which prices were being set. Though this produces an analytically neater model it is neither easy to justify on *a priori* grounds nor productive of good empirical results. It is worth pointing out that analytic convenience alone is the reason for building a log linear model and that, particularly as far as price formation equation 2 is concerned, the form chosen lacks empirical plausibility. Equation 2 implies that income can rise above its long-run equilibrium level not only without limit but also with a diminishing proportional effect upon the inflation rate, while also implying that the further below equilibrium lies real income the greater the impact on the inflation rate will a given change in its level have. If anything, one would expect just the opposite effects to hold true. The implication is that we cannot expect the empirical content of this model to be accurate except in the neighbourhood of full employment. It might fit post-war data, but it would be surprising if it fitted well for the 1930s.

9   This prediction is, of course, the standard 'quantity theory of money' result. Note, though, that it is derived from a model which has an explicit theory of price formation embodied in it. There is

no implication here that the quantity theory of money, taken by itself, is a satisfactory explanation even of equilibrium inflation.
[10]   [Application of the stability conditions set out in chapter 3 will confirm that this model may be unstable if b should be 'small' relative to g. The model is also capable of generating cycles.]
[11]   Notice that this prediction follows from equations 2 and 3 in isolation and hence is independent of the assumptions about the money market embodied in this model. Phelps (1972) discusses the same prediction, while Laidler (1972b) presents some, on the whole favourable, evidence on the cyclical behaviour of the inflation rate in the British economy. Petersen *et al.* (1971) refer to an equation such as 6 as a 'differential Phillips curve'.
[12]   The model thus bears a resemblance to the simplest version of of that fitted by McCallum (1973). However, it differs crucially in the central role which it accords to adaptive expectations on the inflation rate. McCallum could find no strong evidence to support the presence of adaptive expectations, while, as we shall see, the price formation equation utilised here is quite strongly supported by empirical evidence. The apparent contradiction would be well worth investigating. Note that the time structure of the model is simple enough to make its suitability for use with quarterly data *a priori* implausible. Some preliminary investigations with quarterly data readily confirmed this proposition.
[13]   *Cf.* Laidler (1969a)
[14]   Note that R^2 here measures the explanatory power of the independent variables over the *rate of change* of real income and is not comparable with R^2s, reported above, which deal with variance in the *level* of real income.
[15]   Note that the R^2 is concerned with the goodness of fit for the *rate of change* of the rate of inflation.
[16]   I have chosen the money multiplier parameter here as it is estimated from the first difference regression rather than from that performed upon the levels of the data. This choice was quite arbitrary, and in point of fact the performance of the model in the simulation exercises reported below does improve slightly if the other estimate is used. Nothing important, however, appears to hinge upon this.
[17]   And if the result does reflect the effects of guidelines there is the further question of whether they have affected the actual rate of inflation or the behaviour of the index number that is supposed to measure the actual rate of inflation.
[18]   Indeed, the use of mean absolute errors instead of root mean squared errors would have made the model look somewhat better, as would the arraying of statistics on such matters as the frequency with which the model predicts the direction of error of

the naive hypothesis. However, enough evidence has probably been displayed to convince the reader that the model, though not without predictive power, cannot be regarded as satisfactory.

[19]   To make the demand for money dependent upon permanent income alone would produce a money multiplier of this general form but the by now well known 'overshoot' effects of this hypothesis would require β_2 to take on a negative sign, which it does not. The existence of lags in the impact effects of monetary changes can be reconciled with the permanent income hypothesis of the demand for money by postulating lags in the transmission mechanism through which monetary policy works, and in particular lags in the response of aggregate demand to change in interest rate variables, as I have shown in Laidler (1973b). Whether this is in fact what is going on here is a question that would clearly repay further investigation. Such an investigation would, however, require the construction of a quite elaborate structural model that paid explicit attention to the transmission mechanism of monetary policy and hence would involve the sacrifice of the simplicity which I have tried to achieve in the analysis contained in this paper.

[20]   It might also be noted that, when the change in real balances was decomposed into a change in nominal balances and a change in the price level, it was not possible to conclude that the coefficients on these two variables were not equal in magnitude but opposite in sign. As with the unlagged formulation of the money multiplier equation, however, the coefficients were sufficiently badly determined that not too much importance can be attached to this.

[21]   The results presented here are not the last word. When an intercept was permitted to appear in this regression it turned out to be significantly positive and tended to knock the twice lagged value of y out of the regression. This suggests that the price formation model which I am utilising would repay further investigation, and I would conjecture that the source of the difficulty which seems to be turning up here will turn out to lie in the expectation formation mechanism being utilised in the present work.

[22]   But all the results presented in table 7.5 should be taken with a large pinch of salt. They probably tell us more about the consequences of the model's log. linear form than about the properties of the United States economy. In particular, were some property introduced in the model that would limit the ability of real income to exceed its equilibrium level I suspect that this would introduce a strong damping effect into the model's cyclical behaviour (*cf.* note 8 above).

8 Some current issues concerning the international aspects of inflation[1]

written jointly with A. R. Nobay

I

The recent world-wide inflation is not altogether without historical precedent. There have been previous periods in which the price levels of many countries have moved together, and not always in an upward direction: witness the price decline in the latter years of the Nineteenth century that at one time was known as the 'Great Depression'. One salient difference between the present episode and previous ones lies in the relative lack of agreement among economists as to its causes. Though there were always dissenting voices in the past, the dominant view was that the behaviour of prices was largely to be explained in terms of the time path of the supply of money, which in its turn was to be explained by the behaviour of the output of the precious metals.

The current inflation certainly may be—and indeed by some economists is—explained in monetary terms, but it is far from clear that this is a majority viewpoint.[2] Indeed, far more influence upon policy has been accorded to alternative explanations that invoke such sociological concepts as 'relative deprivation' and postulate that inflation is the outcome of a struggle between social groups (perhaps, but not necessarily, the traditional Marxist socio-economic classes) for increasing shares of real income. Within this framework the international aspect of inflation is explained in terms of demonstration effects which lead to real income aspirations becoming co-ordinated across national boundaries.

The two views to which we have alluded here were captured in the contributions of Johnson and Marris to the 1971 Dauphine conference, and the vigour with which the debate continues is reflected in the programme for the 1974 conference.[3] In this paper we shall outline the economic analysis whose failure has forced so many economists to adopt a non-economic explanation of inflation and contrast this analysis with a framework which, because it accords a much more prominent role to money in the economic system, does seem capable of providing an economic explanation of inflation. Then we shall proceed to bring out and discuss what seem to us to be some important unresolved issues concerning the international transmission of inflationary impulses that are present in the monetary explanation of the pheonomenon. In this way we hope to strike a useful compromise between providing a survey of previous literature and making some contribution to moving the debate, or at least one side of it, a little further forward.

II

The events of the 1920s and 1930s, and the developments in economic analysis that accompanied them, seemed to overturn (but, we shall argue, in some ways merely interrupted) an intellectual tradition that had been dominant for a century and a half. That tradition can be summed up in the two phrases 'quantity theory of money' and 'price specie flow mechanism'; its dominant analytic property was to link the behaviour of the domestic price level of any country through the balance of payments to events in the rest of the world. In retrospect it seems incredible that a world-wide monetary contraction and an associated world-wide deflation should have been regarded as providing a definitive refutation of this point of view, but that is what happened. The inability of the quantity theory to provide an explanation of output fluctuations distracted attention from the other things that it could explain, and a new body of doctrine grew up to replace it.

The quantity of money was replaced by the level of autonomous expenditure as the central variable in this new analysis, and it emphasised the determination not of prices but of the level of income and employment. The price level was not ignored altogether, however. The level of money wages was usually taken as an exogenous variable and the price level was treated either, in simpler versions, as determined by a mark-up on money wages or, in more complex versions of the model, as a result of the profit-maximising pricing behaviour of perfectly competitive firms, each experiencing diminishing returns to labour. The quantity of money influenced the price level only as one of the several variables that might influence aggregate demand and hence output and thus was accorded no key role in determining prices.[4]

As to the balance of payments, its monetary aspects were totally ignored by the new approach, for it was assumed, more often implicitly than explicitly, that the monetary authorities could always completely sterilise these by appropriate open market operations. Exports came into the picture as an injection of real expenditure and imports as a leakage. The levels of real exports and imports were both characterised (though not necessarily exclusively so) as depending upon relative prices, and

those relative prices in turn were regarded as being open to
influence by exchange rate changes. The 'elasticities approach'
to the balance of payments was thus a natural complement to the
income expenditure approach to domestic income determination.

Whatever the virtues of this body of doctrine as a means
of dealing with the policy problems of the 1930s, it would be hard
to devise a framework less suited to those which emerged in the
1950s and have been dominant ever since. If the principal determinant of prices in a model is an exogenous money wage rate,
that model is not going to be much help in explaining inflation;
if the principal consequence of a devaluation in a model is to
produce a net injection of aggregate demand into the system—an
injection which has to be met with an output change if the balance
of payments is to be improved—then it is not going to be much
help in dealing with the balance of payment problems of a
country which finds itself operating at full employment. That the
'absorption approach' to the balance of payments represents an
attempt to remedy the latter defect is well known; this body of
analysis need not detain us here because our main concern is with
the economics of inflation. The Phillips curve was the analytic
device introduced to cope with inflation, and for nearly a decade
it seemed capable of doing so.[5]

The Phillips curve hypothesis in its original and simplest
form stated that the rate of money wage inflation varies inversely
with the level of unemployment, the latter variable being a proxy
for the level of excess demand for labour. When one's basic
economic model postulates that the principal determinant of price
level changes is money wage variation, a simple hypothesis about
what changes money wages is obviously very attractive, particularly when it has as much empirical support as the Phillips
curve appeared to command.[6] These factors alone explain the,
at first sight, curious phenomenon that, though price inflation
was always the policy problem, it was wage inflation that had most
analytic and empirical attention paid to it in the orthodox macro-
economics of the 1960s. Understand wage inflation, control it, and
price inflation is automatically under control in a world of simple
mark-up or competitive pricing.

In policy discussions the excess demand for labour quickly
became regarded as a variable susceptible to control through
demand management policy. Thus it seemed as though the rate
of wage and hence price inflation could be brought under the control of the domestic authorities by using such a policy. The
introduction of import price inflation alongside wage inflation as
a determinant of domestic price inflation did introduce a variable
not under the direct control of the domestic authorities, but one
whose effects could nevertheless still be offset by appropriate
domestic demand management.[7]

Evidence generated in the late 1960s and 1970s has, of
course, thoroughly undermined this view of the world. In all
countries, whatever semblance of a stable smooth inverse relationship between unemployment and wage inflation there might have
been in the past, it has completely vanished over the last five or
six years. This evidence is widely regarded as demonstrating that
the economics of a competitive market economy no longer apply
to the world in which we are living: hence the search for sociological and socio-psychological explanations of inflation and
policy prescriptions of wage-price controls.[8] Another important
matter is the international character of the current inflation.
For want of an economic explanation of inflation, its international
character must be attributed to demonstration effects. Hence the
call, heard particularly from OECD, not just for wage and price
controls but for international co-ordination of wage and price
controls as the appropriate means of countering inflation.

Now if it was indeed the case that recent experience showed
that economics was incapable of explaining inflation, one might
have to go along with all this. However, this evidence shows no
more than that a particular body of economic doctrine—albeit
widely accepted—is incapable of dealing with the problem. If
we look to see what the salient characteristics of this failed body
of doctrine are, one factor above all stands out. It is permeated
by the view that economic agents are incapable of distinguishing
between real and nominal values of economic variables. Inflation
of course, would not worry anyone if they could not make this
distinction; indeed they would be unaware of it! What has broken
down is a body of doctrine that tried to explain inflation while
simultaneously assuming that economic agents were incapable
of noticing it. When a theory contains as massive an internal
inconsistency as this it is hardly surprising that it is found
wanting in the face of evidence.

It would be as well to point out the places where money
illusion plays a vital role in the analysis we have been describing,
for the removal of that assumption whenever it occurs is an
important ingredient of recent work in the so-called 'monetarist'
tradition that is attempting to build up a coherent *economic*
analysis of the inflationary process. This is not the only distinguishing feature of monetarist analysis, of course, but it is a vital
one.

The most obvious place in which the macro-economics of the
1960s rested on money illusion was in the Phillips curve itself.
Elementary market economics says that the rate of change of
real wages reacts to changes in the excess demand for labour.[9]
The Phillips curve is concerned with the behaviour of money
wages and hence rests on the implicit assumption either that
prices are constant or that their behaviour is irrelevant. Since

an explanation of wage inflation is required as a prelude to an explanation of price inflation, it must be the latter, and the presence of the rate of price inflation as an extra variable in some formulations of the Phillips curve does not detract from this point: it invariably entered with a fractional coefficient in the relevant empirical work.

However, it is not just in the Phillips curve itself that money illusion turns up. An analysis of inflation which has causation running unidirectionally from demand management policy to unemployment and wage inflation and thence to price inflation also rests implicitly on this premise. A given demand management policy must involve picking a given time path either for the nominal money supply or for nominal interest rates. Given such time paths, what happens to prices influences the real money supply and real interest rates. Hence there is a two-way interaction between price inflation and aggregate demand. This interaction was widely ignored in discussions of inflation in the 1960s, and this must mean that one of two implicit assumptions was being made. Either it was assumed that the time path of money and interest rates had no effect on aggregate demand, or it was assumed that it was the nominal magnitudes of these variables that were important.[10]

The elasticities approach to balance of payments theory similarly rests on a form of money illusion. If it is possible to make a permanent difference to the volume of imports and exports by devaluation—a fundamental postulate of this doctrine (and of the absorption approach)—then the value productivity of resources employed in export industries in terms of foreign goods must rise more than payments to them measured in the same terms; real factor incomes measured in terms of world prices are thus lowered by devaluation. Only if this is not noticed by resource owners would one expect no further repercussions. In short, the effect of devaluation on the domestic price level and hence on domestic money wage bargaining—to say nothing of its effects on the real value of the domestic stock of nominal balances—are ignored. Again, we have an implicit assumption of money illusion, and of a type that is not obviously consistent with that alluded to in our discussion of the Phillips curve.

Now none of this necessarily means that the late 1960s did not see a major change in the social forces operating to determine wages and prices in the developed world. All it means is that a body of economics which accorded the quantity of money a minor role and which rested heavily on the assumption that economic agents were unable to distinguish between real and nominal values proved, not surprisingly, incapable of explaining the relevant evidence. It remains to show that a theory which puts money in the centre of matters and does not rely on money illusion is capable of so doing, and it is to that task which we now turn.

III

The revival of interest in monetary economics began, of course, in the mid-1950s, long before orthodox macro theory was widely regarded as having been discredited by events. Though Friedman himself restated the quantity theory not as a theory of income determination or price level determination but as a theory of the demand for money, it is nevertheless true that much of his early empirical work, and that of his associates, dealt with the determination of the time path either of prices or of money income.[11] To this extent, however much Friedman's theoretical work might owe to the *General Theory* of Keynes, a good deal of the related empirical work harked back to an earlier tradition which had apparently disappeared with the 1930s.[12]

The focal point of the quantity theory regarded as a theory of the level of prices or the rate of inflation is the interaction of a demand for real balances function with a nominal stock of money. The determinants of the demand for real balances are regarded as some sort of real income variable and an opportunity cost of holding money variable. With these two given, the price level adjusts to ensure that, whatever the stock of nominal money, the volume of real money is equal to the amount demanded. Thus if the nominal money supply is exogenously given, it determines the price level. With the exception of the relatively minor complication of the inclusion of an opportunity cost variable in the demand for money function, this is, of course, pure David Hume.

A major contribution of modern monetary literature is the demonstration that the stable demand for money function postulated by Hume and his successors (though not in these terms) does indeed exist for a wide variety of different countries and historical periods, and that its characteristics are independent of the means whereby the nominal money supply is generated.[13] Given a stable demand for money function, the time path of prices is determined by the time path of the nominal money supply, provided that the other arguments in the demand for money function are constant. As is well known, to consider the determinants of the money supply is an open economy operating in a world of fixed exchange rates involves us in looking at the balance of payments. Hence the rest of the world, rather than being tacked on to an essentially closed-economy model as it was in orthodox post-Keynesian macro-economics, is accorded a potentially central role in the monetary approach to inflation theory. In terms of the monetary approach, the international character of inflation in a world of fixed exchange rates between convertible currencies is not a puzzle to be explained; it is something to be taken for granted as following naturally from the analysis. A puzzle would arise for the exponent of monetary theory if inflation turned out not to be international by nature in such a world. Let us now see why this is so.

The nominal money supply in any country is equal, by accounting identity, to the sum of the foreign exchange holdings of, and the domestic credit extended by, the banking system (including the central bank). An appropriate definition of the phrase 'balance of payments' will ensure that the change in a country's foreign exchange reserves is identical to it, and thus, unless domestic credit outstanding always varies systematically to offset changes in reserves, the balance of payments will affect the nominal money supply.

This, of course, is not to say very much. The balance of payments is just one factor that influences the nominal money supply. Moreover what happens to prices when the money supply changes depends on what happens to the other arguments in the demand for money function. At this level the monetary approach provides not an hypothesis about the international transmission mechanism for inflation but a framework in terms of which more detailed discussion can now proceed. It is helpful here to distinguish between theories of the long-run equilibrium characteristics of economies and those that have to do with the way in which economies behave when out of equilibrium—even though some of the literature with which we are here dealing is not always careful about this distinction.

The following would seem to be what modern monetary theory postulates to be the characteristics of the long-run equilibrium of a set of small open economies operating in a world of fixed exchange rates.[14] First, whatever might be the case in the short run, in the long run each economy's output is determined at full employment level by the application of given technology to available productive resources, the level of which is independent of the behaviour of the nominal money supply. The real interest rate is also given to each economy, for, whatever barriers there might be to the international mobility of capital in the short run, these are of no importance in the long run. Thus the forces of 'productivity and thrift' on a world-wide basis determine the real rate of interest, and our small open economy takes this variable as exogenously given to it.

A similar, though more complex, argument is advanced to deal with the determination of the price level. Whatever scope is available for individual countries to indulge in product differentiation in the short run, in the long run every country is a price-taker in the world market for every good. With fixed exchange rates operating, the world money supply is simply equal to the sum of domestic money supplies, and its rate of change is the rate of change of this sum.

In each country, and hence in the world, we have a given level of real income, while a determinate rate of inflation in the world price level is implied by the rate of expansion of the world money supply. In long-run equilibrium this inflation rate is fully anticipated. Thus the world demand for real balances is determined and hence, given the world money supply, so is the equilibrium level of world prices at any moment.

Each individual country then takes this price level as its own and also takes its rate of inflation as that ruling in the world market. If the rate of domestic credit expansion changes in one country, in the long run this affects the country's inflation rate only to the extent that it influences the rate of expansion of the world money supply and hence the world inflation rate. Its principal effect on the individual country is to change the balance of payments, for this is the route whereby a change in domestic credit expansion in one country finds its way into world markets.

Now we have presented here an account of the long-run equilibrium relationships between variables. We have said nothing about the transmission mechanism whereby a change in the domestic credit expansion rate of one country alters that country's balance of payments and raises the world inflation rate. All we have done is to assert that in the long run these things must happen. It is in the answers to the questions about short-run behaviour implicit here that the analysis of most relevance to the conduct of economic policy might lie; but it is also the case that, within the tradition of monetary analysis, there is ample room for disagreement about what factors are important here. There is room for disagreement not only because more than one model of short-run behaviour is compatible with the same long-run equilibrium, but also because as yet we have no fully articulated and satisfactory short-run model.

The description of long-run equilibrium which we have just given would, with suitably amended institutional detail to allow for the role of gold as an international and national money, and suitable changes in vocabulary, be recognisable to David Hume, or indeed to any other writer who contributed to the international aspects of the quantity theory tradition. An economy with full employment and an interest rate determined by real as opposed to monetary forces does, after all, lie at the background of all their work. However, from the French revolutionary wars onwards monetary economics always developed in the context of the discussion of current policy problems; hence the relevant literature had a good deal to say about short-run adjustment processes as well. The dominant viewpoint, at least in British discussions, evolved as a development of Hume's price-specie-flow mechanism, and its essentials may be set out as follows.[15]

The level of prices in any country at a particular moment is determined solely by the quantity of money in circulation in that country. In turn, the country's balance of trade, which dominates the balance of payments, depends upon the relationship between domestic prices and those ruling abroad. Thus a country whose money stock is higher than that required for long-run equilibrium will also have too high a price level, an adverse trade balance, a contracting money stock and hence a falling price level. The chain of causation here, as far as the transmission of price level changes between countries is concerned, is clear. An increase, for whatever reason, in the domestic money stock of one country bids up prices there, and not until domestic prices have risen does the balance of trade change and money begin to flow out to bid up prices elsewhere. It is the flows of money that are the central factor in the transmission of price changes between countries, and these are triggered by relative price level discrepancies.

More complicated versions of this analysis bring international capital flows into the picture but do not alter its fundamentals. At that point in the process at which too high a price level is leading to an outflow of money on the trade account, an increase in interest rates can produce an offsetting capital inflow. This will slow down and hence smooth out the consequences of monetary stringency, thus turning a potential crisis into an orderly contraction. However, this does not alter the basic, trade-dominated interaction of prices, the balance of payments and the money supply.

The mechanism just described, though *a priori* plausible, does not square with the facts even of the late nineteenth and early twentieth centuries, let alone with those of more recent history. It would lead one to expect that, if a particular country experienced an increase in the rate of expansion of the domestically generated portion of its money supply, this would result in an increase in the rate of growth of the money supply itself, an increase in the rate of inflation, eventually a growing balance of payments deficit and hence, again eventually, a slowdown in the rate of monetary expansion. Then there would be a deceleration of the inflation rate as domestic prices returned towards a level compatible with long-run equilibrium. This is not what seems to have happened in such circumstances. Payments deficits followed increases in domestic credit expansion rates, to be sure, but apparently without the intervention of important changes in relative price levels; in particular the sensitivity of capital flows to small changes in international interest differentials seems to have played an important role here. In short, it is hard to find evidence of the relative price level changes that are so central to the price specie flow theory of short-run international monetary disequilibrium, so that the empirical validity of this particular approach to the problems under discussion becomes hard indeed to defend.

Now there was, of course, always a strong body of thought that dissented from the dominant orthodoxy, albeit within the monetary tradition. This is worth mentioning if only to show how deeply rooted in past work is much modern thought on the subject at hand. When the national currency of a country is convertible on demand into specie at a fixed price, and the specie price of commodities is determined on world markets, it is hard to see how the price of commodities in terms of any national currency could get very far out of line. This point lay at the root of the banking school's insistence that, even in the short run, it made more sense to think of the price level as determining the quantity of money in circulation in a particular country than vice versa, for, unlike their anti-bullionist predecessors, they were extremely careful to confine this proposition to the case of money convertible into specie and hence to a case where the arbitrage necessary to preserve the relevant price structure was possible.[16] Wicksell's analysis of monetary disequilibrium and inflation drew heavily on the banking school work, and centred upon the behaviour of interest rates. He always took a high degree of international capital mobility for granted and regarded his 'cumulative process' as something that would work out in a world economy with the time period over which interest rates could differ between countries being relatively short. Hence there is no suggestion in his work that prices in individual countries would ever move in anything but close harmony.[17]

This dissenting viewpoint underlies much recent work and amounts to saying that the long-run equilibrium situation, whose properties we described earlier, is one from which the world does not deviate very far even in the short run, and one that is quickly reached after any disturbance. Thus it may actually be a better approximation to reality to treat the world as if it was always in long-run equilibrium that to treat it as if the specie flow mechanism was operative in the short run. Hence, this alternative viewpoint has the domestic inflation rate of any country determined on the world market even in the short run. Flows of money between countries are therefore looked upon not as the vital link that transmits price level fluctuations between countries but simply as the means whereby the consequences of domestic credit expansion are adjusted to the rate of change in the quantity of money demanded in each country, the determinants of the demand for money being given independently of any domestic monetary policy (except to the extent that domestic credit expansion in an individual country contributes to inflation on a world-wide basis).

However, we cannot stop at this point. If inflation rates do not differ between countries in the short run in a manner compatible with the price specie flow mechanism, they do nevertheless differ for significant time periods, and probably by more than can be explained simply by measurement problems. Moreover in the long run the world may be at full employment but a major policy problem as far as the control of inflation is concerned involves the interaction of inflation and unemployment rates.

If inflation rates do indeed differ between countries, then it cannot be the case that the prices of all goods are always given by the equilibrium properties of world markets. Recent efforts to deal with discrepancies between national inflation rates take this observation as their starting point and postulate the existence of two types of goods: 'tradables' and 'non-tradables'. Tradables are simply goods for which there exists a world-wide market and non-tradables those which are confined to national markets. The world market determines the time path of the price level of tradables, which must always be the same for every country. Persistent discrepancies between national inflation rates are explained in terms of different productivity growth rates in the two sectors, while shorter-term discrepancies are explained by delays in the transmission of inflationary impulses from the tradables sector in any economy to its non-tradable sector.[18] We shall concentrate on the latter point here.

Two, by no means mutually exclusive, routes whereby changes in the inflation rate in world markets can be transmitted to non-tradables may be identified. First, an increase in the rate of inflation in world markets ought to result in an increase in the rate of change of money wages in the tradable sector. Given labour mobility between the tradable and non-tradable sectors, money wage inflation, and hence price inflation, in the non-tradable sector could also be expected to increase. Second, an increase in the rate of price inflation in the tradable sector will initially lead to a changing structure of relative prices and a switch of demand towards non-tradables, and hence will generate pressure towards an increase in the inflation rate there.

In the long run one would expect a given relative price structure to be consistent with equilibrium in the two sectors (or a given time path of relative prices if productivity is growing at different rates in the two sectors) so that marked discrepancies in inflation rates between one country and the rest of the world are to be explained in terms of lags in the mechanism whereby inflation is transmitted from one sector of the economy to the other. Thus, in this view, the transmission of inflation goes directly from world prices into the domestic prices of tradables

and thence, either through the labour market of through a tendency
to substitution between goods, to the prices of non-tradables.
Meanwhile the balance of payments provides whatever change in
reserves is needed, given domestic monetary policy, to generate
the rate of monetary expansion that will support the rate of inflation thus determined.[19]

Such analysis as this does not tell us anything about the
determinants of real income fluctuations. It simply assumes that
these will not take place; but of course they do. It is here that
monetary analysis borrows from the now discredited orthodoxy,
for a version of the Phillips curve free of the assumption of
money illusion provides a vital link in the argument at this point.
The development in question is the so-called ' expectations--
augmented' or 'sophisticated' Phillips curve of Friedman and
Phelps. In essence this analysis has wage and price inflation
rates being determined not 'by markets' but by the price-setting
activities of firms, each one of which sets its rate of wage and
price change equal to the rate it expects its competitors to choose,
these expectations being largely extrapolated from past experience. Firms then modify their initial price and wage decisions
in response to market excess demand. Variations in excess demand manifest themselves in output changes so that fluctuations
in income and employment become an integral part of the mechanism whereby the inflation rates of both prices and wages can
be changed.

Though developed in the context of a closed economy model,
this type of analysis is readily transferable to the open economy
case when a non-tradable sector which does not take its prices
directly from the outside world is postulated. Fluctuations in output and employment may be accorded a role in the transmission
of changes in the world inflation rate from the tradable sector
to the rest of the economy. Though analytically possible, the
introduction of the expectations-augmented Phillips curve into the
monetary analysis of international inflation in this way is nevertheless theoretically awkward. The device belongs to the 'new
micro-economics', while the postulate that firms in the tradable
sector take their prices from world markets comes from the
'old micro-economics'.[20]

The coexistence of the two theories of price formation, one
for the tradable sector and one for the non-tradable sector, in
one model is not easy to justify, but then nor is the distinction
between tradable and non-tradable goods. One might think that
the distinction could roughly correspond to one between goods
which can physically be transported from their place of production
to other locations before being consumed, and those which must
be consumed, as they are produced, at the point of production
However, the existence of a large-scale tourist industry which

can take people to the point of production of any good makes it difficult indeed to think of anything that could not be marketed at some price on a world-wide basis.

Instead of having one sector of the economy for which world market conditions are all-important and another on which world market conditions have no direct influence it seems more reasonable to postulate a spectrum of goods lying across the entire range between these two extremes.[21] Moreover there is no reason to persist with two theories of pricing behaviour. One will do. The whole spirit of the monetary approach is to treat the world as if it was a single closed economy, and there is no reason why we cannot have world-wide fluctuations in income and employment as a necessary accompaniment to changes in the world-wide inflation rate. Fluctuations in the output of all industries, and not just those operating in isolation from world markets, then become part of the mechanism whereby changes in the world inflation rate are brought into any one economy.

To make this argument more precise would carry us beyond the bounds of the current state of knowledge of the economics of inflation in open economies, and it is the current state of knowledge that is the main focus of this paper. We shall therefore not carry this argument any further here but rather turn to summarising the analysis developed in the last few pages, arguing that it accords well with the broad outlines of recent economic history, and then raise questions about the extent to which changes in the exchange rate regime affect its relevance to the future.

IV

The monetary theory of inflation which we discussed in the last section of this paper is not, of course, a radically new departure. Rather, as we have stressed, it represents a continuation of an analytic tradition that goes back to Hume, though it has more in common with the dissenting banking school-Wicksellian branch of that tradition than with its predominating orthodoxy. Moreover it draws on the new micro-economics in order to integrate the analysis of output fluctuation with that of inflation.

In essence it treats the world as a large, highly integrated closed economy in which there is no sharp product differentiation between individual countries. This lack of product differentiation is essential to the proposition that each country takes it price level from the world economy and to the accompanying emphasis on monetary aspects of the balance of payments. Thus the model seems *a priori* better adapted to deal with a world in which international trade is dominated by trade among industrial countries than to a world in which exchange is predominantly between, say, agricultural and industrial economies, where outputs are more sharply differentiated. But this also means that it is a model well adapted to deal with the international economy of the 1960s, which was indeed dominated by trade between industrial countries.[22]

Just as world goods markets are viewed as being highly integrated, so too are world capital markets, and, again, the 1960s saw an enormous increase in the international mobility of capital and in the volume of internationally mobile capital. Thus the preconditions for a monetary view of international inflation to have empirical content would seem to have been approximately met until recently, for a regime of fixed exchange rates between convertible currencies also underlies the foregoing analysis, and such a regime existed, approximately, among major Western nations until 1971 or thereabouts.

The theory would then tell us to look for one factor to explain an increase in the international inflation rate: a marked increase in the world-wide rate of monetary expansion. This did indeed take place, originating in the United States, whose monetary authorities essentially played the role accorded to gold miners in nineteenth century monetary theory. The increase in the rate of monetary expansion originated, as is well known, in the budget deficits that resulted from the attempt to finance the Vietnam war without tax increases—indeed, alongside tax cuts—and was accentuated on a world-wide basis by the once-and-for-all phenomenon of the development of the Eurodollar market, where the United States' balance of payments deficit provided a reserve base for the creation of further additions to the world money supply.

At the same time, the theory would tell us to expect world-wide variations in the inflation rate to be associated with world-wide fluctuations in real income and employment. Again the stylised facts fit the theory, for one of the most striking features of the last few years has been the way in which real output fluctuations have moved together on a world-wide basis. The sharp United States monetary contraction of 1969 was felt throughout the Western world and produced real output contractions and slow-downs in the inflation rate elsewhere over the following three years, while the subsequent expansion preceded the world-wide recovery of real output and inflation rates.

The result of all this, as we know, has been for individual countries to try and cut themselves free of the international monetary system in an attempt to gain control over their own employment and inflation rates.[23] The length of the time lags involved in the transmission of inflationary impulses are almost certainly too long for us to have any idea of whether these attempts have been successful or not, for it can have been only in 1973 that the effects of relatively independent domestic policies taken since 1971 began to dominate the trends inherited from the past. Nor indeed do we know whether the attempts at achieving independence have been successful.

It is true that greater exchange rate flexibility should lead to greater scope for independent national monetary policies, but all our received theories on the way in which flexible exchange rates work seem premissed on a world where international transactions are dominated by the trade account rather than the capital account. The growth in importance of capital movements forced a higher degree of monetary integration on countries than they were willing to live with under the Bretton Woods system. It is not clear what its effects will be on the way in which a system of flexible rates will operate.

Be that as it may, one thing above all should be stressed at the close of this paper. We began by showing how a body of economic theory reasonably well adapted to dealing with the special circumstances of the 1930s broke down when applied to the 1960s. We then went on to show how, suitably adapted, an older theoretical tradition did seem better able to cope with recent economic history. However, the breakdown of the fixed exchange rate system has already removed an essential precondition for that body of theory to be applicable. We must be careful, therefore, not to apply it blindly, and without modification, to current and future policy discussions.

NOTES

[1]   This paper was written jointly with A. R. Nobay, of the University of Southampton, to whom I am most grateful for permission to include it here. We are extremely grateful to George Zis for helpful comments on an earlier draft. Presented at the Third Dauphine Conference on International Monetary Economics, University of Paris (IX), on 28-30 March 1974, the paper is reprinted from the proceedings of the conference by kind permission of the editors, Professors Emil Claassen and Pascal Salin.

[2]   But notice that a monetary explanation of inflation requires an explanation of why it is that the money supply is increasing. Since this cannot now, as it was in earlier times, be attributed to specie discoveries, there is ample scope for those who wish to argue that there are important differences between the current inflation and any of its predecessors. The fact that the behaviour of the world's money supply is now open to political influence is clearly an important factor in understanding what has happened in recent years. Both Serge-Christophe Kolm and Robert Mundell stressed this point when the paper was presented.

[3]   *Cf.* Claassen and Salin (1972).

⁴   But this is not to say, that within the broad framework of post—
Keynesian economic theory, it was not possible to build models
which did accord an important role to money; within that framework the importance of money depends very much upon the interest
sensitivity of both expenditure and the demand for money. The
quantitative judgement of the majority of economists on these
matters, however, seems to have been such as to accord money a
relatively unimportant role. This is particularly the case in
Britain, where the views expressed in the Radcliffe Report (1959)
dominated professional and official thinking on these matters in the
1950s and 1960s.

⁵   Philips' celebrated paper appeared in 1958. The Phillips
curve had already been invented by Irving Fisher in the 1920s,
but the relevant paper was published in a sufficiently obscure
source to make it understandable that this work was overlooked.
Less understandable is the fact that A. J. Brown's (1955) discovery of the same relationship should have been ignored,
particularly by British economists.

⁶   But the major support for the curve came from British
evidence. Samuelson and Solow (1960), for example, showed
clearly that the relationship got much less support from United
States data but nevertheless went on to discuss policy towards
inflation as if the relationship's existence was reasonably firmly
established.

⁷   Phillips was careful in his 1958 paper to refer to the effects
of fluctuations in import prices.

⁸   The interrelationship between non-economic explanations of
inflation and the case for wage price controls is discussed in
Ward and Zis (1974).

⁹   This elementary proposition, is of course, one of the bases of
the expectations-augmented Phillips curve of Phelps (1967) and
Friedman (1968)

¹⁰   Of course, there is nothing inherent in post-Keynesian macro
theory that compels its adherents to assume money illusion.
However, in discussing inflation they seem to have done so. *Cf.*,
for example, Samuelson and Solow (1960), where there is no trace
in the discussion that the authors recognise the two-way nature
of the interaction of aggregate demand and inflation.

¹¹   *Cf.*, for example, Friedman and Meiselman (1963), Friedman
and Schwartz (1963b) or indeed Cagan (1956).

¹²   On the extent of Friedman's debt to Keynes and the relationship of his monetary theory to a pre-Keynesian tradition, *cf.*
Patinkin (1969) and Friedman (1972).

¹³   Much of the relevant evidence is surveyed in Laidler (1969a).
An important source of extra evidence on these matters is Meiselman (1971).

¹⁴   The following passage draws heavily on the work of Mundell

(e.g. 1971), Johnson (e.g. 1972) and Swoboda (e.g. 1974).

[15] The present essay is not concerned with the history of economic thought for its own sake. The development of British monetary theory in the nineteenth century is admirably dealt with by Fetter (1965).

[16] This matter is discussed in detail in Laidler (1972d).

[17] The currency school, whose views came to dominate British monetary thought, never achieved so dominant a position on the Continent. There the banking school position retained a respectable place for itself. For Wicksell's views on the banking school *cf.* Wicksell (1905).

[18] The distinction between tradables and non-tradables bears a close relationship to that between the exposed and sheltered sectors of an economy in the so-called Nordic model of inflation. Here differences in productivity growth rates between sectors play a key role.

[19] The model presented by Parkin (1972) deals with these matters, concentrating in particular on the labour market as a vehicle for the transmission of inflationary impulses.

[20] The model dealt with the Laidler (1972c) uses the expectations-augmented Phillips curve in the manner outlined here in order to produce output fluctuations as an integral part of the mechanism whereby an open economy's inflation rate changes as a result of either domestic or outside impulses. This model is vulnerable to the criticisms levelled here.

[21] But of course one may regard the tradable-non-tradable dichotomy as being a very simple special case of such a spectrum with only two extreme categories. Thus its use may still be defended as a means of achieving analytic simplicity despite the arguments advanced here. We are indebted to Alexander Swoboda for making this point during the discussion following the presentation of this paper.

[22] When countries' outputs are differentiated the elasticities approach to the balance of payments takes on relevance, as does the price specie flow mechanism as an account of the monetary side of balance of payments disequilibrium. We are indebted to Milton Friedman for making this point during the discussion that followed the presentation of this paper.

[23] *Cf.* Bell (1973) for a lucid account of many of the matters raised in the last few paragraphs.

9 Price and output fluctuations in an open economy[1]

I

The recent inflation has been a world-wide phenomenon, and increasingly economists have begun to recognise that a satisfactory explanation of this experience must account for its international character. In particular the so-called 'monetarist' literature on the problem has placed great emphasis on the existence of a regime of fixed exchange rates as a key factor in the international transmission of price level fluctuations.

The theoretical basis of this view is the monetary theory of the balance of payments.[2] This theory as typically presented deals with the behaviour of the price level of an open economy on the assumption that the economy in question is so small a part of the world economy that, given a fixed exchange rate, that economy must simply take its prices from the rest of the world. Domestic monetary policy then determines the rate of change of foreign exchange reserves; moreover once-and-for-all exchange rate changes are viewed as bringing about changes in the domestic quantity of real money balances, thus creating a monetary disequilibrium whose existence can be only temporary. In this theory, then, exchange rate changes have no long-run effects.

As usually presented, the theory in question deals with situations of equilibrium and is silent about the time path that the economy follows between equilibria. Thus the theory is unable to explain why different countries linked by fixed exchange rates nevertheless experience different rates of inflation for significant time periods. Moreover full employment is assumed to characterise the equilibrium situation of the real side of the economy. Nothing is said about what many policy-makers would regard as a key question about inflation, namely the manner in which inflation and unemployment rates interact with each other over time.

In a recent paper Michael Parkin (1972) has dealt with the first of these questions, producing a model in which the usual predictions of the monetary theory of the balance of payments appear as the asymptotic solution to a dynamic system whose characteristics during transition from one steady state to another permit—indeed require—the domestic inflation rate to depart from the world rate. However, Parkin's model is built on the assumption of full employment, and he himself recognises that its failure to deal with output fluctuations is a shortcoming.

In this paper I present a model which, like Parkin's, preserves the predictions of the monetary theory of the balance of payments as characteristics of its steady state solution but permits fluctuations in real income as well as in the inflation rate to characterise its short-run behaviour. In this model full employment is a property of the steady state rather than a state of affairs which is simply assumed to exist at all times. Thus this model extends Parkin's results. It enables us not only to deal with the dynamic properties of the inflation rate between steady states but also to analyse the interaction over time of inflation and unemployment rates. Moreover the model enables us to make a specific analysis of the impact effects on real income and employment of changes in such variables as the rate of domestic credit expansion, the world inflation rate and the exchange rate. It therefore enables us to raise issues about the choice between fixed and flexible exchange rates, issues that have tended to become rather obscured in recent discussions of the monetary theory of the balance of payments.

II

The model which I shall now set out deals with a small open economy operating under a regime of fixed exchange rates which are not expected to change at any time. It produces and consumes two kinds of goods: tradables and non-tradables. The prices of the former are determined exogenously on world markets and those of the latter on domestic markets in a manner I shall shortly describe. At any moment of time there is a level of real national income that corresponds to the existence of a 'natural rate' of unemployment, and this level of income grows at an exogenously given constant rate.[3] Because this level of income is nevertheless associated with less than complete utilisation of all the productive resources available to the economy, it is physically possible for actual income to exceed this level as well as to fall short of it at any moment in time. The significance of the natural unemployment rate is that, when it exists, the supply and demand for productive resources are equal to one another. Hence it corresponds to what would be termed 'full employment' in a simpler and more old-fashioned model.[4]

The level of national income is, of course, an index number measure of the combined outputs of tradables and non-tradables, while the general price level is an index of the prices of these two classes of goods and services. These two variables together determine the demand for cash balances in the economy while the supply of money is identically equal to foreign exchange reserves and domestic credit outstanding,[5] the latter variable being determined exogenously at the discretion of the monetary authorities. Changes in reserves result solely from surpluses and deficits on the balance of trade, for this economy does not participate in international capital markets. The balance of trade falls as the level of income increases and as the price level of non-tradables rises relative to that of tradables; this because a rise in the relative price of non-tradables attracts resources into their production and out of the production of exports and import substitutes.

Finally, the pricing behaviour of firms in the non-tradable sector is of the type suggested by the 'new micro-economics'. Each firm forms expectations about what price it can get for its product and fixes the price initially, revising this price upwards or downwards as excess demand or supply for the good in question reveals itself on the market. In the aggregate this suggests that the rate of change of the price level of non-tradables will be equal to the expected rate of change of the price of those goods plus a function of excess demand.[6] If we assume that the excess demand for non-tradables varies monotonically with the general level of excess demand in the economy, the latter variable may stand as a proxy for the former. Finally we assume that expectations about the rate of change of the price of non-tradables are formed according to a conventional error-learning mechanism.

Formal analysis of an economy such as this is conveniently carried out in terms of a model in which all relationships are log. linear and presented in first difference form. This simplification enables us to derive directly from the analysis propositions about the relationships between the percentage rates of change of variables over time. I have also found it convenient to carry out the analysis in terms of a discrete time formulation of the model.

The symbols to be used are defined as follows: Y = the log of national income, Y^* = the log of that level of income at which the natural level of unemployment prevails, $y' = Y - Y^*$, p = the log. of the price level of non-tradables, π = the log. of the price level of tradables, P = the log. of the general price level, R = the log. of the level of foreign exchange reserves, C = the log. of domestic credit outstanding, M = the log. of the nominal money supply. The superscript e denotes the expected value of a variable, while the subscript $-i$ ($i = 1, 2, 3$) refers to time lags of one period, etc. The prefix, Δ, Δ^2 and Δ^3, etc, denotes the first, etc, difference of a variable, and bars over variables denote that they are treated as exogenously given. The model may now be written as follows:

$$\Delta M = b\Delta Y + \Delta P = b\Delta \overline{Y}^* + b\Delta y + \Delta P \qquad b > 0 \qquad (1)$$

$$\Delta P = w\Delta p + (1 - w)\,\overline{\Delta \pi} \qquad\qquad 0 < w < 1 \qquad (2)$$

$$\Delta p = gy + \Delta p^e_{-1} \qquad\qquad\qquad g > 0 \qquad (3)$$

$$\Delta p^e = d\Delta p + (1 - d)\,\Delta p^e_{-1} \qquad\quad 0 < d < 1 \qquad (4)$$

$$\Delta M = v\Delta C + (1 - v)\Delta R \qquad\quad 0 < v < 1 \qquad (5)$$

$$\Delta R = -ny - m(p - \pi) \qquad\qquad n, m > 0 \qquad (6)$$

The log. linear character of this model is better suited to some of the above equations than to others. Thus it is convenient indeed to have a log. linear demand for money function (equation 1), and a log. linear error-learning equation for the expected rate of inflation on non-tradable goods (equation 4). The balance of trade equation 6 is not hard to swallow in this form once it is realised that we are free to choose the units in which domestic and world prices are measured in order to ensure that, given a zero value for y, the values for the two price levels at which trade is in balance are equal to one another. However, as far as the other three equations are concerned 'realistic' specification is sacrificed in the interests of the analytic simplicity that stems from the log. linearity of the model. Thus equation 5, the money supply equation, is an approximation to an identity: v is the proportion of the money stock backed by domestic credit in some base period, and it is strictly correct to treat it as a constant only if both C and R always expand at the same rate. That the approximation adopted here is one that is quite commonly used should not distract our attention from the limits that its use might impose upon the validity of the analysis that follows.

The price index (equation 2) is similarily an approximation. Its geometric weights imply that, as the price of a good rises, equal changes in it have diminishing impact upon the value of the index. This is an attractive characteristic in a price index for expenditure, since here substitution might be expected to take place against goods with higher prices. However, what we have here is a price index for output, and in this case substitution is towards rather than against the good whose price is relatively high. Again, then, there is an element of approximation involved in using a log. linear formulation. Finally equation 3, which is analogous to a sophisticated Phillips curve, implies that the rate of inflation changes less in response to a change in excess demand the higher is excess demand already and more the lower is excess demand already. It would make much more sense if the relative signs of these responses were just the opposite, and equation 3 must therefore be regarded as an approximation to a more correct relationship, accurate only in the region of full employment.

In this writer's judgement the use of these approximations does not seriously vitiate the qualititive predictions of the model, particularly if we think of these predictions as being applied to the analysis of the consequences of relatively 'small' changes in exogenous variables over relatively 'short' time periods. The reader is, of course, entitled to be sceptical about this, but it is to be hoped that he will at least suspend judgement until these predictions have been derived, and that he will bear in mind the enormous gain in analytic simplicity that the use of the approximations in question gives us.

III

It is convenient to look at this model's steady state characteristics first of all. If the rate of inflation for non-tradable goods is to be constant, it follows from equations 3 and 4 that y must equal zero. Thus full employment is a characteristic of the steady state. As to the rate of inflation, equations 1, 2, 5 and 6 yield:

$$p - \pi = \frac{v}{(1-v)m} \Delta C - \frac{b}{(1-v)m} \Delta Y^* + \frac{w}{(1-v)m} \Delta p$$

$$+ \frac{(1-w)}{(1-v)m} \Delta \pi \tag{7}$$

Every term on the right hand side is a constant, but if $p - \pi$ is to be constant it follows that the rate of inflation of the price of non-tradables, and hence of the domestic price level, must equal that of the world price level. Thus the equilibrium rate of monetary expansion is determined endogenously to the system. Domestic monetary policy, operating through the rate of credit expansion, is in the long run only capable of influencing the rate of change of reserves, and the level—as opposed to the rate of change—of the price of non-tradables. Moreover, given the rate of domestic credit expansion, there is only one equilibrium domestic price level relative to that ruling in the rest of the world; in the long run an exchange rate change can influence nothing except the units in which prices are measured. In short, this model faithfully reproduces, as its steady state properties, the predictions of the monetary theory of the balance of payments.

How interesting all this is depends, of course, upon whether or not the model's dynamic properties are such as to cause it to converge on its steady state solution. We get, on the assumptions that $C, \Delta Y^*$ and $\Delta \pi$ are constant, a third order difference equation of the form

$$y = \alpha_1 y_{-1} - \alpha_2 y_{-2} + \alpha_3 y_{-3} \tag{8}$$

where

$$\alpha_1 = \frac{3b + 2[wg + (1 - v)n] - wdg + (g - dg)(1 - v)m}{b + wg + (1 - v)n + g(1 - v)m} \tag{9}$$

$$\alpha_2 = \frac{3b + wg + (1 - v)n - wdg}{b + wg + (1 - v)n + g(1 - v)m} \tag{10}$$

$$\alpha_3 = \frac{b}{b + wg + (1 - v)n + g(1 - v)m} \tag{11}$$

The necessary and sufficient conditions for the stability of such an equation are[7]

$$\alpha_1 - \alpha_2 + \alpha_3 < 1 \tag{12}$$

$$-\alpha_1 - \alpha_2 - \alpha_3 < 1 \tag{13}$$

$$|\alpha_3| < 1 \tag{14}$$

$$\alpha_3(\alpha_3 - \alpha_1) + \alpha_2 < 1 \tag{15}$$

Inequalities 13 and 14 obviously hold, while 12 gives us

$$\frac{b + wg + (1 - v)n + (g - dg)(1 - v)m}{b + wg + (1 - v)n + g(1 - v)m} < 1 \tag{16}$$

which is also obviously always true.

Inequality 15 is less straightforward, but may be written as

$$bd(1 - v)m < w^2gd + wd(1 - v)n + \left(1 + w + \frac{(1 - v)n}{g}\right.$$

$$\left. + (1 - v)m\right) g(1 - v)m \tag{17}$$

It is possible to conceive in principle of both n and g together being sufficiently small for this inequality to be violated or for b to be sufficiently large, but this, in my judgement, is more a theoretical than a practical possibility. b is the income elasticity of demand for money; we know that this parameter is unlikely to be far above unity in any actual economy, and is much more likely to be less. Moreover the constancy of g is a convenient assumption rather than an accurate reflection of any actual economy's properties. In fact we would expect g to get larger as y increased, approaching infinity at some relatively small positive value for y. As to the cyclical properties of the model, it has proved too complex and general to permit their analysis.[8]

The dynamic properties of this model are such that it is virtually certain to converge upon its steady state. Thus it seems that the predictions of the monetary theory of the balance of payments, embodied as they are in this steady state, are of some relevance to the long-run behaviour of the kind of economy being analysed.

The foregoing analysis by no means exhausts the information that can be culled from this model. Thus it is of considerable interest to ask what it implies about the interaction of the inflation rate and the level of excess demand over time. Equations 3 and 4 imply

$$\Delta p = g\Delta y + dgy_{-1} + \Delta p_{-1} \tag{18}$$

The rate of change of the rate of inflation of non-tradables depends on both the level and the rate of change or excess demand.[9] Thus the rate of inflation is given by

$$\Delta P = wg\Delta y + wdgy_{-1} + w\Delta p_{-1} + (1-w)\Delta\pi \tag{19}$$

Clearly, in an open economy, even in disequilibrium, it is only the rate of domestic inflation relative to the world rate that is determined by domestic excess demand. Thus the tendency of domestic inflation rates to move with the world rate, even in disequilibrium, is present in this model, while it is quite specific in its predictions about what determines the time path of short-run deviations from the world rate.

IV

Now equation 8 was derived on the assumption that ΔC, $\Delta\pi$ and ΔY^* were all constant. Relaxing this assumption yields

$$y = \gamma_1\Delta^3 C + \gamma_2\Delta^2\pi + \gamma_3\Delta^2\pi_{-1} - \gamma_4\Delta^3 Y^* + \alpha_1 y_{-1}$$
$$- \alpha_2 y_{-2} + \alpha_3 y_{-3} \tag{20}$$

where

$$\gamma_1 = \frac{v}{b + wg + (1-v)n + g(1-v)m} \tag{21}$$

$$\gamma_2 = \frac{(1-v)m - (1-w)}{b + wg + (1-v)n + g(1-v)m} \tag{22}$$

$$\gamma_3 = \frac{1-w}{b + wg + (1-v)n + g(1-v)m} \tag{23}$$

$$\gamma_4 = a_3 = \frac{b}{b + wg + (1-v)n + g(1-v)m} \tag{24}$$

and α_1, α_2 and α_3 are defined as before.

The interpretation of the coefficients in equation 20 has to be undertaken with considerable care. The particular time pattern of impact effects implicit there is completely dependent on the time structure of the original model, and that is both highly specific and very simple.

The impact effect of a change in the rate of domestic credit expansion is positive, but it is followed immediately by an equal and opposite effect. This does not, of course, mean that the results of such a change cancel out after two periods. Rather it means that there is a tendency for the effects on domestic variables of changes in the rate of domestic credit expansion to be damped down even in the short run. The mechanism of restoring monetary equilibrium in a closed economy involves changing real income and prices; in an open economy the possibility of 'exporting' real balances through the balance of payments reduces—but in this model does not in the short run cancel out—the need for such domestic changes. This seems to be the underlying economics of this model's response to changes in the rate of domestic credit expansion. The precise time pattern of that response is clearly very much a matter of the structure of lags embodied in the model and hence is probably of little general significance.

Exactly the same point may be made about the influence of a change in the full employment growth rate. Compared with a closed economy, the balance of payments provides an extra source for the more rapid rate of expansion of real balances made necessary by an increase in the rate of growth of real income. Again, this general tendency of the openness of the economy to damp down the domestic impact of exogenous changes shows up as equal but opposite impact effects occurring in successive periods.

Perhaps the most interesting exogenous variable in equation 20 is the world inflation rate. Again, the impact of variations in it is spread over two periods, but in this case it is only the second-period impact that is unambiguously positive in sign. The initial effect is ambiguous. Again, there is some economics underlying the model's behaviour here that is more general than the specific behaviour embodied in equation 20. An increase in the world inflation rate must lead in the long run to an equal increase in the domestic inflation rate. Thus the level of excess demand for goods must, during the impact stage, be predominantly positive. However, the initial effect of such a change on aggregate demand is ambiguous. In as much as an acceleration in the world inflation rate causes the rate of change of the demand for nominal balances to move ahead of the rate of change of their supply, the result must be a fall in aggregate demand for real goods and services. This effect is reflected in the negative sign on $(1 - w)$ in the coefficient of $\Delta^2 \pi$ in equation 20. However, an increase in the world inflation rate also means an increasing incentive to divert re-

sources to the production of traded goods, and hence, through the
balance of payments, to an increase in the rate of growth of the
money supply; hence the positive sign on the term $(1 - v)m$ in the
same coefficient. The particular time pattern where an ambiguous
impact effect is succeeded by a definitely positive one is a property
of this specific model. However, the preponderance of positive
signs reflects the more general characteristic, noted earlier, that
the level of excess demand would have to go positive at some
stage in order to get the domestic inflation rate up to the world
rate. The initial ambiguity, however, suggests that, for example,
if the demand for money responded more rapidly to changes in
the world inflation rate than did the allocation of factors of production between the tradable and non-tradable sectors, then the
overall expansionary impact of an increase in the world inflation
rate might nevertheless be preceded by a tendency for real income to drop away from full employment as prices began to rise.
This conjecture—which, of course, goes far beyond the simple
time structure of the model set out above—raises interesting
empirical and theoretical questions that surely would merit further
investigation.

Now the model under discussion may also be used to get
some idea about the impact effects of devaluation or rather of a
completely unanticipated devaluation. In this model a discrete
devaluation may be characterised as a one-period increase in
the world inflation rate followed by an immediate return to the
old rate, while a downward float of a currency manipulated by a
central bank would appear as an increase in the world inflation
rate followed after a while by a return to the old rate. Of course,
a devaluation unaccompanied by other policy changes leaves the
equilibrium inflation rate unchanged; hence the shocks transmitted
to the system simply involve introducing fluctuations in real income and the inflation rate that ultimately leave the economy
exactly where it was initially, except with a higher *level* of
reserves. This is well known, as it is that the effects in question
are similar to those of a contraction in the rate of domestic
credit expansion followed by the restoration of the initial rate.

It might seem, if the object of a devaluation is simply to
increase the *level* of reserves, that there is no reason to prefer
it to a temporary reduction in the rate of domestic credit
expansion. However, the similarity in impact effect of these two
policy measures is qualitative and not quantitative. A temporary
contraction in the rate of domestic credit expansion restores
reserves by the pressure which the resulting monetary disequilibrium puts on domestic aggregate demand and hence on the
price of non-tradables. A devaluation involves this same effect
but also engineers an initial change in the relative price of non-
tradables that is independent of a change in domestic aggregate

demand. In both cases fluctuations in output and relative prices are the mechanism whereby an increase in reserves is brought about, but devaluation puts more weight on price fluctuations and hence requires smaller output fluctuations for a given change in reserves. Again, the particular time pattern of these effects as embodied in the above model is totally dependent on the specific structure of that model, and hence is a lot less interesting than the more general considerations just discussed. But even our analysis of these general considerations must be treated with care. The devaluation which we have considered is both completely unanticipated and completely without direct influence on the expected rate of inflation for non-tradables. Neither characteristic is very realistic, and we cannot be sure how our model would behave if it was modified to be more readily applicable to an actual devaluation.

V

The immediate implications of the foregoing analysis have already been derived and discussed. They need no further discussion here. However, there are some rather broader implications that do merit a few comments. I have taken the essentially neo-classical monetary theory of the balance of payments and have combined it with one 'Keynesian' assumption.[10] The assumption in question, contained in equations 3 and 4, is that, in a world of less than perfect certainty, when markets are not clearing at full employment, quantity changes must occur to signal the need for price changes to firms. Another simple way of stating the same assumption is to say that complete price flexibility, whether it is a long-run phenomenon or not, is certainly not a short-run one. The effect of introducing this assumption has been to produce a model in which only prices change in the long run in response to exogenous shocks, but in which short-run responses involve both prices and quantities.

An important consequence of renewed interest in the monetary theory of the balance of payments has been a swing among monetary economists towards advocacy of complete fixity of exchange rates. The grounds for this advocacy are that, in the long run, exchange rate flexibility is important only in permitting an economy to enjoy a different inflation rate from that ruling elsewhere. Since in the same long run the inflation rate in question is perfectly anticipated and hence irrelevant to any real economic magnitude, exchange rate flexibility is also irrelevant. Indeed, to clinch the matter it is argued that, in adopting exchange rate flexibility, the real gains in terms of minimising transaction costs in international trade that are available from the maintenance of fixed exchange rates are sacrificed.

Advocates of flexible exchange rates—and notably that most monetarist of all monetarists, Milton Friedman—have always readily conceded that complete exchange rate fixity is preferable in a world of complete price flexibility. Because recent developments in international monetary economics have concentrated on the long-run equilibrium properties of economic models the case for flexible rates has gone by default. The model developed in this paper does deal with short-run phenomena in a world of less than complete price flexibility and, perhaps not surprisingly, finds that external monetary disturbances—here manifesting themselves in the shape of variations in the world inflation rate —can have short-run (but not necessarily unimportant for that reason) consequences for real income and employment. It also suggests that the deflationary impact of a devaluation, through it may be equivalent to the deflationary impact of a cut in the level of the money supply in the long run, allocates its short-run effects on prices and output in different and, from the point of view of output stability, preferable proportions.

The case for exchange rate flexibility has always rested on the belief that the short-run gains from such a system outweigh the admitted long-run losses. There has of late been a tendency to overlook this fact. Perhaps the most important and general implication of the model discussed in this paper is the reaffirmation that exchange rate flexibility confers short-run benefits. This is not to say that the case for exchange rate flexibility is re-established by this paper, but it *is* to say that the case still exists and needs answering even in the context of the monetary theory of the balance of payments.

NOTES

1   An earlier version of this paper was given to a Money Study Group seminar held at the London School of Economics on 24 November 1972. The helpful criticism received then has made a considerable contribution to the revision incorporated in this draft.

2   Johnson (1971, 1972) provides most useful surveys of this literature.

3   This concept of a 'natural unemployment rate' is, of course, Friedman's (1968).

4   In an earlier paper (1973b) I have dealt with a model in which full employment puts a ceiling on output.

5   The absence of an 'opportunity cost of holding money' variable from the demand for money function might seem a little strange. One may defend its absence by postulating the existence of a competitive banking system which pays interest on its deposit liabilities at a rate that varies with the expected rate of inflation.

It is more to the point, in some respects, to note that the introduction of such a variable further complicates the lag structure of what is already quite a complicated model and renders its analysis virtually impossible.

6   This hypothesis about pricing behaviour simply adapts the theory of price formation first set out by Phelps (1967) to the specific structure of the model under consideration. The reader might note that the division of the economy into firms producing tradables and non-tradables is a device used by Parkin (1972).

7   These conditions are taken from Box and Jenkins (1970), p. 114.

8   However, it is easy to derive a closed-economy model of inflation as a special case of the one under analysis here. To do this one sets v and w to one and m and n to zero. The model then produces a second-order system in which cycles may occur, and it is hard to believe that the more complex open economy model dealt with here cannot encompass such behaviour. The simpler model is analysed in Laidler (1972a).

9   This is a special case of a general prediction yielded by 'sophisticated' Phillips curve analysis. Its implications have been discussed elsewhere, *cf.* Laidler (1972b, 1973b) and Phelps (1972).

10   The extent to which this assumption is to be found in the *General Theory* is a matter about which one might argue: hence the quotation marks.

10 The current inflation: the problem of explanation and the problem of policy[1]

I

Up to the mid-1960s the broad facts of British economic life were a low level of unemployment, a moderate rate of inflation, and an increasing tendency towards balance of payments deficits. The widely accepted interpretation of these facts was that they reflected an excess aggregate demand for goods and services which simultaneously resulted in pressure on the labour market — hence the low unemployment level — pressure on wages and prices — hence the moderate inflation rate — and, as a result of wage and price inflation, a gradual loss of competitiveness on the part of British exports and import substitutes which produced the balance of payment problem.

The period since the devaluation of 1967 and particularly the years since 1969 have seen a large, and until recently [summer 1972] increasing, balance of payments surplus, a high, and until recently increasing, level of unemployment and an inflation rate far more rapid than any experienced since the end of the Korean war. It is widely held that this recent experience contradicts the orthodox economist's view that variations in the price level have their origins in variations in aggregate demand and hence can be dealt with by the traditional monetary and fiscal tools of demand management. The coexistence of rapid inflation and high unemployment is seen as evidence that the nature of the inflationary process has changed and that the source of price increases must be sought on the supply side of the economy. From this it follows that anti-inflation policy must concentrate upon holding down cost, and particularly wage, increases; hence the widespread belief that a prices and income policy of some sort is essential to the solution of the current problem.

In this paper I shall argue that recent experience is far from being unique, and that there is nothing in that experience to contradict the orthodox view that inflation is caused by excess demand, once it is realised that this orthodox view tells us not only that expectations are of prime importance but also, and more important, that we should look to the world at large, and particularly the

United States, if we wish to find the source of the current British inflation. It follows from this view that traditional demand management policies are perfectly capable of dealing with inflation, provided they are co-ordinated with policy towards the exchange rate. Indeed, inflation will not be cured without resort to such policies, though the cure cannot be expected to be costless. Thus I shall conclude the paper with a brief discussion of the factors that ought to be considered in designing an appropriate anti-inflation policy.

II

The view that the same theory cannot account for the course of inflation before and since 1969 stems from the fact that since 1969 both the inflation rate and the level of unemployment have increased dramatically. This evidence appears to be totally inconsistent with the theory that higher rates of inflation are associated with higher levels of excess demand for goods and services and hence with lower unemployment levels. But this theory, like any other in economics, makes its predictions on an 'other things equal' basis. In the 1950s and 1960s many of its staunchest proponents failed to state explicitly the circumstances under which one ought to expect its predictions to be true. In particular they failed to note that an important determinant of the rate at which any firm would raise its prices—and for that matter at which any firm and trade union would between them raise wages—must be the rate at which prices in general are expected to increase in the economy. Thus they failed to state explicitly that variations in the level of excess demand cause variations in the rate of inflation *relative to the rate which is expected* and hence are systematically related to variations in the inflation rate only when expectations are not changing.[2] Thus there is scope for at least two views about the recent course of inflation: that the nature of the inflationary process itself has changed, and that the basic process has remained the same but the general public's expectations about the inflation rate have changed.

Now expectations are not directly observable. Virtually any price level behaviour, however unlikely, can be rationalised *ex post* by saying that expectations must have changed. However, it is possible to specify what variables other than the inflation rate itself change with inflationary expectations. It is also possible to formulate precise hypotheses about the factors which influence expectations. To be specific on these two counts is to turn the postulate that expectations must have changed from an **ex post** rationalisation of no scientific value into a potentially falsifiable hypothesis.

Economic theory does predict that inflationary expectations affect matters other than wage and price setting. Indeed, the concept made its first appearance in economics — close to a century ago — not in the context of the theory of wages and prices at all, but as part of a theory of the behaviour of interest rates.[3] The prediction then, as now, was that the rate of interest on those assets whose value is fixed in nominal terms — typically bonds — would tend to exceed that on those assets which represent a claim on real physical assets — typically equities — by the expected rate of price inflation. I say 'tend' here because the yields would differ exactly by the expected rate of inflation only if the assets in question were otherwise exactly alike; even so, on the basis of this theory one may predict that increases in the expected rate of inflation will lead to a relative increase in the rate of interest on nominal assets. Inspection of figure 10.1 reveals that the difference between the yield on equities and that on preference stocks began to widen in late 1966 and opened up dramatically between the final quarter of 1968 and about half-way through 1969, the very same time that the 'wage explosion' was getting under way. This behaviour is certainly consistent with

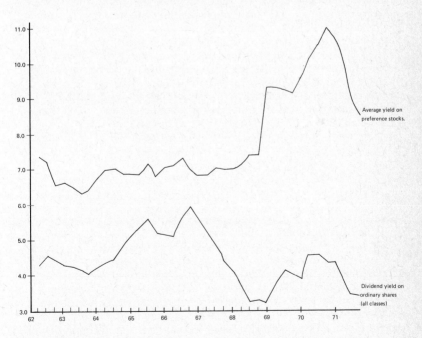

Figure 10.1 Yields on preference and ordinary shares, UK, 1962(2)—1971(4)

the prediction of the expectations hypothesis, and, if it stops a
long way short of establishing the truth of that hypothesis as an
explanation of the increase in the inflation rate, it does at least
raise it above the status of a mere *ex post* rationalisation.

Now let us turn to the question of the manner in which
expectations are formed. For well over a decade economists have
found that a surprisingly simple theory of expectations get them
a long way in interpreting aggregate economic phenomena. The
theory is that people form their expectation of the future value:
of some economic variable, in due course observe the actual
value of the variable, and make their next prediction about it by
revising their initial one by a fraction of the amount by which it
was in error. This so-called 'error-learning hypothesis' has
been applied to income and interest rate expectations, but its
original application was to inflation theory and specifically as a
component of an extremely successful attempt to explain the time
path of prices during hyper-inflation.[4]

Now if people form their expectations by adjusting to their
last error, and if past expectations have been similarly formulated,
it will be intuitively obvious that the currently expected rate of
inflation will depend upon all past values of the actual inflation
rate. Recent values will have more influence than more distant
ones; indeed, it is easy to show that the error-learning hypothesis
implies that the expected rate of inflation is equal to a weighted
average of current and past inflation rates, where the weights
decline geometrically with time.[5] Thus it has the great advantage
of enabling us to express a variable that cannot be directly observed in terms of observable phenomena, hence making the
expected inflation rate an empirically useful concept. In particular, as I shall now show, it enables us to answer the question
'What relationship ought we to observe between the rate of inflation
and the level of excess demand when the expected inflation rate
is not held constant?'

III

I mentioned at the outset of this essay that I believe the openness
of the British economy and events abroad to be crucial in any explanation of recent events. The easiest way to see that this is the
case is first to consider what the relationship between the rate of
inflation and excess demand ought to be in a closed economy in
which the expected rate of inflation is generated solely by the
error-learning mechanism sketched out above, and in which the
actual inflation rate departs from the expected rate solely in response to variations in the level of excess demand. A comparison
of this extremely simple and abstract economic model's behaviour
with that of the British economy yields what I believe are vital

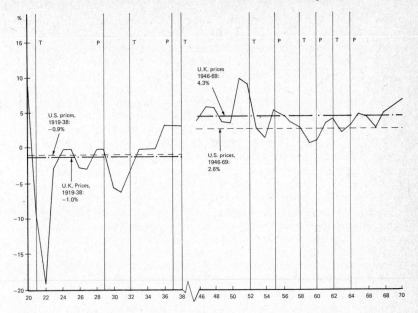

Figure 10.2 The rate of change of retail prices in the UK, 1920-69 (per cent). P = business cycle peak, T = business cycle trough

clues to understanding recent, and indeed not so recent, economic history.

This theory in fact tells us that the *rate of change* of the rate of inflation ought to be related not only to the size of the gap between aggregate demand and potential full employment output, but also to the rate at which that gap is changing. According to this theory, when the level of economic activity is falling away from full employment the rate of inflation will slow down and, as it rises towards full employment, the rate of inflation will at first continue to slow down but will begin to speed up as expansion continues.[6] Thus this extremely simple and orthodox model in which inflationary expectations respond only to past experience of inflation, and current inflation responds only to expectations and excess demand, tells us that it is the rate of change of the inflation rate and not its level that ought to be related to swings in output and employment, and makes reasonably precise prediction about the nature of that relationship.

In figure 10.2 I have plotted the time path of the rate of change of prices as it relates to the course of the business cycle in Britain [since the first world war]. Now it would be surprising indeed if an extremely simple model of a closed economy were not to make some erroneous predictions about the rate of inflation

in a complicated open economy such as Britain, particularly when
it is granted a fifty-year time span in which to make errors.
In fact the model goes badly wrong in its predictions for 1925-27,
when the rate of inflation failed to continue its upward trend; for
1931-35, when it first began to rise too soon and then stopped
rising at the very time when it should have begun to rise; and for
1949-50, 1960-62 and 1967-68, when in each case it was rising
when the model predicts that it should have been falling.[7]

There seem to me to be two major lessons to be learnt from
figure 10.2. First, the period since 1967 is by no means the first
time that orthodox inflation theory has failed to predict events
in the British economy. This seems to me to go a long way towards undermining the view that recent experience is the result
of some new causative mechanism that has never been at work
before. Second, with the exception of 1960-62 (which I am unable
to explain at present), every other false prediction comes in the
wake of a major exchange rate change.[8] The pound was revalued
in 1925, devalued in 1931, effectively revalued by the American
devaluation and realignment of exchange rates of 1933-35, devalued in 1949 and again in 1967. It would be hard to find a more
striking confirmation than this of the importance of the openness
of the British economy. Let us therefore see how our basic model
can be modified to deal with an open economy.

Both components of the model must be altered somewhat when
we come to consider an open economy with fixed exchange rates.
In a closed economy, if demand exceeds supply, the rate of inflation
rises relative to expectations, and if it falls short it falls. The
same is true of an open economy with a flexible exchange rate.
Inflation drives down the exchange rate, ensuring both that import
prices keep up with those of home-produced goods and that the
prices in terms of domestic currency received by exporters rise
also. Deflation has exactly opposite effects.

The existence of fixed exchange rates means that the foreign
trade sector provides an alternative source of both supply and
demand for goods at prices fixed by world market conditions.
If demand exceeds domestic output, then an increase in imports
and a diversion of goods from exports is a possible substitute
for domestic inflation, while a shortfall of demand may equally be
diverted into a 'favourable' change of the balance of payments.
For a 'small' economy with a 'large' foreign sector where there
were negligible costs of switching output between foreign and
domestic markets the tendency just outlined would be sufficient
to ensure that domestic prices never deviated from world prices,
so that, whatever the world inflation rate, that would be the
domestic one too. Such an economy is, of course, very much a
limiting case, though not an empirically irrelevant one, for we
can get considerable insight into the problems of particular

regions of Britain, for example, by regarding them as small open economies of this kind. For Britain as a whole there probably are significant costs of moving between domestic and foreign markets which mean that the openness of the economy limits, rather than completely overwhelms, the tendency of the inflation rate to vary in the short run with the level of aggregate demand.

In the long run, though, it is surely unreasonable to expect the British inflation rate to move too far from that ruling in general in the rest of the world. British producers of exportables cannot be expected to hold domestic prices constant when the price of their goods on world markets is increasing, nor can the suppliers of British imports and import substitutes be expected to sell them below world market prices for any length of time.

Now all this amounts to saying that the openness of the British economy means that the domestic inflation rate is less sensitive to purely domestic disturbances than it would be were the economy closed, and that in the long run the inflation rate ruling in the rest of the world is going to have an important — perhaps dominant — influence. This at least is likely to be true so long as the fixed exchange rate remains fixed.[9]

If there is a devaluation the domestic price of imports must rise, while the domestic price of exports too will rise as producers divert output towards the overseas markets made more profitable by the devaluation. Moreover these effects will spread through factor markets and will influence the prices of goods not directly involved in foreign trade. These are the inevitable and obvious consequences of a devaluation, and it is reasonable to suppose that those involved in fixing wages and prices will anticipate a period of accelerated inflation in the wake of a devaluation. Thus exchange rate changes under a fixed-rate regime must introduce an extra factor — independent of past experience — into the determination of the expected inflation rate, as well as setting in motion the events whereby the expectations in question are validated. This is surely a plausible hypothesis with which to explain the systematic failure of a closed-economy model to predict the direction of change of the inflation rate in the period following exchange rate changes.[10]

Though it was the behaviour of the inflation rate after exchange rate changes that first prompted consideration of the openness of the economy, the foregoing argument also tells us to look for another characteristic in the data charted in figure 10.2. It tells us that in the absence of exchange rate changes the British inflation rate would on average in the long run follow the world rate. If we take a long-run average of the United States inflation rate as an approximate measure of that world rate—and this is surely permissible, given the dominance of the US in world trade—then we may compare the average levels of the British and US inflation

rates to see whether the prediction has any empirical content.
Inspection of figure 10.2 will certainly confirm that, systematic
though variations in the British inflation rate may have been, it
has fluctuated around quite different average levels at different
times. These average levels have not deviated far from the long-
run world inflation rate, as represented by the United States rate,
as is also apparent from inspection of figure 10.2; the average
US and British rates over various time periods are there super-
imposed upon the annual series for the British inflation rate.[11]
Since 1949 the British inflation rate has been systematically
above the US rate, but it has taken two devaluations to permit
this.

   To summarise the argument, then: the long-run trend in the
British inflation rate is given from the outside so long as Britain
maintains a fixed exchange rate; most fluctuations about this
trend are to be explained by variations in the domestic level of
aggregate demand which cause the rate of inflation to vary relative to its expected level — which must, of course, normally be
dominated by the world rate. However, changes in the exchange
rate exert a powerful independent effect on the expected and
actual rate of inflation so that a devaluation gives an upward
impetus to the inflation rate and a revaluation a downward
impetus independently of what is happening to aggregate demand
and the level of employment. Furthermore, this analysis explains
the broad pattern of events [since 1919], a pattern into which
events of the last few years are no more difficult to fit than
any others.

   The abnormally high inflation rate of recent years may be
interpreted as resulting from a combination of two circumstances.
First the attempt of the American authorities to finance a war in
Vietnam and a war on poverty while simultaneously cutting
federal tax rates and attempting to keep interest rates down led
to a greatly increased rate of monetary expansion after 1966 and
to a substantial increase in the world inflation rate, an increase
which was bound to affect the British rate of inflation (*cf.* figure
10.3). Second, the devaluation of 1967 led to an upward revision
of inflationary expectations that was independent of and additional
to the effect of the change in the world inflation rate. The combined effects of these two factors swamped the downward pressure being exerted on the inflation rate by the considerable
excess supply in the economy until towards the end of 1971. No
serious problem was noted until 1969, two or three years after
the forces towards which this argument points were set in motion,
but inspection of figure 10.2 confirms that it was 1967 that saw
the trough in the inflation rate. We noticed that we has a problem
in 1969 because it was then that the rate of inflation reached an
unusually high level, but it had already been rising steadily to-

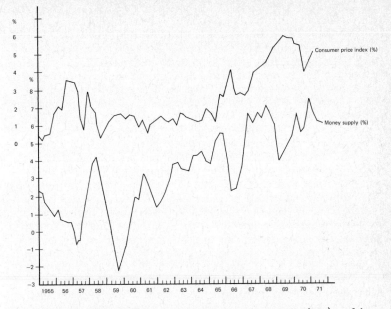

Figure 10.3 Rates of change in the money supply (M_1) and in the consumer price index, US, 1955-71

wards that level for two years; moreover inspection of figure 10.1 suggests that the expected inflation rate began to move up sharply even before, and surely in anticipation of, the devaluation of 1967. These two facts lend further support to the view that one must look to the events of 1967 and before to find the origins of our current problems.

Now if it is the case that the current inflation may be explained in the terms set out in this lecture it follows at once that explanations which look to purely domestic causes of inflation — I am thinking here in particular of those explanations that centre on trade union militancy — are quite simply too parochial in outlook and confuse the description of inflation with the analysis of its causes. Certainly there is ample room within the explanation I have advanced for trade unions to demand large increases in money wages in a period in which large increases in prices are anticipated, and for employers to be willing to concede such increases; I know of no evidence that would compel disbelief in the assertions of trade union leaders that their 'militancy' in recent years has been the result of their desire to protect their members' living standards against erosion by an inflationary process neither of their creation nor under their control.[12]

IV

How, then, are we to cope with inflation both in the long-run sense
of avoiding the problem in future and in the short-run sense of
dealing with the present situation? If my diagnosis of the evidence
is correct, there is precious little Britain can do about inflation in
the long run if she maintains a fixed exchange rate. She must
simply accept the world rate and recognise that her own contribution to the determination of that rate is negligible. It might be
noted in passing that if the enlarged Common Market does form a
currency union, then Britain will, by the same argument, have to
accept the European inflation rate. Whether or not this is the
world rate depends upon whether the Common Market adopts a
floating or fixed rate *vis-à-vis* the rest of the world. However, the
rate of domestic price increase is surely a legitimate matter of
domestic concern, and there can be no presumption that the rest of
the world will generate just that rate of inflation that the British
population finds desirable; and, to repeat, domestic control over
the domestic inflation rate requires the adoption of a flexible exchange rate. However, it ought to be stressed that the adoption of
such an exchange rate regime does not guarantee the achievement
of the desired rate of inflation.[13] It merely makes it possible for
Britain to have any rate of inflation she chooses, regardless of
what is happening elsewhere.

Though I have argued that recent inflation has to a significant
extent been imported, the secular increase in the balance of payments deficit that took place throughout the period 1950-67 is
strong evidence that Britain was importing price stability over
this earlier period. To discuss in any detail what the appropriate
inflation rate to aim for would be and how it might be maintained
would require another paper or two. Suffice it, then, to assert that
I think there would be widespread agreement that the target rate
of inflation should be lower than the present rate, and also to
assert that the maintenance of a steady long-run rate of growth
of the money supply at an appropriate rate must be a *sine qua non*
of the policy that would achieve that rate of inflation. This, of
course, is the one policy that successive British governments
have never tried. Let us now take up the more pressing problem
of how to reduce the current inflation rate.[14]

It is a widely held view that a prices and incomes policy is an
essential ingredient of any policy design to reduce the current
inflation rate, but I would reject this view for two reasons. First,
the premise upon which the case for such a policy is based is that
union aggressiveness is the root cause of the problem, and I have
already rejected that premise. This is not a decisive argument
against an incomes policy, for in as much as large wage and
price increases are a symptom of inflation it is certainly possible

that a policy of attempting directly to control them could relieve
the symptoms, if it did not in and of itself cure the disease. However, the fact remains that quite exhaustive empirical investigation has failed to produce any evidence that such policies have in
the past affected the rate of inflation, with the sole exception of
the Cripps era, when wage and price controls were accompanied
by a battery of quantitative restrictions as well.[15] This, of course,
does not mean that prices and incomes policies have no effects.
Given that they are so much easier to apply to some sectors of
the economy than others, they undoubtedly produce some ineffici-
ency in the use of resources and considerable short-run inequities
in the distribution of income. Thus, like orthodox policies, they
impose costs on the community, but, unlike orthodox policies,
there is no evidence that they succeeed in reducing the overall
rate of change of prices and incomes. In the face of these problems
it is surprising that there is still such wide support for the re-
introduction of prices and incomes policies, but it is worth noting
that their proponents find it much easier to agree that some such
policy should be used than to agree upon even the approximate
form in which it should be implemented.[16]

V

Be that as it may, there is no mystery as to how the rate of inflation may be reduced. Sufficiently stringent demand management
policies can do that. Indeed, in the present state of knowledge
these are the only policies available to us. The problem is that
such policies simultaneously produce unemployment, so that
reducing the rate of inflation is costly. The central prediction of
the expectations theory of wage and price setting advanced earlier
is that it is impossible to reduce the rate of inflation below its
expected rate without simultaneously producing unemployment.
To be sure, this same unemployment produces a downward pressure on wage and price inflation that eventually feeds back into
expectations, so that a lower rate of inflation can be enjoyed in
the long run without a permanent rise in the unemployment
rate; but this does not alter the fact that reducing the inflation
rate is costly while the process of reduction is in progress.
The same theory, though, suggests that the longer we are willing
to take about reducing the inflation rate by a given amount, the
less unemployment need be tolerated in the interim.[17]

Now it is deficient demand for goods and services, and hence
for labour, that simultaneously slows down the rate of price and
wage inflation and brings about unemployment. There is no natural
law that there must be a unique relationship between excess
supply and unemployment. Excess supply is not the only cause
of unemployment. Structural imbalance in the economy, both as

between industries and regions, is a source of unemployment, as is the inevitable and closely related friction involved when the labour force is redeployed in the face of changes in the composition of output. If unemployment must be endured in order to reduce the inflation rate, then it is surely reasonable to expect governments to make an effort to minimise the amount necessary. This requires measures to make labour markets more efficient, both as transmitters of information about where job vacancies are and as providers of incentives and opportunities for individuals to equip themselves with the skills necessary to fill those vacancies, for this is the way in which the frictional and structural components of unemployment can be reduced.

A similar argument must hold about inflation. If we must put up with more inflation than we would like for a significant period in order to minimise the unemployment problem, then there is a great deal to be said for minimising the burden that it places on the population. Now in an economy in which everyone always had perfect information about the future course of prices there would be no cost to inflation.[18] It would simply be one more factor to take into account when making decisions. Problems arise when information is less than perfect and mistakes are made. For example, people enter into private insurance and pension contracts with certain expectations about the future course of prices, the rate of inflation turns out to be higher than expected, and their real wealth is diminished. Or again Parliament sets State pensions and income tax rates presumably with the intention of providing the old with a certain minimum standard of living and imposing a certain pattern of real tax burdens on the working population. Inflation at a faster than anticipated rate ensures that what Parliament intended does not come about; poverty among the old and excessive tax burdens upon the working population are the result.

One could multiply such examples without difficulty, but enough has already been said to illustrate the nature of the problems brought on by the recent increase in the inflation rate. They are essentially distributional problems, and there is nothing inherent in the inflationary process that prevents them being tackled as such. There is no reason in principle why State pensions cannot be pegged to the cost of living, nor tax rates.[19] There is no reason why holders of claims to private pensions cannot be compensated for the losses imposed upon them by the inflation rate's unexpectedly increasing since they entered into their contracts. Similarly, but on the other side of the coin, there is no reason in principle why the debtors who gain from inflation — for example, householders with mortgages — cannot be taxed on the windfalls which unanticipated inflation brings them.

How easy it would be to deal with any particular distributional inequity that has arisen or could in future arise from
inflation cannot be assessed without a detailed study. However,
I raise this general question not because I have ready-made
answers to its many facets but because I find it surprising that,
given that we have been living with inflation for so long, and given
that so many people profess to be deeply disturbed by its adverse
distributional effects, so little work has been done on devising the
means whereby we can minimise these effects. Surely the most
serious side effect of various governments' pursuit of incomes
policies to reduce the inflation rate without increasing unemployment — always a futile pursuit since 1950 — has been to distract
attention from the problems of making labour markets more
efficient and of making it easier for the general public to live with
inflation. After all, if one thinks one has found a ready-made, rapid
and costless cure for inflation there is no need to make the effort
of investigating the means whereby the costs involved in curing it
slowly by other methods may be minimised.

Thus the policy implications of my analysis can be stated very
simply. Adopt a flexible exchange rate and rely on the rate of
monetary expansion to achieve, in the long run, the inflation rate
desired. Recognise that the inflation rate can be reduced only at
the cost of unemployment during the transition, so proceed slowly
towards the target; recognise that the amount of unemployment
required over a given period to reduce the inflation rate by a
given amount is less the more efficient are labour markets, and
the less is the structural imbalance in the economy. Also recognise that much of the harm that inflation can do may be amelio-
rated by policies to compensate the losers; hence pay much more
attention than hitherto to designing policies to deal both with the
structure of the labour market and with the distributional inequities produced by inflation. In short, and above all, face up to the
fact that inflation is not a problem for which some costless
panacea is likely to be found just around the corner; utilise instead the considerable knowledge that we already have of its
nature to cure it at as low a cost as possible, recognising that
this cost will not be zero.

NOTES

1   The Lister lecture given to Section F of the British
Association for the Advancement of Science, September 1972;
reprinted from Joan Robinson (ed.), *After Keynes,* Oxford, Black-
well, 1973. A version also appeared in the *National Westminster
Bank Quarterly Review,* November 1972. This paper is based on
work currently being carried out under the auspices of the SSRC —
University of Manchester Inflation Project. As will be apparent

from the references, it draws not only on my research but on that of other members of the project. In particular I have had many helpful and stimulating discussions with John Foster, Michael Parkin, David Rose and George Zis. I am grateful to John Hargreaves for drawing the charts and collecting the data on which they were based. Nevertheless the author alone is responsible for the points of view expressed here.

2   The view that the inflation rate varies systematically with excess demand is, of course, the basis of Phillips curve analysis. There is no mention of expectations in Phillips's original paper (1958), nor in the work of Lipsey, who developed Phillips's analysis further; *cf.* Lipsey (1960) and Lipsey and Parkin (1970). Note, though, that Parkin (1970b) paid careful attention to expectations, and did find them to be important.

3   *Cf.* Irving Fisher (1896).

4   The hypothesis was first applied to income expectations by Friedman (1957), to interest rates by Meiselman (1963) and to the inflation rate by Cagan (1956).

5   The hypothesis states that, if X^e is the predicted value of some variable, X its actual value, and $-1, -2, \ldots -n$ are time lag subscripts, then

$$X^e - X^e_{-1} = b(X - X^e_{-1})$$

where b is a positive fraction. It follows from this that

$$X^e = bX + b(1 - b)X_{-1} + b(1 - b)^2 X_{-2} \ldots b(1 - b)^n X_{-n} \ldots$$

6   [This prediction is derived in more detail in chapter 6. Empirical work being carried out by my colleagues John Carlson and Michael Parkin ('Inflation expectations', *Economica,* forthcoming) suggests that a slightly modified expectations hypothesis in which people learn from their last two errors is more appropriate for dealing with inflationary expectations in Britain. This hypothesis, which is equivalent to saying that people take note not only of the size and sign of their predictive errors but also of the direction and rate of change of those errors, may be written

$$\Delta P^e - \Delta P^e_{-1} = c(\Delta P - \Delta P^e_{-1}) + h(\Delta P_{-1} - \Delta P^e_{-2})$$

If we substitute this equation into the analysis set out in chapter 6, we get

$$\Delta P - \Delta P_{-1} = g(E - E_{-1}) + cg(E_{-1} - Y^*) + hg(E_{-2} - Y^*)$$

which is not qualitatively different from our earlier prediction. The potential importance of the prediction that the turning point of the cycle in the inflation rate should lag the turning point in the business cycle is, however, accentuated.]

7   My turning points are taken from Matthews (1969). Note that the NBER regards 1924-27 as having constituted a separate downswing, but that Matthews disagrees with this dating. There are no turning points given after 1964 but we are on safe ground, I think, if we assert that the economy was not on a cyclical up-swing in 1967. If anything, this year marked a trough.

8   [I have been reminded since writing this passage that early 1961 saw a small revaluation of the mark and the guilder. Even this false prediction from the simpe closed-economy model is thus associated with an exchange rate change.]

9   A formal version of the foregoing argument is developed in chapter 8 above.

10   The empirical work of Carlson and Parkin mentioned in n. 6 above has addressed itself to this particular hypothesis and provides strong support for it.

11   This is, of course, only a crude first test. The hypothesis in question here would certainly be worth much more careful investigation than this.

12   The classic study of wage inflation that seemed to lend considerable support to the union militancy hypothesis is that of Hines (1964). The results of a recent study by Purdy and Zis (1974) go a long way towards undermining Hines's results.

13   It might seem odd at first sight that I am arguing simultaneously that devaluations are inflationary and that the operations of a flexible exchange rate system will not lead to inevitable inflation when the rate falls. However, there is no inconsistency here. With a fixed exchange rate a balance of payment deficit arises as a consequence of inflationary pressure *and instead of* domestic prices increases. Devaluation may, crudely speaking, be regarded as forcing the price level to rise to the level it would have achieved in the first place had the earlier deficit not occurred. With a flexible rate, inflationary pressure results in rising prices, which lead to a fall in the rate. When a new equilibrium rate has been reached to accommodate the new domestic price level that is the end of the story.

14   The case for a steady rate of growth in the money supply is put most eloquently by Friedman (1960). I have given a non-technical account of the case in Laidler (1971c) and discussed much of the work upon whose results the case is based in Laidler (1971a).

15   For a survey of this evidence *cf.* Parkin, Sumner and Jones (1972).

16   [Since I wrote this paragraph such policies have been adopted again, and appear to have failed again while bringing about a good deal of industrial unrest.]

[17]   I have discussed this issue in more detail in Laidler (1971b).
[18]   This would be true provided that the information was free
and there were no costs to be incurred in adjusting plans in the
light of new information. It is precisely because information is
costly to obtain, and because remaking plans is expensive, particularly when binding contracts have been entered into, that even
predictable inflation is costly. It is worth noting explicitly that
distributional effects of the type discussed here occur at any
time when the rate of change of prices deviates (either upwards
or downwards) from the anticipated rate. They are not peculiarly
the result of rising prices *per se*. I am grateful to John Foster
for helpful discussion on these matters.
[19]   We are beginning to see some movement in this direction,
albeit in an unsystematic way. Old age pension rates are now
reviewed annually, while increases in the minimum money income
at which households become liable for income tax seem to be
becoming more frequent.

11 Thomas Tooke on monetary reform[1]

I

The controversy that surrounded the passage of Sir Robert Peel's
Bank Charter Act of 1844 has already produced a substantial historical literature, and on the whole this literature has awarded the
honours to the currency school.[2] This is perhaps a little strange,
since the banking structure created in 1844 failed to mitigate the
periodic financial difficulties of the type that had plagued Britain
in the 1820s and 1830s, and the very rules under which the system
was supposed to work had to be suspended to cope with several
subsequent crises. Of course, it is always possible that the suggestions of the opponents of the Act could have led to even worse
difficulties, but in this essay it will be argued that the recommendations of Thomas Tooke, the leading member of the banking school,
were based on greater insight into the manner in which the monetary system worked prior to 1844, and were very much what a
modern economist might suggest within the constraint of the
policy goals ruling in the nineteenth century. It will not, however,
be argued that Tooke's analysis was logically complete and
rigorous, for, as we shall see below, there are places where
critical pieces of it are missing or badly set out, and where extra-
neous matters intrude unduly.

In the following pages I shall first discuss the policy goals of
the time and sketch out the differences of opinion about the problems of achieving them. I shall then go into Tooke's analysis of
the banking system in order to show that his assessment of the
policy problem was not without foundation. Finally it will be argued
that, given this analysis, his very moderate practical recommendations are more appealing than those made by the currency
school.

II

One of the more remarkable facets of nineteenth century British
economic doctrine is the almost unanimous agreement that is to be
found on policy goals. With the exception of Attwood and his fol-

lowers, the leading economists of the day all took the view that the overriding aim of monetary policy was to maintain the convertibility, both at home and abroad, of Bank of England notes into gold at a fixed price. Tooke himself referred to this as 'the *sine qua non* of any sound system of currency' (1840, p. 177) and expressed 'unutterable surprise' that 'any well informed person, not of The Birmingham School, could seriously propose to have cash payments suspended, rather than that the mercantile community should be subjected to some inconvenience...' (1844, p. 104). To this goal all others were to be sacrificed, and the debate between the currency school and the banking school took this for granted. The debate, rather, was about the structure of the institutional framework necessary to guarantee the achievement of this end, and about the costs which competing schemes would impose upon the economy in maintaining the convertibility of paper currency. Nor was there disagreement about the nature of the costs involved, for all saw them as arising from the disruption of credit markets, and hence the real side of the economy, that might arise from the monetary measures necessary to correct external drains of specie.[3]

In order to achieve the desired end the currency school proposed that the Bank of England note issue should absorb that of the country banks, and that, apart from a fixed fiduciary issue, it should fluctuate exactly with the specie reserve of the Bank's note issue department, which was to be separated strictly from the department handling the Bank's deposit business. This they proposed because they wished to make the monetary system work along the lines of a strict, not to say automatic, price-specie flow mechanism. They took the view that previous crises, in which the suspension of cash payments by the Bank of England had been a very real threat, had had their roots in an over-issue of bank notes, on the part both of the Bank of England and of the country banks. By linking the note issue directly to specie reserves they hoped that the system would work exactly as it would under a purely metallic money supply so that any incipient specie drain abroad would immediately set up equilibrating forces. Thus not only would the convertibility of notes be guaranteed at all times, since the bullion to meet an internal drain would always be available, but also the correction of disequilibrium would be rapid and, beginning the moment the problem arose, mild in its effects.

It was Tooke's view that this framework, which was, of course, adopted in 1844, would not achieve the desired effect, for though he agreed that it would ensure the convertibility of the note issue, he was convinced that this would be achieved at too high a price in terms of periodic disruption of domestic credit markets. He did not disagree that too high a price level caused by monetary expansion could cause an external specie drain, but he did deny that this was the only cause.[4] In his view such drains could equally well arise from shifts in the real conditions of supply and demand for traded goods. Furthermore such shifts did not have to be permanent. Corn imports in particular were liable to frequent fluctuations, especially given the way in which the corn laws operated, and in such circumstances he suggested that no monetary action was necessary. Rather, he proposed that the Bank of England should hold reserves of sufficient size to be able to finance temporary deficits of this kind without having recourse to domestic deflation to combat them, and he regarded the principal cause of previous difficulties as the Bank's failure to hold adequate amounts of bullion.

It was his view that 'not less than ten millions can ever be considered a safe position of the treasure of the Bank of England seeing the sudden calls to which it is liable'(1838, II, p. 330), and he wanted to see for the reserves 'a latitude for variation between fifteen millions and five millions ...' rather than '... as it has recently been, between ten millions and nothing' (1840, p. 187). Such an increase in the Bank's average level of reserves would enable the economy to ride out temporary disequilibria without serious domestic repercussions, and would also give the Bank ample time to recognise 'the existence of more extensive and deeper seated causes of demand for the metals ...' and to take appropriate action 'without producing alarm and disturbance of the money market on the one hand, or endangering an extreme and unsafe reduction of the Bank treasure on the other' (1840, p. 187).[5]

Now it surely needs little argument that these recommendations of Tooke's would meet with approval among modern economists. The distinction between temporary and more fundamental imbalances is now commonplace in the literature on economic policy, and the current international monetary mechanism is based upon it. Moreover the problems we now face with this system are not ones that could have arisen in the context of nineteenth century policy goals. Debates now are not about the wisdom of financing short-term imbalances without domestic deflation, but arise rather over the choice between deflation and devaluation when disequilibria persist. Since devaluation was out of the question in the 1840s, the problems we face today could hardly have then arisen. Given the overriding need to maintain convertibility at a fixed exchange rate, it is hard to see how modern advice would differ much from that given by Tooke.[6]

This conclusion, however, presupposes a great deal about the monetary institutions existing prior to 1844. Tooke wished to do no more than alter one aspect of the behaviour of one of these institutions, the Bank of England. The currency school thought it necessary to reform fundamentally the institutional framework itself, and in fact succeeded in doing so. Tooke regarded these

reforms as either beside the point, or even likely to worsen rather
than better matters; and so, before any firm conclusions as to the
superiority of his policy proposals can be reached, we must look
at his analysis of the pre-1844 monetary system.

III

The first step in understanding both Tooke's analysis of the banking
system and his objections to the proposals of the currency school
is to realise that the latter regarded the control of the quantity of
currency outside the Bank of England issue department as sufficient to control the level of domestic economic activity. This is a far
narrower range of assets than what we would now call 'money',
and Tooke, stressing the fact that coin and bank notes were but
one component of what he usually referred to as the circulating
medium, saw the importance of this factor. As he put it, 'It appears,
then, that there is neither authority nor reasoning in favour of the
definition which invests Bank notes with the properties of money,
or paper currency *to the exclusion of all other forms of paper
credit*' (1848, p. 163; Tooke's italics). Specifically, he thought it
necessary to regard bank deposits (or rather cheques drawn upon
them, for he was far from clear on this point) and bills of exchange
as forms of paper credit with an equal claim to be considered as
forming part of what we would now call the money supply (*cf.*
Tooke, 1844, p. 32).

It was on the basis of this insight that he argued that control
of the note issue alone would be an inadequate policy tool. Indeed,
he went even further, claiming that the volume of notes in circulation at any time depended upon the demand of the public, and was
beyond the *direct* control of the banking system. We must be careful not to confuse this doctrine with the so-called 'real bills fallacy',
one of whose implications it resembles but to which in this context it is not closely related. Tooke was above all an empiricist,
and he noted, as far as country bank notes were concerned, 'that
their circulation is devoted and confined to local purposes, chiefly
in small amounts, for the retail trade ...'. He further argued that
if country bankers were to refuse to issue their own notes, then
'such refusal must be accompanied by offering Bank of England
notes or coin, and thus local circulation would be equally filled
up' (1844, p. 38). Should notes be issued in excess, on the other
hand, then 'the law of reflux' would take effect in one of three ways:
'by payment of the redundant amount to a banker on a deposit
account, or by the return of notes in discharge of securities on
which advances have been made. A third way is that of a return of
the notes to the issuing bank by a demand for coin' (1848, p. 185).
Of these three methods, only the second has anything to do with the
workings of bank credit, where the real bills doctrine, which states

that the banking system should meet the 'needs of trade' for loans
on goods in process, might be relevant. The other two clearly
have to do with the way in which the non-bank public desire to
hold their assets.[7] The importance of the real bills element here
is very minor, particularly when it is realised that it is only a
direct influence on the note circulation that Tooke denied the
banks. He was perfectly willing to admit that the volume of bank
advances could affect the level of economic activity, and hence the
volume of notes in circulation.[8]

If we interpret the 'law of reflux' as operating with the level
of economic activity given, determined in part by the volume of
bank lending, it becomes part of a theory analogous to the modern
analysis of the public's demand for currency relative to other
assets, rather than a component of some erroneous doctrine of the
effect of bank credit. Tooke's views on the determination of the
quantity of bank notes in circulation then become propositions
about the composition, rather than the size, of what would now be
called the money supply, for they amount to the following. At a
given level of economic activity the public will find it convenient
to hold and use a certain quantity of bank notes. Should these notes
not already be in circulation, the public may obtain them by converting their deposits or coin into notes. Should too many notes
be in circulation they may be exchanged for deposits, used to pay
off debts to the banking system, or should they begin to depreciate
they could be exchanged for gold coin, one of the items relative
to which their depreciation would have to take place.

However, if Tooke was on the whole correct in his analysis of
the demand for currency, his analysis was a good deal less firmly
grounded when he came to deal with the 'circulating medium'
as a whole, for he argued that its quantity also was the effect,
rather than the cause, of the price level. In so arguing he used
reasoning similar to that which he employed in dealing with
currency alone, so that even a charitable reader must attribute
a fallacy of composition to him on this score. The basic line of
the argument was that just as notes could substitute for coin, so
could cheques substitute for notes, and bills of exchange for
cheques. If one instrument was not available, then another would
take its place. Now such substitution was doubtless possible, and
contractions and expansions of the note issue would to some
degree, perhaps a high one, be offset by greater use of other
instruments. However, Tooke overlooked several important factors
in dealing with it.

In the first place, he never really faced the degree of substitutability between assets on the demand side. Though he noted
that coin and small notes would be more difficult to replace with
cheques and bills than large notes, he did not go into this too
deeply, merely expressing the judgement that there would be little

substitution of other forms of paper for £1 notes, but somewhat
more for the notes up to £10 in value. (Notes under £5 circulated
only in Ireland and Scotland in the 1840s). For notes of higher
denomination, the tone of his argument suggests that he regarded
them well nigh perfect substitutes for cheques and bills of exchange
(*cf*. 1844, pp. 32-3).

However, substitutability on the demand side is not necessarily
the most important factor here, for so long as bankers were
willing to permit their customers to draw cheques without limit,
and businessmen were able to issue bills of exchange in any
amount they wished, there would be no reason why a sufficient
amount of other instruments could not be created to maintain any
level of prices. Substitutability on the supply side is the key factor.
Bank of England deposits and notes were substitutes in their
creation as well as in their use, so in this context Tooke was not
so far from the mark. If all that was contracted was the Bank of
England's note issue, but not its liabilities, it is far from clear
that payments previously made in notes could not have been made
almost equally well by cheques on the Bank.

However, with country bank liabilities and bills of exchange it
is a different matter. They were substitutes in use for Bank of
England liabilities, but not in their creation. Though a contraction
of Bank of England liabilities might have produced an incentive
to use county bank liabilities and bills of exchange to finance
transactions, it is also probably true that this same contraction
would have produced incentives to cut their supply. Tooke, stressing that the motive for issuing bills of exchange lay 'in the prospect of resale with a profit' (1844, p. 79), certainly showed insight
into the role of expectations and speculation in private credit
markets but overlooked the fact that emitters of such instruments
would presumably wish to hold some form of reserve against the
time when they fell due to cover the possibility that the goods so
financed might be sold at a loss rather than a profit. Not to have
done so would have amounted to speculation on zero margin,
and it is hard to believe that this was a very common practice.
A similar argument clearly holds for the behaviour of country
banks.[9] Thus Tooke in this instance overlooked the key role of
Bank of England liabilities as a reserve base for other components
of the circulating medium, a factor which the currency school,
with their insistence on the fact that bills of exchange and clearing balances between banks had ultimately to be settled in terms
of some other means of payment, seem to have had some insight
into, albeit perhaps not a very precise one, since the only use to
which they put this observation was as a component of the argument that bills of exchange and cheques were not money but
merely substitutes for money, and hence could not exert an influence on the price level.[10]

If Tooke erred in one direction, however, his opponents erred in another, for it is Bank of England liabilities rather than just notes, as they tended to claim, that were the important factor. No one would argue now that control of the note issue of a central bank, but not of its deposit business, would be an adequate monetary policy tool, but this is precisely what the currency school held. The difficulties that both sides of this debate had in understanding the nature of the circulation, and the determination of its magnitude, lies in their lack of a theory of multiple credit expansion, even though versions of such a theory had already been reasonably well worked out by Joplin and Pennington.[11] Presumably the currency school saw no need for it, since they overemphasised the importance of bank notes, while Tooke and his followers, because they saw cheques rather than bank deposits as the substitute for notes and bills of exchange, never fully realised the importance of the liability side of the banking system's balance sheet.[12] However, Tooke's lack of clarity on this matter did not lead his too far astray. Having tended to deny any great importance to the circulating medium in the determination of prices, he had to provide an alternative theory, and in the context of the theory to which he appears to have adhered the above-noted problems lead to difficulty only in the context of short-run disequilibrium situations, and these are more a matter of confused thought than outright error.

IV

Ricardo's work contains two different but not incompatible theories of the price level. In his policy writings during the period of the bank restriction he relied on the quantity theory of money as a short-run theory of prices, but in the *Principles* the price level was viewed as being determined in the long run by the cost of production of gold relative to the cost of production of other goods. Tooke was willing to admit either of these theories as particularly relevant, depending upon the situation to be analysed. The quantity theory was relevant when the money supply was made up of government issues of paper money, 'inconvertible and compulsorily current' (1848, p. 176), since such paper could clearly depreciate relative to both goods and gold; and the cost of production of gold theory was relevant when the money supply was convertible on demand into gold.

He regarded any permanent depreciation of the currency as impossible so long as the banks stood ready to buy and sell their notes at a fixed price in gold, just as he regarded any permanent appreciation of paper impossible for the same reasons; the 'law of reflux' (*cf.* above p. 214) would prevent this. Though Tooke never explicitly took the step, it is clear that this argument is

readily extendible to other forms of paper credit in the circulation.
Thus, given that the price of money in terms of gold was fixed, in
the long run the price of goods in terms of gold and hence money
was left to be determined by the 'quantity of money ... valued in
gold ... destined for current expenditures' (1844, p. 71) interact-
ing with the cost of production of goods.[13] If the equilibrium value
of gold is given by its cost of production, and so is that of total
output, then the equilibrium price of goods coming out of this
interaction must be the ratio of the cost of production of goods to
that of gold. Tooke, not having any grasp of, or perhaps faith in,
an index number concept, does not, of course, put it in this way,
but his discussion of the determination of the prices of various
individual goods makes it clear that this is the type of mechanism
he had in mind (cf. 1844, pp. 71-2).

This, as a theory of the long-run equilibrium level of prices
in a classical framework, is unimpeachable, and certainly none of
the currency school would have disagreed with it.[14] Indeed,
Torrens agrees explicitly, and attacks Tooke mainly on what we
would now call his 'short-run' theory of the relationship between
the quantity of the circulating medium and the level of prices. It
was Torrens's view that the third method of reflux, the exchange
of notes for specie, could not take place until after an over-issue
of notes had depreciated their value, while Tooke argued that the
fact of the notes' direct convertibility and other assets' indirect
convertibility would prevent them ever depreciating. The debate
here, in terms of modern analysis, is best interpreted as being
about the cost of converting other assets into gold. Their equilibrium price could never fall below their gold redemption value
minus the cost of the redemption transaction. It would take quite
a painstaking piece of econometric research to establish the
exact value of this cost for various assets but it is hard to
believe that it could have been a significant amount. In the case of
bank notes, all that was required was to enter a bank and ask for
their redemption in gold coin. It is this writer's judgement that,
at the very least, the currency school were not on very strong
ground when they argued that the equilibrium gold value of notes
could depreciate significantly in the presence of gold convertibility.
There is another possible interpretation of the currency school's
position here. They could have been arguing about the possibility
of temporary disequilibrium arising owing to a slowness on the
part of the public to realise that notes were depreciating. At best
this could be only a short-run phenomenon, and if this is all they
meant, then a great deal of the debate was about the purely
empirical and not very interesting problem of how long the short
run was in this case.[15]

However, there is more to the debate than this, for one
crucial issue between Tooke and his opponents in this context was

that of the causation of disequilibria. Tooke was far from denying
that it was impossible for the domestic price level to be, from
time to time, too high to maintain external balance. What he did
deny was that making the circulation of bank notes fluctuate
exactly with the Bank of England's specie reserve would prevent
this in any way. If it was true that such disequilibria usually
arose in the first place from an over-issue of bank notes, as the
currency school argued, then the reforms they suggested would
have dealt with the problem. Tooke, however, thought it as likely,
or even more likely, that balance of payments deficits would
arise from bad harvests, or from monetary expansion that arose
quite independently of the note issue. The latter could arise
either from an expansion of the banks' deposit business or from
speculative behaviour in wholesale markets leading to a credit
expansion there. If Tooke was right, then rather than preventing
a disequilibrium arising, relying on making the note issue fluctuate with the specie stock as virtually the sole rule of monetary
policy meant that no contractionary action would be taken by the
banking system until a disequilibrium had been going on long
enough for its effects to manifest themselves in an outflow of
specie. There is quite a modern touch to Tooke's views here, for
he appears to have appreciated, to some extent at least, the
importance of lagged responses in the monetary mechanism.

As we have already noted, Tooke's position on the matter of
credit expansion occurring independently of the Bank of England
is an oversimplified one, since he did not completely appreciate
the role of a reserve base in checking such speculative activity.
However, so long as the banking department of the Bank of England
and the private banks were not subject to any required reserve
ratio against their liabilities, and so long as merchants issuing
bills of exchange were permitted to make up their own minds as
to what size reserve to hold against them, no reserve base could
serve as a mechanical check against such speculation.[16] If, in
the process of a speculative boom, emitters of the circulating
medium permitted their reserve ratios to fall, contraction of the
note issue would not automatically offset a monetary expansion.
The following passage shows clearly that this was Tooke's view.
It also shows his awareness, to which we have alluded earlier,
of the short-run effects that the banking system could have on the
price level through its lending activities.

> The mischief of commercial revulsions from overtrading,
> whenever traceable to the banks, has been from over advances
> of capital, on insufficient or inconvertible securities, or both.
> Banks, whether of issue or not, may, in the competition for
> business, make advances to persons undeserving of credit,
> and may discount large amounts of doubtful bills, thus adding

to the circulating medium, without adding directly to the amount of the circulation, that is of notes ... prices may experience a temporary inflation from credit so unduly extended. A creation of bills of exchange and deposits must be the certain consequence; and while the banks are in credit, might sustain the extended transactions for some time, without the intervention of bank notes. The recoil of the speculation and overtrading would, in most cases, not be caused in the first instance by a want of bank notes, but by a want of demand from a view to the supply and consumption ... Now there is no provision in the proposed measure [i.e. the 1844 Act] to prevent such over advances by banks, whether joint stock or not. [1844, pp. 158-9]

At the same time, Tooke held that a fall in the Bank of England note issue in response to an external specie drain would not immediately cause any smooth contraction of the circulating medium; he regarded the Bank of England's banking operations as a much more important factor here than its note issue. He argued that the bulk of any demand for bullion for export 'would fall almost exclusively upon the deposit department' (1844, p. 108), so that the notes withdrawn would be from that department's reserves rather than from those in the hands of the public. As a consequence of this, and 'unless, and upon this, in my opinion, the question hinges, the deposit or banking department were bound to hold a much larger reserve than seems to be contemplated by any of the plans which I have seen' (1844, p. 105), in the face of any substantial balance of payments deficit the Bank 'must sell securities, or allow the existing ones, if short dated, to run off, and they must inexorably shut their doors to all applications for advances or discounts' (1844, p. 108). The effect of this, thought Tooke, would go far beyond limiting the power of the Bank to 'overtrade in discounts and loans' as Torrens suggested, and 'under certain circumstances of the trade, it would operate with a degree of violence on the state of credit of which, as it appears to me, Colonel Torrens has no adequate idea' (1844, p. 108).

Furthermore, if the demand for bullion came rapidly enough, even a rapid reduction of the Bank's discounts might not be enough to stem the demand, so that 'the deposit department would have no alternative but to stop payment' (1844, p. 109). All this Tooke saw coming about without any large reduction of the quantity of bank notes in the hands of the public, except in as much as the restriction of bank advances affected the state of trade and hence reduced the demand for them, and happening, furthermore, when the issue department would still have large stocks of bullion on hand. Written in 1844, the passage from which the above quotations are taken could easily pass as a slightly exaggerated account of the events of 1847.[17]

V

We have now set out what seem to be the key elements of Tooke's views on monetary theory and its application to the policy problems of the 1840s, but it would be as well to attempt to summarise them here briefly before stating any conclusions.

It has been argued that the underlying theory of the price level in Tooke's work is one which related the cost of production of goods to the cost of production of gold, and that this is a long-run theory which implies, in a classical framework, that, if the prices of other elements of the money supply are pegged to gold, then their quantity must adjust and become the consequence rather than the cause of the price level. It has also been argued that there was no real debate on this matter between Tooke and his opponents, but that rather it was the cause of short-run fluctuations that was at issue. There seem to have been two elements to the point of view which he took here.

First, even if the circulation had been made up purely of bank notes and coin he would have relied on the 'law of reflux' to maintain prices stable over all but quite short periods. Excess notes would either return to the banks in discharge of debts without affecting prices, or, if by any chance they did not, then they would begin to depreciate relative to gold as well as to other goods and would rapidly return to the banks in exchange for coin. In the first of these points there is an element of the real bills doctrine upon which we have commented above (*cf.* n. 7), but the second was accepted by his opponents, who, however, argued that the reflux in this case would not be rapid. To this extent the debate was purely about how long the short run is.

However, in the second element of Tooke's thought there is genuine theoretical disagreement with the currency school, for he saw the problem of the quantity of bank notes in circulation as having to do with the composition rather than the size of what we would now call the total money stock. He denied that the banking system could have any direct influence on the amount of notes in the hands of the public and saw its power to influence this variable as working through the effect of its lending policies on the state of trade. Thus he argued that regulation of the note issue was neither a necessary nor an effective policy tool

He tended to apply the same arguments to the determination of the size of the total circulation, and on this point he appears to have been confused. He argued that bills of exchange and the like would be created in anticipation of future prices, and hence were the effect rather than the cause of these prices. He did, however, see that the issue of bills could provide the conditions which would enable predictions of future prices to be fulfilled in the short run.

The source of the confusion here is his lack of a theory of the
relationship between the lending activities of those institutions and
individuals whose debt makes up the circulation and the quantity
of the circulation, and, closely related, his failure to see clearly
that deposits, rather than cheques, were the relevant substitute
for bills of exchange and bank notes.

However, this confusion did not lead Tooke into serious error.
Its principal effect was to lead him to look at bank advances and
speculative lending by other institutions and individuals as a
source of short-run price fluctuations, rather than to look at the
deposits, notes and bills created in the same process. He may
not have understood the credit multiplier process, but he clearly
did understand the role that banks, and particularly the Bank of
England, could play in altering the level of aggregate demand by
changes in the volume of their loans.[18] Though far from a perfect
statement of the matter, Tooke's emphasis on bank lending as a
key variable in short-run business fluctuations surely put him
closer to the truth than did the currency school's emphasis on the
size of the note issue.

Now the main problem of the time was the maintenance of
the convertibility of the note issue, both at home and abroad, at a
fixed parity, and Tooke did not deny for a moment that the plans
of the currency school would achieve this end. Rather he argued
that there were other ways of achieving the same goal at less
cost. He thought that the structure created in 1844 would work
only at the cost of violent fluctuations in credit conditions, and
possibly even of the loss of convertibility of Bank of England
deposits, unless the government were to intervene. Moreover he
saw such problems arising whenever there was an external specie
drain. Had these consequences been necessary to preserve the
convertibility of the currency it is clear he would not have objected
to them, but he regarded them as avoidable ones.

In the first place, he did not regard it as necessary to counter-
act all balance of payments disequilibria with domestic contraction, since temporary problems, especially those arising from the
need to import corn in the wake of bad harvests, would in no way
endanger convertibility if sufficient reserves were held at the
time they started. As to those disequilibria arising from domestic
over-expansion, they would provide their own cure with the natural
tendency of the banking system to curtail lending in the face of a
decreasing reserve of bullion. Moreover, with an adequate reserve base, this could be done without undue haste, and again
without financial panic and a danger of a suspension of payments.
As to longer-run problems—and Tooke is not very specific as to
their cause—they too could be taken care of by domestic contraction carried out slowly.

Given that modern economists are familiar with the distinction between temporary and fundamental balance of payments problems, given that they are extremely conscious of the disruptive effects of sudden contractions of the money supply brought about by rapid cuts in bank lending, and given that they are well aware that a useful definition of money must be wider in scope than bank notes and coin, they would surely find that Tooke's view, that the key to successfully operating a convertible money supply lay in adequate central bank reserves of bullion, has a great deal to commend it. They might also be willing to concede that there was much that was to the point in the analysis which led to this view, despite the flaws that we have noted, and to admit that on the whole Tooke's programme is a more appealing one than that of the currency school.

NOTES

[1]   This paper is reprinted from M. H. Peston and B. A. Corry (eds.), *Essays in Honour of Lionel Robbins,* London, Weidenfield & Nicolson 1972. I am deeply indebted to Bernard Corry for the many hours he contributed to discussing the subject matter of this essay with me, and to Robert Clower and Harry Johnson for most useful comments on an earlier draft. Nevertheless, all errors, omissions, misinterpretations and quotations taken out of context, are my own responsibility.

[2]   The main contributions to this literature are to be found in Gregory (1928), Mints (1972), Viner (1937), Robbins (1958), and most recently in Fetter (1965). Of these it is Fetter, the latest contributor, who is the most sympathetic to the banking school, and Gregory, the earliest, who goes so far as to refer to the currency school as 'the elect' (1928, p. 77), who is the least so. This literature spans almost forty years, and though it would be a fascinating study in itself to trace the evolution of opinion about nineteenth century monetary controversy over this period, there is hardly room to do so in one brief paper. As far as possible, then, I have tried to avoid debate with these commentators, and to let Tooke's ideas speak for themselves.

[3]   The whole matter of the so-called 'classical' economists' views on the interaction of monetary and real phenomena is discussed in Hicks (1967), chapter 9. On this issue the 'classics' were a good deal more 'Keynesian' than they are often presented.

[4]   It should be noted that by the 1830s the Ricardian practice of defining too high a price level relative to one which would maintain balance of payments equilibrium regardless of what other factors were operating had died out.

[5]   The importance which Tooke attached to these passages is attested to by the fact that he quotes them several years after

they were first written (1844, pp. 114-17). Indeed, the theme of the necessity of the Bank of England holding adequate specie reserves is strongly present in Tooke's early *Consideration on the State of the Currency* (1826), where it is seen, as in his later work, as being the key to preventing disturbances in the balance of payments being transmitted rapidly and violently to the domestic economy. It is worth pointing out that this earlier essay of Tooke's is much closer to a currency school position than is his later work, particularly in the stress it lays on the importance of regulating the note issue. However, stress is laid on the regulation of the note issue in this work not only because special monetary characteristics setting it apart from other forms of paper credit are attributed to it but also because bank notes are viewed as being the principal store of value used by the poorer members of society. These are the least able to foresee, and protect themselves from the consequences of, bank failures. Tooke wished to see notes, particularly low denomination notes, replaced by coin, or backed by much bigger specie reserves than were commonly held against them, as much to protect the poor from the consequences of commercial crises as because he expected such a measure to mitigate the causes of such crises. *Cf.* Tooke (1826), pp. 118-27.

6   There does, of course, exist the rather serious problem of distinguishing in practice between a fundamental disequilibrium on the one hand and a temporary one on the other. In terms of Tooke's analysis, however, the problem is perhaps not so great as it is in a contemporary framework. First, he tended to associate a temporary problem with a bad harvest, not a difficult phenomenon to recognise, and secondly he offered what amounted to a decision rule for deciding when the Bank should act in other cases. Any time when the Bank's specie reserves, having fallen by five million pounds, continued to fall was an occasion for domestic contraction (*cf.* 1844, pp. 115-17).

7   As to the real bills element in Tooke's thought at this point, it clearly exists but, as Fetter (1965, pp. 191-3) notes, unlike Fullarton, Tooke never stepped clearly into the celebrated fallacy. His emphasis on the 'mode of issue' of notes in relation to their effect on prices does suggest that he was not entirely free of erroneous notions on this score, and he clearly attached some importance to this point. Since it does not seem to play a key role in the logic of Tooke's position on policy matters, this writer has chosen not to emphasise the issue. However, *cf.* n. 8.

8   This comes out clearly from his discussion of the evidence of country and Scottish bankers quoted in Tooke (1844), chapters 8-9, and in his discussion of the possible manner in which the principles of the 1844 Act would operate. See below, p. 220. In Fullarton's hands the law of reflux becomes more like a com-

ponent of the real bills doctrine, with his emphasis on the banking
system's need only to discount good short-term paper in order
never to over-extend its issue. As just noted, Tooke certainly
regarded this as good banking practice, but as much because it
maintained the system's liquidity in the face of the possibility of
sudden demands for redemption of both notes and deposits as
because he viewed it as a safeguard against too much monetary
expansion. It was the convertibility of notes into gold that he
regarded as the ultimate safeguard here. The fact that he noted it
to be a method of reflux 'the least in use' is as well interpreted
as evidence that he thought the banking system worked smoothly
under the threat of an internal specie drain as that convertibility
was unimportant.

9   The foregoing point is one also raised by Cramp (1961),
pp. 69-74, though not specifically in the context of Tooke's work.

10   Tooke at one point maintains this distinction between money
and its substitutes, as Gregory points out. However, he did not
carry the argument to the point of assigning all effects on prices
to bank notes, and in fact makes no use of the distinction in any
analysis (*cf.* Gregory, 1928, pp. 77-8).

11   *Cf.* Wood (1939), pp. 35-7. In this context it is interesting to
speculate that English economics had to wait until the twentieth
century to rediscover this analysis, perhaps because of the influence of the currency school's emphasis on bank notes and coin
as money.

12   Wood (1939, pp. 56-8) notes Tooke's lack of a theory to con-
nect Bank advances with Bank liabilities and then goes on to
argue that this omission precludes Tooke from having a monetary
theory of the determination of the level of economic activity.
Unless one defines 'monetary' in a particularly narrow sense this
seems to this writer to be going a little too far.

13   In restating this argument in the summary given at the end
of *The Currency Principle* Tooke omitted the words 'valued in
gold', which are all-important for the interpretation I am here putting on the analysis. Either this was merely a careless slip in the
preparation of a pamphlet which was, after all, put together in a
hurry, or in summarising his argument Tooke became confused
between his analysis of the equilibrium price level and that of the
influence of aggregate demand on short-run fluctuations in the
price level. The latter element of his thought is taken up below.

14   Morgan (1943, pp. 127-43) notes the general agreement that
emerged between the banking school and the currency school as to
the applicability of this theory to the explanation of the long-run
level of prices. The emphasis on cost of production as a determinant of value is undoubtedly responsible for Tooke's apparently
extraordinary statement that a low rate of interest leads to low
rather than high prices. Though he makes it clear that he is

talking of the long-run equilibrium situation here (*cf.* 1844, pp. 124-5, particularly the footnote), the statement would still be true only were gold production less capital-intensive than that of some representative bundle of other goods. Since he never alludes to this point, one can only conclude that his thought was very confused here. However, note that in the already cited footnote he is quite clear that a rise in the Bank of England's discount rate will lead to a depression of prices in the short run.

15   That much of the dispute between the protagonists in this particular debate centres round the question of how long in the short run is a suggestion already made by Corry (1961).

16   Being a staunch advocate of *Laisser-faire,* Tooke would not have countenanced any legal reserve requirements of the type suggested here. He did not, after all, even envisage implementing his own policy proposals by law, but rather sought to persuade the Bank of England to mend their ways by rational argument. Nevertheless, as Fetter notes (1965, p. 191), Tooke's analysis of the evils of over-banking make a very strong case for legal controls on the entire system, let alone on the Bank of England. It is worth noting, though, that legal reserve requirements are always minimum requirements and do not give the central bank complete control over commercial banks' liabilities. Contemporary American evidence suggests that this is particularly the case when there are many small banks in a system. Certainly variations in these banks' excess reserves are significant for the behaviour of the monetary sector of the United States even today.

17   1848, pp. 281-406. Needless to say, so formidable a controversialist as Tooke did not attribute any exaggeration to himself.

Torrens claimed the events of 1847 as evidence of the success of the Act of 1844, apparently on the grounds that the convertibility of notes was never in danger, which was true, and on the grounds that their quantity in circulation had not fluctuated as greatly as in previous crises. Torrens (1847) saw the root of the 1847 crisis in the banking department having held too few reserves rather than as lying in the structure created by the Act of 1844. Though all the evidence he adduces is true, and the arguments he provides are logical, to this writer at least they appear to be beside the point of Tooke's criticism. The latter had, after all, never denied that convertibility would be guaranteed by the Act, and had been arguing for a decade that inadequate reserves were the key factor that had to be cured in order to rid England of financial crises. For a modern account of the events of the 1847 crisis, see Morgan (1943), pp. 147-57.

18   There are two aspects of this element of Tooke's thought that are worth noting. It must be apparent that he comes quite close to recognising the role of Bank of England deposits as a reserve base for the credit structure of the economy, so that we

must conclude that he was unclear about, rather than totally inno-
cent of, this factor as he sometimes gave the impression. Nevertheless, it is changes in the Bank's discounting operations that receive the greatest stress. The volume of its liabilities is not seen
as a key variable, except in as much as the public's drawing down
these will cause changes in Bank lending. The stress on bank
lending as the key factor in short-run fluctuations, here confined
to the Bank of England but elsewhere, as we have seen, extended
to the country banks, issuing and non-issuing alike, is also of
interest from the point of view of the history of doctrine, since it
seems to be one of the roots of Wicksell's thought on the problem
and hence of a great deal of twentieth century monetary theory.
Wicksell discusses Tooke in some detail in 1898a, pp. 168-90,
and 1905, pp. 81-7.

Bibliography

Alchian, A. A. (1969), 'Information costs, pricing and resource unemployment', in E. S. Phelps (ed.), *Microeconomic Foundations of Employment and Inflation Theory*, New York, Norton.

Alford, R. F. G. (1960), 'A taxonomic note on the multiplier and income velocity', *Economica*, XXVI, February, pp. 53-62.

Andersen, L. C., and Jordan, J. L. (1968), 'Monetary and fiscal actions: a test of their relative importance in economic stabilisation', *Federal Reserve Bank of St Louis Monthly Review*, L, November.

Ando, A., and Modigliani, F. (1965), 'The relative stability of monetary velocity and the investment multiplier', *American Economic Review*, LV, September, pp. 693-728.

Archibald, C. G. (1969), 'The Phillips curve and the distribution of unemployment', *American Economic Review*, LIX, Papers and proceedings, May.

Artis, M. J., and Nobay, A. R. (1969), 'Two aspects of the monetary debate', *National Institute Economic Review*, August, pp. 33-51.

Bailey, M. J. (1956), 'The welfare cost of inflationary finance', *Journal of Political Economy*, LXIV, pp. 93-110.

Barret, C. R., and Walters, A. A. (1966), 'The stability of Keynesian and monetary multipliers in the United Kingdom', *Review of Economics and Statistics*, XLVIII, November, pp. 395-405.

Barro, R. J. (1972), 'A theory of monopolistic price adjustment', *Review of Economic Studies*, XXIX, pp. 17-26.

Barro, R. J., and Grossman, H. I. (1971), 'A general disequilibrium model of income and employment', *American Economic Review*, LXI, March, pp. 82-93.

Bell, G. (1973), *The Eurodollar Market and the International Financial System*, London, Macmillan.

Box, G. E. P., and Jenkins, G. M. (1970), *Time Series Analysis: Forecasting and Control*, New York, Holden Day.

Brainard, W. C., and Tobin, J. (1968), 'Pitfalls in financial model building', *American Economic Review*, LVIII, Papers and proceedings, May, pp. 99-122.

Breton, A. (1968), 'A stable velocity function for Canada?', *Economica*, XXXV, November, pp. 451-53.

Brown, A. J. (1939), 'Interest, prices and the demand for idle money', *Oxford Economic Papers* 2, May, pp. 46-69.

— (1955), *The Great Inflation, 1939-1951*, London, Oxford University Press.

Brunner, K. (1951), 'Inconsistency and indeterminacy in classical economics', *Econometrica*, XIX, April, pp. 152-73.

Brunner, K., and Meltzer, A. H. (1970), 'A monetarist hypothesis of economic fluctuations' (mimeo), paper given at the first Konstanz Conference on Monetary Economics, June.

— (1971), 'The uses of money: money in the theory of an exchange economy', *American Economic Review,* LXI, December, pp. 784-805.

Cagan, P. (1956), 'The monetary dynamics of hyperinflation', in M. Friedman (ed.), *Studies in the Quantity Theory of Money*, Chicago University Press.

— (1965), *Determinants and Effects of Changes in the Stock of Money, 1870-1960*, New York, Columbia University Press for the National Bureau of Economic Research.

— (1968), 'Theories of mild continuing inflation: a critique and extension', in S. W. Rousseas (ed.), *Proceedings of a Symposium on Inflation — its Causes, Consequences and Control*, Wilton, Conn., Calvin K. Kazanjian Economics Foundation.

— (1969a), 'The influence of interest rates on the duration of business cycles', in P. Cagan and J. M. Guttentag (eds.), *Essays on Interest Rates,* I, New York, National Bureau of Economic Research.

— (1969b), 'A study of liquidity premiums on federal and municipal government securities', in P. Cagan and J. M. Guttentag (eds.), *Essays on Interest Rates*, I, New York, National Bureau of Economic Research.

Carlson, J. A. (1972), 'Elusive passage to the non-Walrasian continent', University of Manchester Inflation Workshop (mimeo).

Carlson, J. A., and Parkin, J. M. (forthcoming), 'Inflationary expectations', *Economica*.

Christ, C. F. (1968), 'A simple macroeconomic model with a government budget constraint', *Journal of Political Economy*, LXXVI, February, pp. 53-67.

Claassen, E., and Salin, P. (eds.)(1972), *Conference on Stabilisation Policies in Interdependent Economies,* Amsterdam, North-Holland.

Clower, R. W. (1965), 'The Keynesian counter-revolution: a theoretical appraisal', in F. H. Hahn and F. P. R. Brechling (eds.), *The Theory of Interest Rates*, London, Macmillan.

Coppock, D. J., and Gibson, N. J. (1963), 'The volume of deposits and the cash and liquid assets ratios', *Manchester School*, XXXI, September, pp. 203-22.

Corry, B. A. (1961), *Money, Saving and Investment in English Economics*, London, Macmillan.

Cramp, A. B. (1961), *Opinion on Bank Rate, 1822-60*, London School of Economics.

Crouch, R. (1967), 'A model of the United Kingdom's monetary sector', *'Econometrica'*, XXXV, July-October, pp. 398-418.

Deane, P., and Cole, W. A. (1967), *British Economic Growth, 1688-1959*, second edition, Cambridge University Press.

DeLeeuw, F. (1965), 'A model of financial behaviour', in J. F. Duesenberry et al. (eds.), *The Brookings Quarterly Econometric Model of the United States*, Chicago, Rand McNally.

DePrano, M., and Mayer, T. (1965), 'Tests of the relative importance of autonomous expenditure and money', *American Economic Review*, LV, September, pp. 729-52.

Feige, E. (1967), 'Expectations and adjustments in the monetary sector', *American Economic Review*, LVII, Papers and proceedings, May, pp. 462-73.

Fetter, F. W. (1965), *The Development of British Monetary Orthodoxy, 1797-1875*, Cambridge, Mass., Harvard University Press.

Fisher, D. (1968), 'The demand for money in Britain: quarterly results, 1951 to 1967', *Manchester School*, XXXVI, pp. 329-44.

Fisher, I. (1896), 'Appreciation and interest', *Publications of the American Economic Association*, third series, II, August, pp. 331-442.

Friedman, M. (1956), 'The quantity theory of money: a restatement', in M. Friedman (ed.), *Studies in the Quantity Theory of Money*, Chicago University Press.

— (1957), *A Theory of the Consumption Function*, Princeton University Press for the National Bureau of Economic Research.

— (1958), 'The supply of money and changes in prices and output', in *The Relationship of Prices to Economic Stability and Growth*, Eighty-fifth Congress of the US, Joint Economic Committee, Washington, D.C.; reprinted in M. Friedman (ed.), *The Optimum Quantity of Money*, London, Macmillan, 1969.

— (1959), 'The demand for money: some theoretical and empirical results', *Journal of Political Economy*, LXVII, June, pp. 327-51.

— (1960), *A Programme for Monetary Stability*, New York, Fordham University Press.

— (1968), 'The role of monetary policy', *American Economic Review*, LVIII, March, pp. 1-17.

— (1970), 'A theoretical framework for monetary analysis', *Journal of Political Economy*, LXXVIII, March-April, pp. 193-238.

— (1972), 'Comments on the critics', *Journal of Political Economy*, September-October, pp. 906-50.

Friedman, M., and Meiselman, D. (1963), 'The relative stability of monetary velocity and the investment multiplier in the United

States, 1898-1958', in Commission on Money and Credit, *Stabilization Policies*, Englewood Cliffs, N. J., Prentice-Hall.

— (1965), 'Reply to Ando and Modigliani and to DePrano and Mayer', *American Economic Review*, LV, September, pp. 754-85.

Friedman, M., and Schwartz, A. J. (1963a), *A Monetary History of the United States, 1867-1960*, Princeton University Press for the National Bureau of Economic Research.

— (1963b), 'Money and business cycles', *Review of Economics and Statistics*, XLV, February, supplement, pp. 32-64; reprinted in M. Friedman (ed.), *The Optimum Quantity of Money*, London, Macmillan, 1969.

— (1970), *Monetary Statistics of the United States*, New York, National Bureau of Economic Research.

Goodhart, C. A. E., and Crockett, A. D. (1970), 'The importance of money', *Bank of England Quarterly Bulletin*, X, June, pp. 159-98.

Gregory, T. E. (1928), *An Introduction to T. Tooke and W. Newmarch's 'A History of Prices'*, London; reprinted 1962.

Grossman, H. I. (1972), 'Was Keynes a 'Keynesian'? A review article', *Journal of Economic Literature*, X, March, pp. 26-30.

Grossman, H. I., and Dolde, W. (1970), 'The appropriate timing of monetary policy' (mimeo), paper given at the World Congress of the Econometric Society, Cambridge, September.

Gupta, S. B. (1970), 'The portfolio balance theory of the expected rate of change of prices', *Review of Economic Studies*, XXXVII, April, pp. 187-204.

Hamburger, M. (1967), 'Interest rates and the demand for consumer durable goods', *American Economic Review*, LVII, December, pp. 1133-53.

— (1968), 'Household demand for financial assets', *Econometrica*, XXXVI, January, pp. 97-118.

Harris, L. (1968), 'Regularities and irregularities in monetary economics', in C. R. Whittlesey and J. S. G. Wilson (eds.), *Essays in Money and Banking in Honour of R. S. Sayers*, Oxford, Clarendon Press.

Hester, D. J. (1964), 'Keynes and the quantity theory: comment on Friedman and Meiselman's CMC paper', *Review of Economics and Statistics*, XLVI, November, pp. 354-86.

Hicks, J. R. (1950), *A Contribution to the Theory of the Trade Cycle*, Oxford, Clarendon Press.

— (1967), *Critical Essays in Monetary Theory*, London, Oxford University Press.

Hines, A. G. (1964), 'Trade unions and wage inflation in the United Kingdom, 1893-1961', *Review of Economic Studies*, XXXI, pp. 221-52.

— (1971), 'The determinants of the rate of change of money wage rates and the effectiveness of incomes policy', in H. G.

Johnson and A. R. Nobay (eds.), *The Current Inflation*, London, Macmillan.

Hutchinson, T. W. (1968), *Economics and Economic Policy in Britain, 1946-66*, London, Allen & Unwin.

Hynes, A. (1967), 'The demand for money and monetary adjustments in Chile', *Review of Economic Studies*, XXXLV, July, pp. 285-94.

Johnson, H. G. (1962), 'Monetary theory and policy', *American Economic Review*, LII, June, pp. 335-84.

— (1967), 'Recent developments in monetary theory', in H. G. Johnson, *Essays in Monetary Economics*, London, Allen & Unwin.

— (1970), 'Recent developments in monetary theory — a commentary', in D. R. Croome and H. G. Johnson (eds.), *Money in Britain, 1959-69*, London, Oxford University Press.

— (1971), 'The monetary approach to balance of payments theory', lecture delivered to the Graduate Institute of International Studies, Geneva, Switzerland, February.

— (1972), *Inflation and the Monetarist Controversy*, the de Vries Lectures, 1971, Amsterdam, North-Holland.

Jorgenson, D. W. (1963), 'Capital theory and investment behaviour', *American Economic Review*, LIII, Papers and proceedings, May, pp. 247-59.

Kaldor, N. (1970), 'The new monetarism', *Lloyd's Bank Review*, July, pp. 1-18.

Kareken, J., and Solow, R. (1963), 'Lags in monetary policy', in Commission on Money and Credit, *Stabilization Policies*, Englewood Cliffs, N. J., Prentice-Hall.

Keynes, J. M. (1930), *A Treatise on Money*, London and New York, Macmillan.

— (1936), *The General Theory of Employment, Interest and Money*, London and New York, Macmillan.

Khusro, A. M. (1952), 'An investigation of liquidity preference', *Yorkshire Bulletin of Economic and Social Research*, IV, January, pp. 1-20.

Klein, J. J. (1956), 'German money and prices, 1932-44', in M. Friedman (ed.), *Studies in the Quantity Theory of Money*, Chicago University Press.

Knight, F. H. (1933), 'Social economic organisation', in F. H. Knight, *The Economic Organisation*, Harper & Row, New York, 1951 edition; reprinted as reading 1 in Breit and Hochman, *Readings in Microeconomics*, London, Holt Rinehart & Winston, 1969.

Laidler, D. E. W. (1966), 'The rate of interest and the demand for money', *Journal of Political Economy*, LXXIV, February, pp. 55-68.

— (1968), 'The permanent income concept in a macroeconomic model', *Oxford Economic Papers,* XX, March, pp. 11-23.

— (1969a), *The Demand for Money — Theories and Evidence,* Scranton, Pa., International Textbook Co.

— (1969b), 'The definition of money: theoretical and empirical problems', *Journal of Money, Credit and Banking,* I, August, pp. 508-25.

— (1970), 'Recent developments in monetary theory — discussion paper', in D. Croome and H. G. Johnson (eds.), *Money in Britain, 1959-69,* London, Oxford University Press.

— (1971a). 'The influence of money on economic activity: a survey of some current problems', in G. Clayton, J. Gilbert and R. Sedgwick (eds.), *Monetary Theory and Monetary Policy in the 1970s,* London, Oxford University Press; reprinted here as chapter 2.

— (1971b), 'The Phillips curve, expectations and incomes policy', in H. G. Johnson and A. R. Nobay (eds.), *The Current Inflation,* London, Macmillan; reprinted here as chapter 4.

— (1971c), 'Monetarism, stabilisation policy and the exchange rate', *Bankers' Magazine,* No. 1531, October, pp. 163-8.

— (1972a), 'A monetarist model of simultaneous fluctuations in prices and output' (mimeo). (This paper sets out the analytic basis of chapter 7 of this book.)

— (1972b), 'The current inflation: explanations and policies', *National Westminster Bank Review,* November, pp. 6-21; reprinted here as chapter 10.

— (1972c), 'Price and output fluctuations in an open economy' (mimeo), University of Manchester Inflation Workshop; printed here as chapter 9.

— (1972d), 'Thomas Tooke on monetary reform', in M. Peston and B. Corry (eds.), *Essays in Honour of Lord Robbins,* London, Weidenfelt & Nicolson; reprinted here as chapter 11.

— (1973a), 'Expectations, adjustment and the dynamic response of income to policy changes', *Journal of Money, Credit and Banking,* V, February; reprinted here as chapter 3.

— (1973b), 'Simultaneous fluctuations in prices and output: a business cycle approach', *Economica,* XL, February, pp. 60-72; reprinted here as chapter 6.

Laidler, D. E. W., and Parkin, J. M. (1970), 'The demand for money in the United Kingdom, 1956-67: preliminary estimates', *Manchester School,* XXXVIII, September, pp. 187-208.

Lee, T. H. (1967), 'Alternative interest rates and the demand for money: the empirical evidence', *American Economic Review,* LVII, December, pp. 1168-81.

Leijonhuvfud, A. (1968), *On Keynesian Economics and the Economics of Keynes: a Study in Monetary Theory,* London and New York, Oxford University Press.

Lipsey, R. G. (1960), 'The relation between unemployment and the rate of change of money wage rates in the United Kingdom, 1862-1957', *Economica,* XXVII, February, pp. 1-31; reprinted in R. A. Gordon and L. R. Klein (eds.), *Readings in Business Cycles,* Homewood, Ill., 1965.

Lipsey, R. G., and Parkin, J. M. (1970), 'Incomes policy: a reappraisal', *Economica,* XXXVI, May, pp. 115-38; reprinted in J. M. Parkin and M. T. Sumner (eds.), *Incomes Policy and Inflation,* Manchester University Press, 1972.

Lucas, R. E., Jr., and Rapping, L. A. (1970), 'Real wages, employment and inflation', in E. S. Phelps (ed.), *Microeconomic Foundations of Employment and Inflation Theory,* New York, Norton.

Matthews, R. C. O. (1969), 'The post-war business cycle in the UK', in M. Bronfeurbrenner (ed.), *Is the Business Cycle Obsolete?* New York, Wiley.

Mayer, T. (1967), 'The lag effect in monetary policy: some criticisms', *Western Economic Journal,* V, September, pp. 324-42.

— (1968), *Monetary Policy in the United States,* New York, Random House.

McCallum, B. T. (1973), 'Friedman's missing equation: another approach', *Manchester School,* XLI, September, pp. 311-28.

Meiselman, D. (1963), *The Term Structure of Interest Rates,* Englewood Cliffs, N. J., Prentice-Hall.

— (ed.) (1971), *The Varieties of Monetary Experience,* Chicago University Press.

Mints, L. A. (1948), *A History of Banking Theory,* Chicago University Press.

Morgan, E. V. (1943), *The Theory and Practice of Central Banking, 1797-1913,* Cambridge University Press.

Morrison, G. (1966), *Liquidity Preferences of Commercial Banks,* Chicago University Press.

Mortenson, D. T. (1970), 'A theory of wage and employment dynamics', in E. S. Phelps (ed.), *Microeconomic Foundations of Employment and Inflation Theory,* New York, Norton.

Motley, B. (1970), 'Household demand for assets: a model of short-run adjustments', *Review of Economics and Statistics,* LII, August, pp. 236-41.

Mundell, R. A. (1971), *Monetary Theory: Inflation, Interest and Growth in the World Economy,* Pacific Palisades, Cal., Goodyear.

Norton, W. E. (1969), 'Debt management and monetary policy in the United Kingdom', *Economic Journal,* LXXXIX, September, pp. 475-94.

Parkin, J. M. (1970a), 'Discount houses' portfolio and debt selection', *Review of Economic Studies,* XXXVII, October, pp. 469-99.

— (1970b), 'Incomes policy — some further results on the determination of the rate of change of money wages', *Economica,* XXXVII, November, pp. 368-401; reprinted in J. M. Parkin and M. T. Sumner (eds.), *Incomes Policy and Inflation,* Manchester University Press, 1972.

— (1971), 'The Phillips curve—a historical perspective: lessons from recent empirical studies and alternative policy choices', in H. G. Johnson and A. R. Nobay (eds.), *The Current Inflation,* London, Macmillan.

— (1972), 'Inflation, the balance of payments, domestic credit expansion and exchange rate adjustments' (mimeo), University of Manchester.

Parkin, J. M., Gray, M., and Barrett, R. (1970), 'The portfolio behaviour of commercial banks', in K. Hilton and D. F. Heathfield (eds.), *The Econometric Study of the United Kingdom,* London, Macmillan.

Parkin, J. M., and Sumner, M. T. (eds.) (1972), *Incomes Policy and Inflation,* Manchester University Press.

Parkin, J. M., Sumner, M. T., and Jones, R. A. (1972), 'A survey of the econometric evidence on the effect of incomes policy on the rate of inflation', in J. M. Parkin and M. T. Sumner (eds.), *Incomes Policy and Inflation,* Manchester University Press.

Patinkin, D. (1965), *Money, Interest and Prices,* second edition, New York, Harper & Row.

— (1969), 'The Chicago tradition, the quantity theory and Friedman', *Journal of Money, Credit and Banking,* I, February, pp. 46-70.

— (1972), *Studies in Monetary Economics,* New York, Harper & Row.

Pesek, B., and Saving, T. (1967), *Money, Wealth and Economic Theory,* New York, Macmillan.

Petersen, D. W., Lerner, E. M., and Lusk, E. J. (1971), 'The response of prices and incomes to monetary policy: an analysis based upon a differential Phillips curve', *Journal of Political Economy,* LXXXIX, September-October, pp. 857-66.

Phelps, E. S. (1965), 'Anticipated inflation and economic welfare', *Journal of Political Economy,* LXXIII, February, pp. 1-17.

— (1967), 'Phillips curves, expectations of inflation and optimal unemployment over time', *Economica,* XXXIV, August, pp. 254-81.

— (ed.) (1970), *Microeconomic Foundations of Employment and Inflation Theory,* New York, Norton.

— (1972), *Inflation Policy and Unemployment Theory: the Cost-Benefit Approach to Monetary Planning,* London, Macmillan.

Phelps, E. S., and Winter, S. G., Jr. (1970), 'Optimal price policy under atomistic competition', in E. S. Phelps (ed.), *Microeconomic Foundations of Employment and Inflation Theory,* New York, Norton.

Phillips, A. W. (1954), 'Stabilization in a closed economy', *Economic Journal,* LXIV, June, pp. 290-323.

— (1958), 'The relation between unemployment and the rate of change of money wage rates in the United Kingdom', *Economica,* XXV, November, pp. 283-99.

Poole, W. (1970), 'Optimal choice of monetary policy instruments in a simple stochastic macro-model', *Quarterly Journal of Economics,* LXXXIV, May, pp. 197-216.

Purdy, D. L., and Zis, G. (1974), 'Trade unions and wage inflation in the UK — a reappraisal', in D. E. W. Laidler and D. L. Purdy (eds.), *Inflation and Labour Markets,* Manchester University Press.

Radcliffe committee (Committee on the Working of the Monetary System) (1959), *Report,* London, HMSO.

Robbins, L. C. (1935), *An Essay on the Nature and Significance of Economic Science,* second edition, London, Macmillan.

— (1958), *Robert Torrens and the Evolution of Classical Economics,* London, Macmillan.

Samuelson, P. A., and Solow, R. M. (1960), 'Analytical aspects of anti-inflationary policy', *American Economic Review,* L, May, pp. 177-94.

Schwartz, A. J. (1969), 'Short-term targets of three foreign central banks', in K. Brunner (ed.), *Targets and Indicators of Monetary Policy,* San Francisco, Chandler.

Shackle, G. S. (1967), *The Years of High Theory,* Cambridge University Press.

Sheppard, D. (1970), 'Money, encashable assets, private institutional credits and private expenditure in the UK, 1860-1962' (mimeo), Graduate Centre of Management Studies, University of Aston in Birmingham.

Sims, C. A. (1972), 'Money, finance and causality', *American Economic Review,* LXII, September, pp. 540-52.

Smith, D. L. (1968), 'Incomes policy', in R. E. Caves *et al., Britain's Economic Prospects,* Washington, D.C., Brookings Institution, and London, Allen & Unwin; reprinted in J. M. Parkin and M. T. Sumner (eds.), *Incomes Policy and Inflation,* Manchester University Press, 1972.

Solow, R. M. (1968), 'Recent controversies on the theory of inflation: an eclectic view', in S. W. Rousseas (ed.), *Proceedings of a Symposium on Inflation — its Causes Consequences and Control,* Wilton, Conn., Calvin K. Kazanjian Economics Foundation.

Stigler, G. C., (1961), 'The economics of information', *Journal of Political Economy,* LXIX, June, pp. 213-25.

Swoboda, A. K. (1974), 'Monetary policy under fixed exchange rates: effectiveness, the speed of adjustment and proper use', in H. G. Johnson and A. R. Nobay (eds.), *Issues in Monetary Economics,* London, Oxford University Press.

Tanner, J. E. (1969), 'Lags in the effects of monetary policy: a statistical investigation', *American Economic Review*, LIX, December, pp. 794-805.

Tobin, J. (1972), 'Inflation and unemployment', *American Economic Review*, LXII, March, pp. 1-18.

Tobin, J., and Swan, C. (1969), 'Money and permanent income: some empirical tests', *American Economic Review*, LIX, May, pp. 285-95.

Tooke, T. (1826), *Considerations on the State of the Currency*, London.

— (1838), *A History of Prices*, I-II, London.

— (1840), *ibid.*, III, London.

— (1848), *ibid.*, IV, London.

— (1844), *An Inquiry into the Currency Principle*, second edition, London.

Torrens, R. (1847), *Sir Robert Peel's Act of 1844 Explained*, London.

Tucker, D. (1966), 'Dynamic income adjustment to money supply changes', *American Economic Review*, LVI, June, pp. 433-49.

Viner, J. (1937), *Studies in the Theory of International Trade*, New York, Harper.

Walters, A. A. (1965), 'Professor Friedman on the demand for money', *Journal of Political Economy*, LXXIII, October, pp. 545-51.

— (1969), *Money in Boom and Slump*, Hobart Paper 44, London, Institute of Economic Affairs.

— (1970), 'The Radcliffe report — ten years after: a survey of empirical evidence', in D. R. Croome and H. G. Johnson (eds.), *Money in Britain, 1959-69*, London, Oxford University Press.

Ward, R., and Zis, G. (1974), 'Trade union militancy as an explanation of inflation: an international comparison', *Manchester School*, LII, March, pp. 46-65.

Wicksell, K. (1898a), *Interest and Prices*, trans. R. F. Kahn, London, Royal Economic Society, 1936.

— (1898b), 'The influence of the rate of interest on commodity prices', in *Selected Papers on Economic Theory*, reprinted London, 1956.

— (1905), *Lectures on Political Economy*, II, trans. E. Claassen, ed. L. C. Robbins, London and New York, Routledge, 1935.

— (1907), 'The influence of the rate of interest on prices', *Economic Journal*, XVII, p. 213-20.

Williamson, J. (1970), 'A simple neo-Keynesian growth model', *Review of Economic Studies*, XXXVII, April, pp. 151-71.

Wood, E. (1939), *English Theories of Central Banking Control, 1819-1958*, Cambridge, Mass., Harvard University Press.

Wright, C. (1969), 'Saving and the rate of interest', in A. C. Harberger and M. J. Bailey (eds.), *The Taxation of Income from Capital*, Washington, D.C., Brookings Institution.

Index of names

Subject index

Government debt, 40, 59
Great Depression
    1930's, 36-8, 58, 167-8
    nineteenth-century, 166
Growth models, 62

Hicks—Hansen model, *see* IS—LM model
Hicksian economics, 125, 127
Hyperinflation, 55, 198

Income, vii, xi, 24, 27, 28, 30, 31, 32, 47, 51, 54, 65, 74, 79, 101, 122,
    134-65, 177, 184
Incomes policy, ix, xii, 82-100, 121, 131, 132, 145, 169, 181, 204-5,
    207, 209
Industrial disputes, 209
Inflation
    accelerating rate of, 100, 126, 127-9, 130, 131, 133, 201
    anticipated, 112
    equilibrium, 9, 10, 14
    expectations, vii, ix, xi, 10, 11, 12, 17, 48, 49, 62, 63, 64, 82-100,
        105, 117, 120-1, 124, 125, 127, 128, 131, 132, 133, 136, 137-8,
        142, 151, 156, 162, 163, 173, 177, 181, 182, 185, 193, 196, 197,
        198, 199, 202, 203, 205, 208
    international aspects, 18, 166-82
    Nordic model of, 182
    policy against, vii, ix, 83, 87, 88, 91, 92-3, 195-210
    price, vii, viii, ix, x, 9, 49, 63, 136, 170, 176, 205
    research on, vi, 19
    'sociological' theories of, vii, 1, 7, 13, 166, 169
    structuralist theory of, 11
    wage, vii, viii, ix, x, 9, 49, 63, 82, 85, 87, 88, 93-4, 98, 110, 120,
        125, 136, 168, 169, 170, 176, 205, 209
Inflationary gap, 26
Information, xi, 1-18, 115, 116, 210
Interest rate, ix, x, 11, 12-13, 21, 22, 23, 24-5, 28, 29, 30, 31, 32, 34-5,
    39, 40, 44, 50, 51, 54, 55, 56, 57, 59, 60, 61, 66, 71-3, 77, 102-5,
    106, 107, 109, 110, 117, 122, 123, 128, 130, 136, 140, 142, 155,
    170, 173-4, 181, 193, 197, 198, 202, 208, 225
    natural, 12, 110-1, 133
    real, ix, 112, 123, 125, 133, 170
Inventories, 114-5, 124
Investment, 23, 24, 26, 29, 53, 57, 63, 122, 126, 128, 129, 132, 133
IS—LM model (Hicks—Hansen model), vii, x, xi, 4, 15, 17, 20, 21,
    23, 28, 29, 30, 34, 39, 41, 42, 43, 48, 53, 59, 60, 65, 75, 81, 134,
    155